Android Apps for Absolute Beginners

Wallace Jackson

Apress®

Android Apps For Absolute Beginners

Copyright © 2011 by Wallace Jackson

ISBN-13 (pbk): 978-1-4302-3446-3

ISBN-13 (electronic): 978-1-4302-3447-0

Printed and bound in the United States of America (POD)

Trademarked names, logos, and images may appear in this book. Rather than use a trademark symbol with every occurrence of a trademarked name, logo, or image we use the names, logos, and images only in an editorial fashion and to the benefit of the trademark owner, with no intention of infringement of the trademark.

The use in this publication of trade names, trademarks, service marks, and similar terms, even if they are not identified as such, is not to be taken as an expression of opinion as to whether or not they are subject to proprietary rights.

President and Publisher: Paul Manning
Lead Editor: Matthew Moodie
Technical Reviewer: Kunal Mittal
Editorial Board: Steve Anglin, Mark Beckner, Ewan Buckingham, Gary Cornell, Jonathan Gennick, Jonathan Hassell, Michelle Lowman, Matthew Moodie, Jeff Olson, Jeffrey Pepper, Frank Pohlmann, Douglas Pundick, Ben Renow-Clarke, Dominic Shakeshaft, Matt Wade, Tom Welsh
Coordinating Editor: Corbin Collins
Copy Editors: Marilyn Smith, Sharon Terdeman, Tracy Brown
Compositor: MacPS, LLC
Indexer: BIM Indexing & Proofreading Services
Artist: April Milne
Cover Designer: Anna Ishchenko

Distributed to the book trade worldwide by Springer Science+Business Media, LLC., 233 Spring Street, 6th Floor, New York, NY 10013. Phone 1-800-SPRINGER, fax (201) 348-4505, e-mail orders-ny@springer-sbm.com, or visit www.springeronline.com.

For information on translations, please e-mail rights@apress.com, or visit www.apress.com.

Apress and friends of ED books may be purchased in bulk for academic, corporate, or promotional use. eBook versions and licenses are also available for most titles. For more information, reference our Special Bulk Sales–eBook Licensing web page at www.apress.com/info/bulksales.

The source code for this book is available to readers at www.apress.com. You will need to answer questions pertaining to this book in order to successfully download the code.

In loving memory of all of our wonderful furry companions who graced our lives with unconditional love for decades here on our ranch in the La Purisima State Historic Park on the Point Conception Peninsula in Northern Santa Barbara County.

Contents at a Glance

Contents

About the Author

 **Wallace Jackson** is the CEO of Mind Taffy Design, a new media content design and production company founded in 1991. Mind Taffy specializes in leveraging free for commercial use open source technologies to provide an extremely compact data footprint, royalty-free, digital new media advertising and branding campaigns for the leading international brands and manufacturers worldwide.

Wallace has been pushing the cutting edge of i3D and Rich Media Application Design via viral digital content deliverables, using under 512KB of Total Data Footprint, for over two decades. He has worked for leading international brands to create custom new media digital campaigns for industry-leading companies, including brand marketing, PR, product demonstration, digital signage, e-learning, AdverGaming, logo design, and end-user training for top Fortune 500 companies.

He has produced new media projects in a number of digital media "verticals" or content deliverable areas, including: interactive 3D [i3D], Rich Internet Applications (RIA) content production, virtual world design, user interface (UI) design, user experience (UX) design, multimedia production, 3D modeling, sound design, MIDI synthesis, music composition, image compositing, 3D animation, game programming, mobile application programming, BrandGame creation, website design, CSS programming, data optimization, digital imaging, digital painting, digital video editing, special effects, morphing, vector illustration, IPTV Programming, iTV application design, interactive product demos, and tradeshow multimedia.

Wallace has created new media digital campaigns for leading international branded manufacturers, including Sony, Samsung, Tyco, Dell, Epson, IBM, Mitsubishi, Compaq, TEAC, KDS USA, CTX International, ADI Systems, Nokia, Micron, ViewSonic, OptiQuest, SGI, Western Digital, Sun Microsystems, ProView, Sceptre, KFC, ICM, EIZO, Nanao, Digital Equipment [DEC], TechMedia, Pacific Digital, ArtMedia, Maxcall, Altrasonic, DynaScan, EZC, Smile, Kinoton GMBH, and many others.

Wallace holds an MSBA post-graduate degree in Marketing Strategy from USC, an MBA degree in Management Information Systems Design and Implementation from the USC Marshall School of Business, and a Bachelor's degree in Business Economics from UCLA Anderson School of Management. He is currently the #2 ranked All Time Top Expert on LinkedIn, out of more than 90,000,000 executives that use that social media business web site.

About the Technical Reviewer

 **Kunal Mittal** serves as an Executive Director of Technology at Sony Pictures Entertainment, where he is responsible for the SOA, Identity Management, and Content Management programs. He provides a centralized engineering service to different lines of business and leads efforts to introduce new platforms and technologies into the Sony Pictures Enterprise IT environment.

Kunal is an entrepreneur who helps startups define their technology strategy, product roadmap, and development plans. Having strong relations with several development partners worldwide, he is able to help startups and even large companies build appropriate development partnerships. He generally works in an advisor or consulting CTO capacity, and serves actively in the project management and technical architect functions. He has authored and edited several books and articles on J2EE, cloud computing, and mobile technologies. He holds a Master's degree in Software Engineering and is an instrument-rated private pilot.

Acknowledgments

My sincere thanks go to:

Matthew Moodie, my lead editor, for his patience and thoughtful guidance in shaping this first edition of *Android Apps for Absolute Beginners*. Matthew, thanks for guiding me as a new Apress author, and I look forward to future collaborations with you.

Kunal Mittal, my esteemed technical reviewer, for his hard work and insightful suggestions in shaping this edition of the book.

Steve Anglin, my acquisitions editor, for bringing me into the Apress family to write this book. I wouldn't have done it at all if it were not for you!

Dominic Shakeshaft, editorial director, for overseeing the editorial process while I wrote. I appreciate your help with the higher-level issues involved.

Corbin Collins, my coordinating editor, for listening to all of my miscellaneous and sundry problems during the writing of this book and helping to get them all sorted out.

Marilyn Smith, **Sharon Terdeman**, and **Tracy Brown**, my copy editors, for their excellent editing and book-polishing skills and for all the great suggestions for making this a fantastic Android book.

My Editorial Board, including Steve Anglin, Mark Beckner, Ewan Buckingham, Gary Cornell, Jonathan Gennick, Jonathan Hassell, Michelle Lowman, James Markham, Matthew Moodie, Jeff Olson, Jeffrey Pepper, Frank Pohlmann, Douglas Pundick, Ben Renow-Clarke, Dominic Shakeshaft, Matt Wade, and Tom Welsh, for making sure this is the best book for beginners about the esteemed open source Android operating system.

The many loved ones and clients who patiently awaited my return to i3D content production from the "professional sidetracker" commonly known as writing a programming book.

Introduction

Over the last two years, Google's Android operating system (OS) has gone from a virtually unknown open source solution to the current mobile OS market leader among all mobile handsets, with over one-third of the market share, and it's still climbing rapidly. Android has even started to dominate the tablet OS marketplace, and is also the foundation for the popular iTV OS known as GoogleTV. There seems to be no end in sight for Android's rocketing success, which is great news for owners of this book.

I've heard a great many people say, "I have a really phenomenal idea for a smartphone application! Can you program it for me!?" Rather than sit back and code all of these applications for everyone, I thought it might be a smarter idea to write a book about how an absolute beginner could code an Android application using open source tools that cost nothing to download and that are free for commercial use, and then leverage that new found knowledge to reach their dream of making their application idea a revenue-generating reality.

Thanks to open source and Google's Android development environment, Oracle's Java programming Language, Linus Torvald's Linux operating system, the Eclipse code editing software, and this book, vaporizing a software product out of thin air, and at no production cost other than your PC and "sweat equity," is now a complete reality.

The Target: The Programming Neophyte

As you may have inferred from the title, this book assumes that you have never programmed before in any programming language. It is written for someone who has never written a single line of code before, and who is thus unfamiliar with object-oriented programming (OOP) languages such as Oracle's Java and mark-up languages such as XML. Both of these open source languages are used extensively in creating Android applications.

There are lots of Java and Android books out there, but all of these books assume you have programmed before, and know all about OOP. I wanted to write a book that takes readers from knowing absolutely nothing about programming or knowing how to install a Software Development Kit (SDK) and Integrated Development Environment (IDE) all the way to being able to program Android applications using Java and XML.

The Weapon: Android, the Innovative Mobile Code Environment

Android is my Internet 2.0 development weapon of choice, because it allows me to develop highly advanced applications for the primary Internet 2.0 devices, including the main three where revenue potential is by far the greatest:

- Smartphones

- Tablets

- iTV or Interactive Television

The other reason I place my bets on Android is because it is open source, and thus free from royalties and politics. I do not have to submit my Android application to any company and ask permission to publish it, as long as it is not harmful in any way to others. For this reason, and due to the free for commercial use nature of open source software, there is little external risk involved in developing an application for the Android Platform.

How This Book Is Organized

Because this is a book for absolute beginners, we start at the very beginning, showing where to download and how to install the various Android, Java, and Eclipse environments, as well as how to configure these environments and how to set them up for application development and testing. This in itself is no easy task, and must be done correctly, as these tools provide the foundation for all of our Android development, debugging, and testing for the remainder of the book.

Next I will provide you with an overview of where Android came from, why, how, and when Google acquired it, and how it is uniquely structured among software development platforms. I will introduce XML, Java, OOP, and Android concepts soon after that, as well as cover how Android manages its screen layout. We will then move these concepts into use in later chapters in the second half of the book; these chapters explain the most important concepts in Android in their most logical order as they pertain to applications development.

In that second half of the book, we'll start getting into developing a user interface (UI), as that is the front-end or interface for your user to your Android application. Soon after we'll cover how your UI talks to your application via events processing. To spice up your application's visual appearance, we'll get into graphics, animation, and video, and then get into even more advanced topics after that, such as databases and communications.

Finally we will look at some of the advanced features of Android that you will want to visit after finishing the book; these are topics that are too advanced for a first book on Android but which provide some of the coolest features in smartphone development today.

We'll walk you through all of these topics and concepts with screenshots of the IDE and visual examples and then take you though step-by-step examples reinforcing these concepts. Sometimes we will repeat previous topics to reinforce what you have learned and apply these skills in new ways. This enables new programmers to re-apply development skills and feel a sense of accomplishment as they progress.

The Formula for Success

Learning to develop an Android application is an interactive process between you and the tools and technologies (Eclipse, XML, Java, Android, and so on) that I cover in this book. Just like learning to play a sport, you have to develop skills and practice them daily. You need to work through the examples and exercises in this book, more than once if necessary to become comfortable with each concept.

Just because you understand a concept that doesn't necessarily mean you will know how to apply it creatively and use it effectively; that takes practice, and ultimately will happen when the "ah-ha" moment occurs, when you understand the concept in context with the other concepts that interconnect with it.

You will learn quite a bit about how Android works from this introductory book. You will glean a lot of insight into the inner working of Android by working through all of the exercises in this book. But you will also learn new things not specifically mentioned in this book when you compile, run and debug your programs. Spending time experimenting with your code and trying to find out why it is not working the way you want, or trying to add new features to it, is a learning process that is very valuable.

The downside of debugging is it can sometimes be quite frustrating to the new developer. If you have never wanted to put a bullet in your computer monitor, you will soon. You will question why you are doing this, and whether you are savvy enough to solve the problem. Programming can be very humbling, even for the most experienced of developers.

Like an athlete, the more you practice, the better you will become at your skill. You can do some truly amazing things as an Android programmer. The world is your oyster. It is one of the most satisfying accomplishments you can have, seeing your app in the Android App Store. However, there is a price, and that price is time spent practicing your coding.

Here is our formula for success:

- Trust that you can pull it off. You may be the only one who says you can't do this. Don't tell yourself that.

- Work through all the examples and exercises in this book, twice if necessary, until you understand them.

- Code, code some more, and keep coding – don't stop. The more you code, the better you'll get.

- Be patient with yourself. If you were fortunate enough to have been a star pupil who can memorize material simply by reading it, this will not happen with Java and XML coding. You are going to have to spend lots of time coding in order to understand what is happening inside the OS.

- Whatever you do: DON'T GIVE UP!

Required Software, Materials, and Equipment

One of the great things about Java, Android and Eclipse is they are available in both 32-bit and 64-bit versions on the three primary operating systems in use today:

- Windows

- Mac

- Linux

The other great thing about Java, Android and Eclipse is that they are free. You can download Android at `http://developer.android.com/SDK/`. For equipment, any modern computer will do. Fortunately they are only $250 to $500 brand new on `www.PriceWatch.com` and an OS such as SUSE Linux is free and an amazing development operating system. SUSE Linux V11 can be downloaded at `www.OpenSUSE.com` and is currently at version 11.4 and very stable.

Operating System and IDE

Although you can use Android on many platforms, the Eclipse integrated development environment (IDE) that developers use to develop Android apps is most commonly used on an Intel-based Windows or Linux PC. The Eclipse IDE is free and is available on the Internet at `www.eclipse.org`. The operating system should be Windows XP or later or SUSE Linux 11.4 or later to run Eclipse most effectively.

Software Development Kits

You will need to download the Eclipse IDE from Eclipse and the Android SDK from Google. This is available at http://developer.android.com/SDK/.

Dual Monitors

It is highly recommended that developers have a second monitor connected to their computer. It is great to step through your code and watch your output window and Android emulator at the same time on dual, independent monitors. Today's PC hardware makes this easy. Just plug your second monitor in to the second display port of any Intel-based PC or laptop, with the correct display port adapter, of course, and you're able to have two monitors working independently from one another. Note it is not required to have dual monitors. You will just have to organize your open windows to fit on your screen if you don't.

Chapter 1

Preliminary Information: Before We Get Started

This chapter introduces the Android operating system, giving you a little background information to put things into perspective. We'll visit just how expansive this platform has become in today's Internet 2.0 environment of portable consumer electronic devices. *Internet 2.0* here refers to the consumption of the Internet over a wide variety of different types of data networks using highly portable consumer electronic devices, including smartphones, tablets, e-book readers, and even new emerging consumer electronic products such as interactive television (iTV).

As this is an introductory book on the subject, not all of the advanced new media-related areas, such as 3D and video streaming, will be covered. Some specifics of what the book will and will not cover are outlined in this chapter.

At the end of the chapter, you'll learn which tools you need to obtain in order to develop for the Google Android platform, with instructions on how to download them.

Those of you who already recognize the significance of the Android revolution and know which tools are needed to develop Android applications development may want to skip this chapter. However, may be some tidbits in here that could spawn development ideas —so skip along at your own risk!

Just a bit of fair warning: developing reliable applications for Android is not in any way a trivial task. It takes a fair amount of knowledge of both high-level programming languages such as Java and markup languages like XML. Building useful and engaging new media applications also requires a deep knowledge of related new media technologies such as 2D imaging, 3D rendering, audio processing, video streaming, GPS localization, and database design.

Don't expect to learn all of this at one sitting. Becoming a top-notch Android programmer will take years of dedication and practice, as well as diligent research and trial and error. In this book, you will gain the foundation that you need to build future expertise, as well as learn the work process for eventually building your Android masterpeice.

Some History: What Is Android?

Android was originally created by Andy Rubin as an operating system for mobile phones, around the dawn of this twenty-first century. In 2005, Google acquired Android Inc., and made Andy Rubin the Director of Mobile Platforms for Google. Many think the acquisition was largely in response to the emergence of the Apple iPhone around that time; however, there were enough other large players, such as Nokia Symbian and Microsoft Windows Mobile, that it seemed like a salient business decision for Google to purchase the talent and intellectual property necessary to assert the company into this emerging space, which has become known as Internet 2.0.

Internet 2.0 allows users of consumer electronics to access content via widely varied data networks through highly portable consumer electronic devices, such as smartphones, touchscreen tablets, and e-books, and even through not so portable devices, such as iTVs, home media centers, and set-top boxes. This puts new media content such as games, 3D animation, digital video, digital audio, and high-definition imagery into our lives at every turn. Android is one of the vehicles that digital artists will leverage to develop media creations that users have never before experienced.

Over the past decade, Android has matured and evolved into an extremely reliable, bulletproof, embedded operating system platform, having gone from version 1.0 to stable versions at 1.5, 1.6, 2.0, 2.1, 2.2, 2.3, and, recently, 3.0. An embedded operating system is like having an entire computer on a chip small enough to fit into handheld consumer electronics, but powerful enough to run applications (commonly known as *apps*).

Android has the power of a full-blown computer operating system. It is based on the Linux open source platform and Oracle's (formerly Sun Microsystems's) Java, one of the world's most popular programming languages.

> **NOTE:** The term *open source* refers to software that has often been developed collaboratively by an open community of individuals, is freely available for commercial use, and comes with all of the source code so that it can be further modified if necessary. Android is open source, though Google develops it internally before releasing the source code; from that point on, it is freely available for commercial use.

It is not uncommon for an Android product to have a 1GHz processor and 1GB of fast, computer-grade DDR2 memory. This rivals desktop computers of just a few years ago and netbooks that are still currently available. You will see a further convergence of handheld operating systems and desktop operating systems as time goes on. Some examples are the Windows Mobile 7 and iPhone 4 mobile platforms.

Once it became evident that Android and open source were forces to be reckoned with, a number of major companies—including HTC, Samsung, LG Electronics, and T-Mobile—formed and joined the Open Handset Alliance (OHA). This was done in order to put some momentum behind Google's open source Android platform, and it worked.

Today, more brand manufacturers use Android as an operating system on their consumer electronic devices than any other operating system.

This development of the OHA is a major benefit to Android developers. Android allows developers to create their applications in a single environment, and support by the OHA lets developers deliver their content across dozens of major branded manufacturer's products, as well as across several different types of consumer electronic devices: smartphones, iTV sets, e-book readers, home media centers, set-top boxes, and touchscreen tablets. Exciting possibilities—to say the least.

So, Android is a seasoned operating system that has become one of the biggest players in computing today, and with Google behind it. Android uses freely available open source technologies such as Linux and Java, and standards such as XML, to provide a content and application delivery platform to developers as well as the world's largest consumer electronics manufacturers. Can you spell O-P-P-O-R-T-U-N-I-T-Y? I sure can ... it's spelled *ANDROID*.

Advantage Android: How Can Android Benefit Me?

There are simply too many benefits of the Android platform to ignore Android development.

First of all, Android is based on open source technology, which was at its inception not as refined as paid technologies from Apple and Microsoft. However, over the past two decades, open source software technology has become equally as sophisticated as conventional development technologies. This is evident in Internet 2.0, as the majority of the consumer electronics manufacturers have chosen Linux and Java over the Windows and Macintosh operating systems. Therefore, Android developers can develop not only for smartphones, but also for new and emerging consumer electronic devices that are network-compatible and thus available to connect to the Android Market. This translates into more sales onto more devices in more areas of the customer's life, and thus more incentive to develop for Android over closed and PC operating systems.

In addition to being free for commercial use, Android has one of the largest, wealthiest, and most innovative companies in modern-day computing behind it: Google. Add in the OHA, and you have more than a trillion dollars of megabrand companies behind you supporting your development efforts. It seems too good to be true, but it's a fact, if you are an Android developer (which you are about to be, in about a dozen chapters).

Finally, and most important, it's much easier to get your Android applications published than those for other platforms that are similar to Android (I won't mention any names here to protect the not so innocent). We've all heard the horror stories regarding major development companies waiting months, and sometimes years, for their apps to be approved for the app marketplace. These problems are nearly nonexistent on the open source Android platform. Publishing your app on Android Market is as easy as paying $25, uploading your *.apk* file, and specifying free or paid download.

The Scope of This Book

This book is an introduction to developing applications on Android. It's intended for absolute beginners—that is, people who have never created an application on the Android platform for a consumer electronic device. I do not assume that you know what Java is or how XML works.

What's Covered

This book covers the basic and essential elements of Android development, including the following:

- The open source tools required to develop for this platform
  - Where to get these free tools
  - How to properly install and configure the necessary tools for applications development
  - Which third-party tools are useful to use in conjunction with the Android development tools
  - Which operating systems and platforms currently support development for the Android using these tools
- The concepts and programming constructs for Java and XML, and their practical applications in creating Android applications
- How Android goes about setting up an Android application
  - How it defines the user interfaces
  - How it writes to the display screen
  - How it communicates with other Android applications
  - How it interfaces with data, resources, networks, and the Internet
  - How it alerts users to events that are taking place inside and outside the application
- How Android applications are published
- How Android applications are ultimately sold, downloaded, and updated automatically through the Android Market

Realize that Android has more than 44 Java packages that contain over 7,000 pieces of programming code functionality to allow you to do just about anything imaginable—from putting a button on the screen to synthesizing speech and accessing advanced smartphone features like the high-resolution camera, GPS, and accelerometer.

> **NOTE:** A *package* in Java is a collection of programming utilities that all have related and interconnected functionality. For example, the `java.io` package contains utilities to deal with input and output to your program, such as reading the contents of a file or saving data to a file. Later chapters describe how to organize your own code into packages.

What does this mean? It means that even the most advanced Android books cannot cover the plethora of things that the Android platform can do. In fact, most books specialize in a specific area in the Android APIs. There is plenty of complexity in each API, which ultimately, from the developer's viewpoint, translates into incredible creative power.

What's Not Covered

So, what *isn't* covered in this book? What cool, powerful capabilities do you have to look forward to in that next level book on Android programming?

On the hardware side, we will not be looking at how to control the camera, access GPS data from the smartphone, and access the accelerometer and gyroscope that allow the user to turn the phone around and have the application react to phone positioning. We will not be delving into advanced touchscreen concepts such as gestures, or accessing other hardware such as the microphone, Bluetooth, and wireless connections.

On the software side, we will not be diving into creating your own Android MySqLite Database Structure, or its new media codecs for digital video and digital audio, and its real-time 3D rendering system (called OpenGL ES). We will not be exploring speech synthesis and recognition, or the universal language support that allows developers to create applications that display characters correctly in dozens of international languages and foreign character sets. We will not be getting into advanced programming such as game development, artificial intelligence, and physics simulations. All of these topics are better suited to books that focus on these complex and detailed topical areas.

Preparing for Liftoff: SDK Tools to Download

In Chapter 3, you'll learn how to set up a complete Android development environment. We'll focus on Windows, because that's what I use to develop for Android, but the process on Mac or Linux systems is similar, and I'll make sure you can follow along if you prefer either of those systems.

Here, we'll look at where to go to download the tools you'll need, so that you are ready for action when the time comes to install and configure them. This is because each of these development tools is hundreds of megabytes in file size, and depending on your connection speed, may take anywhere from ten minutes to ten hours to download.

There are three major components of an Android development environment:

- Java
- Eclipse
- Android

In Chapter 3, when you install and configure the packages you are downloading now, you will see that Eclipse requires the Java package to be installed in order to install and run. Therefore, we will walk through downloading them in the order of installation, from Java to Eclipse to Android.

Java

Let's start with the foundation for everything we are doing, the Java Platform, Standard Edition (Java SE). Java SE contains the core Java programming language.

To download Java SE, simply go to the Java SE Downloads section of Oracle's web site, which is in the Technology Network section under the Java directory, at this URL:

`http://www.oracle.com/technetwork/java/javase/downloads/index.html`

Figure 1–1 shows the Java SE Downloads site.

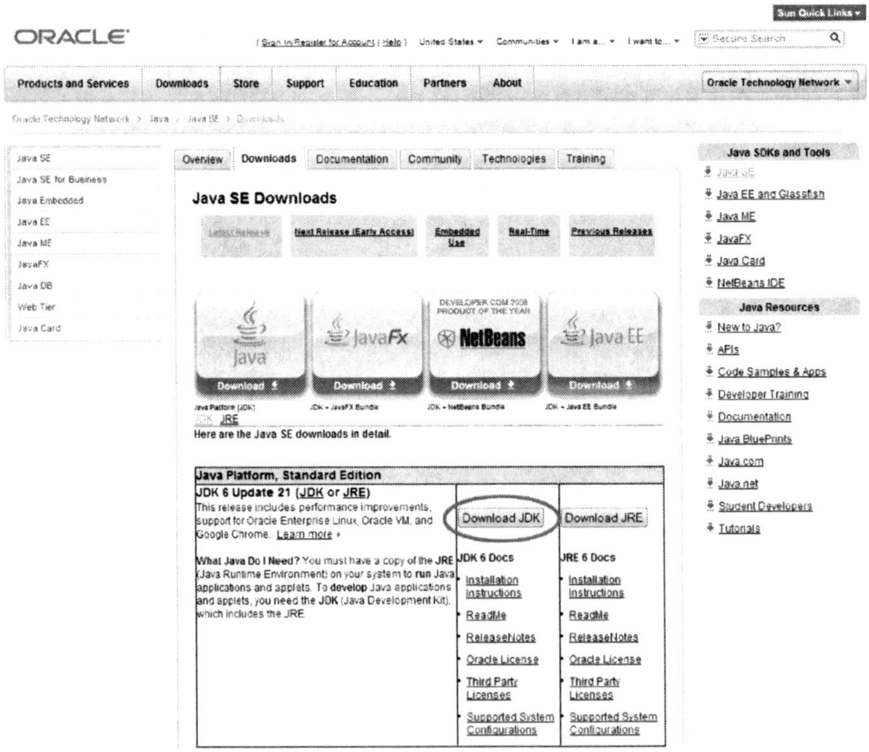

Figure 1–1. *Download the Java SE JDK.*

Click the Download JDK button to start downloading the Java SE Java Development Kit (JDK). Then choose your platform from the drop-down menu that appears, accept the license, and click the Continue button. You will be shown a link to the download that you selected. Click that link to start the download.

> **NOTE:** Make sure *not* to download Java Platform, Enterprise Edition (Java EE), JavaFX, or Java with NetBeans.

Eclipse

Eclipse is an *integrated development environment* (IDE), which is a piece of software dedicated to allowing you to more easily write programming code, and run and test that code in an integrated environment. In other words, you write all your code into its text editor, before running and testing that code using commands in Eclipse, without ever needing to switch to another program.

Currently, Android requires the Galileo version of Eclipse (*not* Helios). You should download the version of Eclipse that supports Java—Eclipse IDE for Java Developers. Go to the Eclipse web site's Downloads section at this URL:

`http://www.eclipse.org/downloads/packages/release/galileo/sr2`

Figure 1–2 shows the Galileo package you want to download.

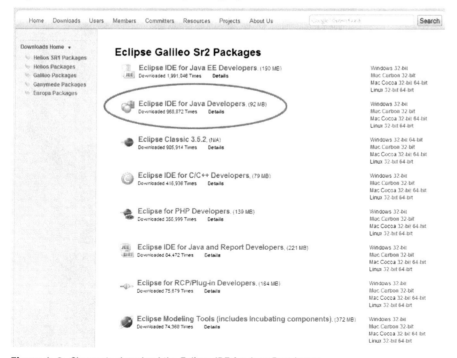

Figure 1–2. *Choose to download the Eclipse IDE for Java Developers.*

Click the link in the right-hand column that matches your system, and then choose the site from which to download.

Android SDK

The Android Software Development Kit (SDK) is a collection of files and utilities that work hand in hand with the Eclipse IDE to create an Android-specific development tool.

To dowload the Android SDK, go to the Android Developers web site, located at this URL:

```
http://developer.android.com/sdk/index.html
```

Figure 1–3 shows the Android SDK packages available. Download the latest SDK for the platform you are using.

Figure 1–3. *Download the Android SDK.*

> **NOTE:** We will walk through installing the other minor packages (shown on the left side of Figure 1–3) using Eclipse in Chapter 3. For now, you don't need to worry about anything except downloading the main SDK.

Once the Eclipse and Android SDKs are installed and configured, you can further enhance them by installing phone emulators and other add-ins, which are covered in Chapter 3. In that chapter, we will go through the detailed setup of the Eclipse IDE for Android development.

Summary

Andy Rubin's creation called Android was purchased by Google in 2005 and made freely available to developers to create mobile device applications using Java and XML. Since then, the Android phenomenon has grown to encompass an open industry alliance of the leading manufacturers and become the fastest growing mobile platform today. It is the horse to bet on for the future of not only mobile devices, but also other types of consumer electronic devices, including tablets and iTV.

What you will learn about in this book spans from how and where to get the Android development environment to how to set it up properly, how to configure it optimally, and how to use it to create applications that employ the powerful features of Android.

The three basic components you'll need for Android development are Java, Eclipse, and of course, Android. You can download these various components for free, as described in this chapter. Once the Android SDK is installed in Eclipse, that IDE becomes a comprehensive Android application development environment.

The next chapter provides an overview of what you will learn in this book, and then we'll get started with setup in Chapter 3.

Chapter 2

What's Next?
Our Road Ahead

Before getting into the details of Android development, we'll take a look at our "road ahead." This chapter provides an overview of what is covered in this book, and why it's covered in the order we will cover it.

You will see the logical progression throughout the book of how each chapter builds upon the previous ones. We'll move from setting up the IDE in Chapter 3, to learning how Android works in Chapters 4 and 5, to adding exciting visuals and user interfaces (UIs) in Chapters 6 through 8, to adding interactivity and complexity in Chapters 9 through 11. The final chapter inspires you to keep learning about the more advanced features of the Android platform.

Your Android Development IDE

In Chapter 1, you downloaded the Java SE, Eclipse, and Android SDK packages you need to build an environment for creating Android applications. In Chapter 3, you'll learn how to set up the tools you'll use throughout the rest of the book. You'll do this by creating, step by step, from scratch, the very latest Android IDE out there—right on your very own development workstation.

Note that part of this process must be done while online, so be sure to have your Internet connection active and firing on all cylinders. We'll be connecting in real time, via Google's Android Developers web site, to the latest Android application development tools, plug-ins, drivers, and documentation.

Although it might seem that the setup of Java SE, Eclipse IDE, Android's SDK, and an Android Virtual Device (an emulator that mimics the behavior of a real Android smartphone) is a topic too trivial for an entire chapter, that task is actually one of the most critical in this book. If your IDE does not work 100% perfectly, your code will not work 100% perfectly. In fact, without a robust and properly configured IDE, you may not be able to develop any code at all!

The Eclipse IDE is a sophisticated programming environment that features code highlighting, device emulation, logic tracing, debugging, and a plethora of other features. Figure 2–1 shows an example of working in Eclipse, and Figure 2–2 shows an Android Virtual Device in action.

NOTE: An Android Virtual Device is an emulator that mimics the behavior of a real Android smartphone, as shown in Figure 2–2.

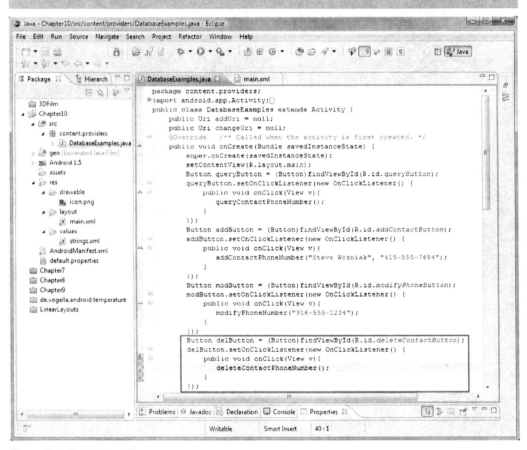

Figure 2–1. *The Eclipse IDE*

Figure 2–2. *An Android Virtual Device (AVD) in action*

In Chapter 3, you will learn how to customize the Eclipse IDE with Android plug-ins, which will morph the tool into one tailored to the particular needs of an Android developer like you. As you will see, setting up this IDE for your specific development goals is not a trivial undertaking.

Java, XML, and How Android Works

As you'll learn in Chapter 4, an Android application is "stratified." Its functionality is spelled out in Java code, XML markup, and the Android manifest in a way that is truly unique. This adds a great deal of extensibility, or development flexibility, to applications. Android makes heavy use of an XML-based markup language to define the basic components of an application, especially its visual components. Markup is not technically code, but rather consists of tags, similar to the HTML tags web developers use to format their online documents. XML is used in Android to define everything from UIs to data access, and even programmatic constructs like Java object definitions and configurations.

XML markup tags are easier for beginners to comprehend than a complex programming language like Java. For this reason, you'll use XML throughout this book whenever possible, as Google recommends. Here, you'll get a basic beginning knowledge of

Android application development, yet this will still give you the ability to make your apps look very elegant and professional. I call it getting the maximum return on your investment, and XML makes this possible.

The Android Application Framework

By the time you reach Chapter 5, you'll have built a rock-solid integrated Android software development environment and acquired a basic understanding of the components that make up an application development project (images, text, layout, buttons, code, audio, video, animation, XML, and so on).

In Chapter 5, you'll learn the unique lingo of Android application design—that is, what the various components of an Android application are called.

I'll outline how Java programming code and XML, along with any new media resources, are compiled, compressed, and bundled into Android's signature *.apk* file type (APK stands for *Android PacKage*), and how logical Android components talk to each other in an application.

The chapter also provides an overview of Android *activities*, which define the user experience on the screen, and explains how they operate. You'll learn about Android *services as well*, which run in the background, separate from the application's activities, and provide the user with advanced functions through the UI.

You'll also take an initial look at *broadcast receivers,* which alert an Android application to events of interest, such as the activation of a camera on an Android device or an incoming phone call. In fact, your app can even send out its own broadcasts, if there is some reason to let other applications know of a change in state in one of your application's data constructs.

The chapter finishes up with a look at *content providers*, which are often databases filled with information, such as a contact list, that applications may want to access to provide functionality of their own. Android ships with a number of preconfigured content providers, and you can also write your own.

Screen Layout Design

By Chapter 6, you will have a better idea of how the Android operating system works internally, and how it wants to see applications put together. You'll be ready to design graphics, UIs, and even user experiences for your applications.

You'll do all of this using screen constructs called *views* and *view groups* (grouped views) and flexible *layout* containers, which can all be nested within each other to create the UI your application needs.

Chapter 6 explains how the display screen—the way most users interact with an Android application—is handled in Android with a mixture of Java code and XML markup that controls the hierarchy of View and ViewGroup objects and Layout containers. You can also extend these classes to create your own custom View objects and Layout containers when you need a more complex design. These containers ultimately hold the other visual and UI content in your application in its proper place, and thus are the foundation of your application design. You'll want to learn these screen view and layout concepts thoroughly, as they are core to implementing everything else that Android can do.

You'll revisit XML yet again in this chapter, and learn how it allows you to define complex screen layouts and UI designs *without writing a single line of Java code*. You'll learn about the different types of layout containers, and how each can be useful in different UI design scenarios, and even code a really cool application that is written almost completely with XML.

User Interface Design

In Chapter 7, we'll start building usable UI designs, using the XML foundation of the previous chapters, via your screen layout and view control.

We'll cover the three main screen resolutions that you can design UIs for under Android and which options you have for providing high-, medium-, and low-resolution graphics to allow Android to fit your application to each major screen size. We'll also cover the creation of standardized Android icons for use in your UI designs.

Android has a large number of UI elements, such as buttons, text fields, radio buttons, check boxes, menus, alert dialogs, and all of those familiar controls that allow users to interface with application software. These items can be implemented both in Java and in XML.

In Chapter 7, we'll design and code a usable application. We'll design views, layouts, and UI elements, as well as attach their XML design elements to Java code that performs some simple functions when the UI elements are used by the application's users.

We'll look at the differences between option menus and context-sensitive menus, as well as submenus for both of these types of menu constructs. We'll also review different types of dialog boxes, such as alert dialogs, progress dialogs, and dialogs for picking dates and times.

Graphics and Animation Design

In Chapter 8, we'll start adding application media elements through images, video, and animation. These elements are key to making your application look great across all Android phones.

The Android smartphone Active-Matrix Organic Light-Emitting Diode (AMOLED) half-size video graphics array (HVGA) and wide video graphics array (WVGA) screens on current products are impressive enough these days to allow some amazing experiences to be created, so this is where it starts to get interesting as far as the visuals are concerned.

In Chapter 8, we'll explore the following:

- How to use bitmap images in Android applications
- How to animate bitmaps and vectors to create some pretty realistic effects
- The different screen sizes, and how to create icons and graphics that scale between widely varying screen resolutions
- An interesting user-controlled image-scaling technology called 9-patch
- The Android media player functionality, which allows you to control both video and audio with minimal programming logic
- How Android allows you to control images directly
- How to draw directly to the underlying canvas via Java code

Interactivity

In Chapter 9, we'll talk about adding interactivity to applications, so that they respond to user input and actually do something. You do this by handling UI *events*. We'll look at the most efficient way of handing events that are triggered by your users using the UI elements that are attached to the views and layouts defined in your XML files.

The following topics are covered:

- *Event listeners*, which execute the proper code in response to an event that is triggered when a UI element is used by the user (for instance, you can run some code when a user touches a UI element or presses a key on the keyboard)
- Default event handlers that allow you to build event handling right into your UI elements
- Touch mode and navigation via the directional keys and the trackball, and the differences between these, mainly having to do with a concept called *focus*
- How focus movement is handled in Android
- How the operation of focus in Android can be controlled via Java code
- How focus preferences can be set in your XML files

Content Providers

In Chapter 10, we'll be ready to get into the complexity of accessing data structures and Android *content providers*. These content providers allow you to access databases of system information that are available through the Android operating system, as well as your own databases of information.

Content providers are the only method Android provides for sharing data across applications, which is why they are important enough to merit their own chapter. We'll take a close look at the features of Android that allow you to query data from items common to the Android platform, such as images, video, audio, and contacts.

Additionally, you can create your own content providers or add data to one. You'll see how to create a *content resolver* so that you can interface with whatever content providers you choose (and have permissions to access).

You'll learn about how content providers expose their data via data models similar to databases, and how to use cursors to traverse the database in various ways.

Finally, we'll investigate URI objects and how to use them to identify and access data sets. Each set of data in the database will have its own Uniform Resource Identifier (URI), which is similar to an HTTP URL.

Intents and Intent Filters

In Chapter 11, we are going to tackle one of the more complex concepts in the Android environment: intents. *Intents* are asynchronous messages (members of the Intents class) that travel between Android's activities, services, and broadcast receiver components. *Asynchronous* means not synchronized; that is, messages can be sent and received independently (not in sync, but without pattern or reason) from each other.

Using intents allows you to take your current Android applications to an entirely new level of complexity. Prior to this chapter, you'll have added functionality to your application by accessing the cool functions that Android provides. But all easy things must come to an end, so they say.

Armed with intents (no pun intended), you can create advanced programming logic of your own that ties together everything you have learned in the previous chapters. This allows for far more powerful and useful programming constructs, and takes you from beginner to intermediate.

You'll learn how to spawn Intent objects that can carry highly customized messages back and forth between your Android UI (activities) and your programming logic (services) for instance, as well as to and from broadcast receiver components.

We'll also look at *intent resolution* and *intent filters*. These allow you to filter out events that your apps do not need to be concerned with, allowing you to optimize the progress of internal communications.

The Future of Android

In the final chapter, I will expose you to all of those fascinating areas within the Android development environment that we did not have the bandwidth to cover in this book. There may be a lot of unfamiliar names and acronyms in this description, but that's the nature of the future of Android.

The 3D engine inside Android is called OpenGL ES 1.2. You'll see how it allows you to create real-time rendered 3D games and applications. And I'll give you some great resources to find out more about this powerful 3D engine.

The SQLite database exists inside the Android operating system. We'll uncover the power it offers in allowing client-side databases to be created and used as content providers.

Smartphone hardware such as the high-definition camera, GPS, accelerometer, and microphone can be used to capture and digitize real-world events around us as images, audio, and gestures, and turn them into data that can be used in your applications. Computer programming has never been so powerful and innovation-oriented.

Inter-Android communication is another hot area, especially since Android devices can be used as wireless hubs, giving access to many. We will look at Android's integrated Bluetooth APIs, which allow Android applications to wirelessly connect with any Bluetooth device, and even provide for multiple connections.

We'll cover the concept of creating app *widgets*, or miniature applications that can be embedded in other applications (think: the Android home screen) and receive real-time updates (for things like clocks, radios, and weather stations).

Finally, we'll consider the popular area of locations and maps using the Android location package and Google Maps as an external data library. These tools are valuable for Android application development, due to the mobile nature of the smartphone and the fact that it has a built-in GPS.

Summary

As you can see from this chapter, this book will take you on a wild journey through the various parts and components of the Android operating environment—from UI design, to new media assets, to database access, to more complicated background services and interapplication messaging. We'll be dealing with adding some pretty cool elements to Android applications, mainly by leveraging the power of "design via XML" and some of Android's built-in features.

In the next chapter, you'll build an Eclipse-based Android IDE using the software that you downloaded at the end of Chapter 1. After that, you'll learn about how the Android development environment is modularized and how to set it up to create applications using this diverse mobile operating system.

Chapter **3**

Setting Up Your Android Development Environment

It's time to get your hands dirty. In this chapter, starting from scratch, you'll equip a computer system to develop Android applications. You'll first install Oracle's (formerly Sun's) Java SE JDK and the Java Runtime Environment, then the Eclipse IDE, and finally the Android SDK, the tool set that provides Eclipse with the tools you'll need to create Android apps. Sound convoluted? It is. After all, this is high-end software development, remember. What these are and how they relate to each other will become clear as you proceed through this chapter.

Once the installation is complete, you'll finish up by fine-tuning your Android environment within Eclipse to include smartphone emulators, which let you test your app with a representation of an Android phone on your workstation. You'll also have USB driver support, which makes it possible for you to test your applications on a real-live Android smartphone. With these tools in place, you'll be ready to rock and roll, and can begin to explore how Android does things.

Installing Java, Eclipse, and Android

If you have not downloaded the required software as described in Chapter 1, you will need to do that before proceeding, so those packages are ready to install. Here, we will walk through installing Java SE and the JRE, Eclipse 3.5 (Galileo) or 3.6 (Helios)both of which are supported by the Android SDK, the Android SDK, and the Android Development Tools. For the examples in this chapter (and book), we will install the software on a Windows system.

> **NOTE:** Versions of the Java Runtime Environment, the Eclipse IDE, the Android SDK, and the Android Eclipse plug-in are also available for Macintosh and Linux computers. The steps to install them are nearly identical to those described in this chapter, and you will have no problems following along. For more information, see
> `http://developer.android.com/guide/developing/eclipse-adt.html`.

Java SE and JRE: Your Foundation for Application Development

In Chapter 1, you downloaded the latest JDK from the Oracle web site, so the file *jdk-6u24-windows-i586.exe* (or a similarly named file) is on your desktop and ready to install.

The installation includes the Java Runtime Environment (JRE), which is the environment that allows Java programs such as Eclipse to run, or execute, under the Java runtime engine. Indeed, this is the reason it is called a *runtime*—it is the environment, or software process, that is active while a Java application is running.

Oracle has made the installation of the Java SE environment relatively painless. The installation package is itself a software program (an executable, or *.exe* file type) that will create the necessary folder structure on your hard disk drive and install all the files precisely where they need to go.

Follow these steps to install Java SE and the JRE:

1. Double-click the JDK icon on your desktop (or in whatever folder you downloaded it to) to launch the setup application. If your operating system asks if it is OK to run the installation software, tell it to go right ahead.

2. The legal agreement dialog appears, asking if you agree to the terms of use for Oracle's Java software. Read these, and then select Accept to continue with the installation.

3. The next dialog tells you which files and features will be installed and lets you turn off features that you do not wish to include. We are not going to touch anything in this dialog, so simply click Next to copy the 300MB of development files onto your hard drive, as shown in Figure 3–1.

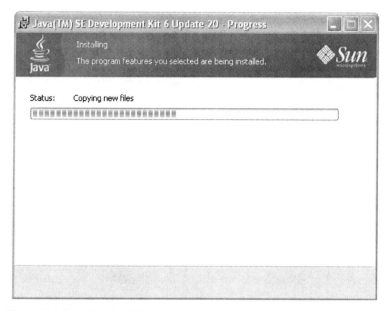

Figure 3–1. *Installing the JDK*

4. After installing the JDK files, the installer will suggest a folder for the JRE, usually in *C:/ProgramFiles/Java/jre6*. Simply hit the Next button to accept the default setting.

5. Once the JDK and JRE have finished installing, the final screen will tell of a successful installation and provide a button for you to register the product online if you are connected to the Internet. It is most likely a good idea to register JDK (as well as the Eclipse and Android SDK), so that you can receive updates regarding its development progress.

Eclipse IDE: The Development Environment

Now that you have successfully installed Java on your computer, you can install Eclipse Galileo (Version 3.5) or Helios (Version 3.6), which is the IDE you will use for your Android projects. You need to have Java installed before you install and run Eclipse because Eclipse is written in Java.

> **NOTE:** An IDE is a software package somewhat like an advanced text editor, but with features specifically fine-tuned for writing computer programs rather than publishing text documents. If you want to get up to speed on all the amazing features of the Eclipse IDE, run through the Help or Tutorials section once you have installed it.

In Chapter 1, you downloaded Eclipse from the Eclipse web site, so the Eclipse *.zip* file is on your desktop and ready to install. Eclipse is a little harder to install than Java, because it does not have an installation program (an *.exe* file in the case of Windows), but instead has a folder structure of files inside a *.zip* archive. The trick is to extract this file structure properly onto your hard drive, so that Eclipse can find the files it needs, and they are in the folders where it is going to look for them.

Follow these steps to install Eclipse:

1. Double-click the Eclipse Galileo or Helios *.zip* file to launch WinZip extractor, as shown in Figure 3–2 (notice that the Extract button is highlighted).

> **TIP:** If you don't have WinZip, a free alternative called PKZIP is available for Windows, Mac, and Linux. Simply Google "PKZIP" and download the free version for your operating system type now. Got it? Good. If you have Windows Vista or Windows 7, you can also open *.zip* files natively using the Windows Explorer application, so you don't need to download an extractor utility.

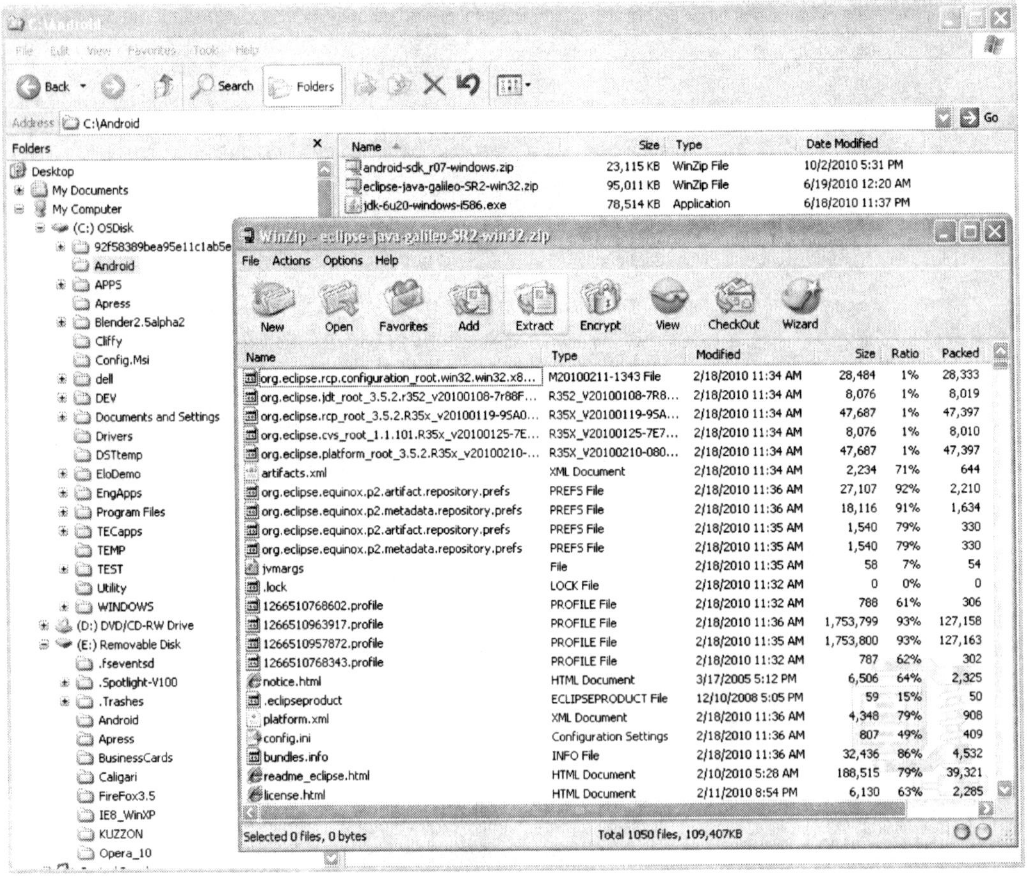

Figure 3–2. *Looking inside the Eclipse .zip file*

2. Click Extract, and make sure that the location to extract the Eclipse file structure is the root of your *C:* disk drive, as shown in Figure 3–3. This will put Eclipse into a folder structure (defined in the *.zip* file) under *c:\eclipse*, which is exactly where other software (in the case the Android SDK) is going to look for (and find) it. Note that you must leave the Use folder names check box checked for this to work properly.

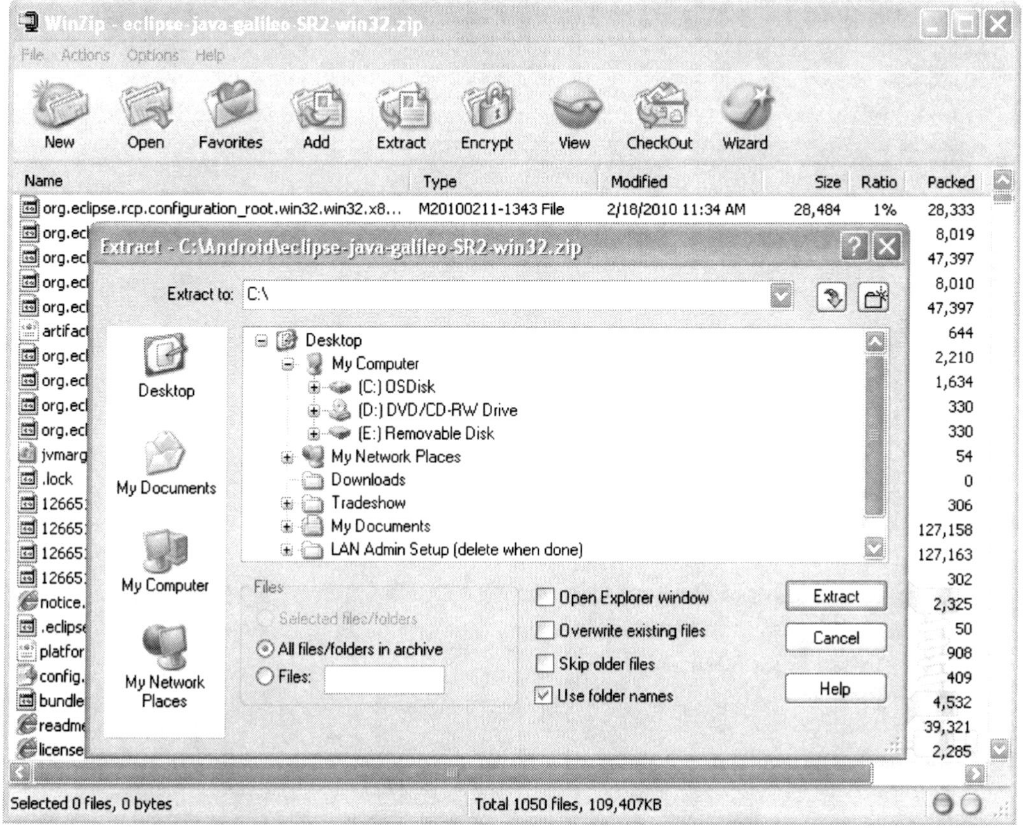

Figure 3–3. *Unzipping your Eclipse package with "Use folder names" checked*

3. Go to Windows Explorer and click the *c:\eclipse* folder to view its file structure. Look for a file called *eclipse.exe*, which is the actual Eclipse program "executable" (hence .exe) file that you'll want to use to launch the IDE.

4. Right-click the *eclipse.exe* file and select the **Create Shortcut** option, as shown in Figure 3–4.

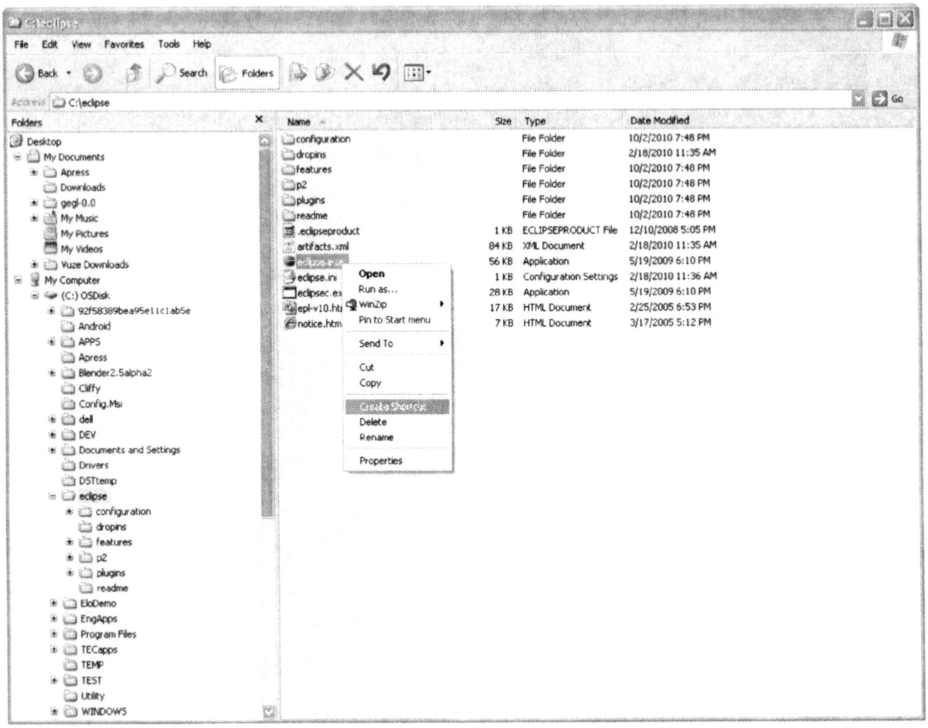

Figure 3–4. *Creating a shortcut for Eclipse*

5. Drag the *eclipse.exe* shortcut file onto your Quick Launch bar, and *voila*, you now have an icon that requires only a single-click to launch the IDE, as shown in Figure 3–5.

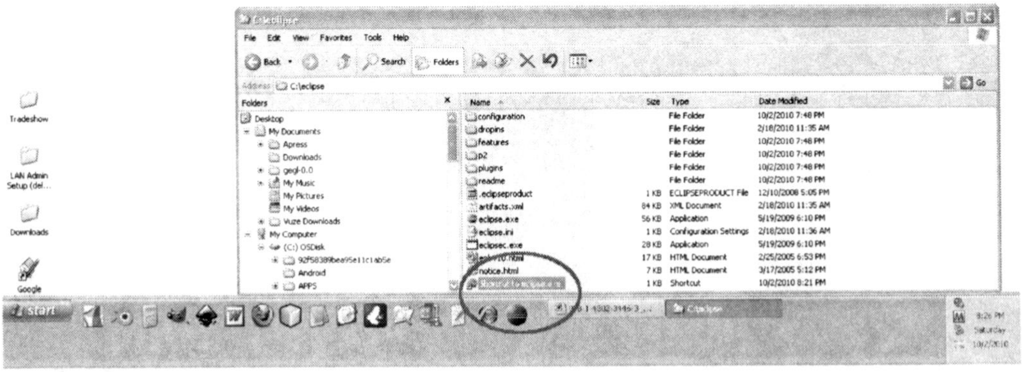

Figure 3–5. *Dragging the Eclipse shortcut onto the Quick Launch bar*

Congratulations, you now have one of the most powerful open source IDE software packages ever written, installed with Java SE, ready to launch at a moment's notice and use to develop Java software. Now, all you need to do is install Android and configure it inside Eclipse, and you'll be ready to develop Android applications *ad infinitum*. Cool beans.

Android SDK: The Android Tool Kit for Eclipse

The last major step in putting together an Android development environment is to install the latest Android SDK (currently, version 10).

In Chapter 1, you downloaded the Android SDK from the Android web site, so the file *android-sdk_r10-windows.zip* is on your desktop and ready to extract. This process is quite similar to the installation of the Eclipse IDE. As you did with Eclipse, extract the Android SDK to your *C:* root folder now, as shown in Figure 3–6.

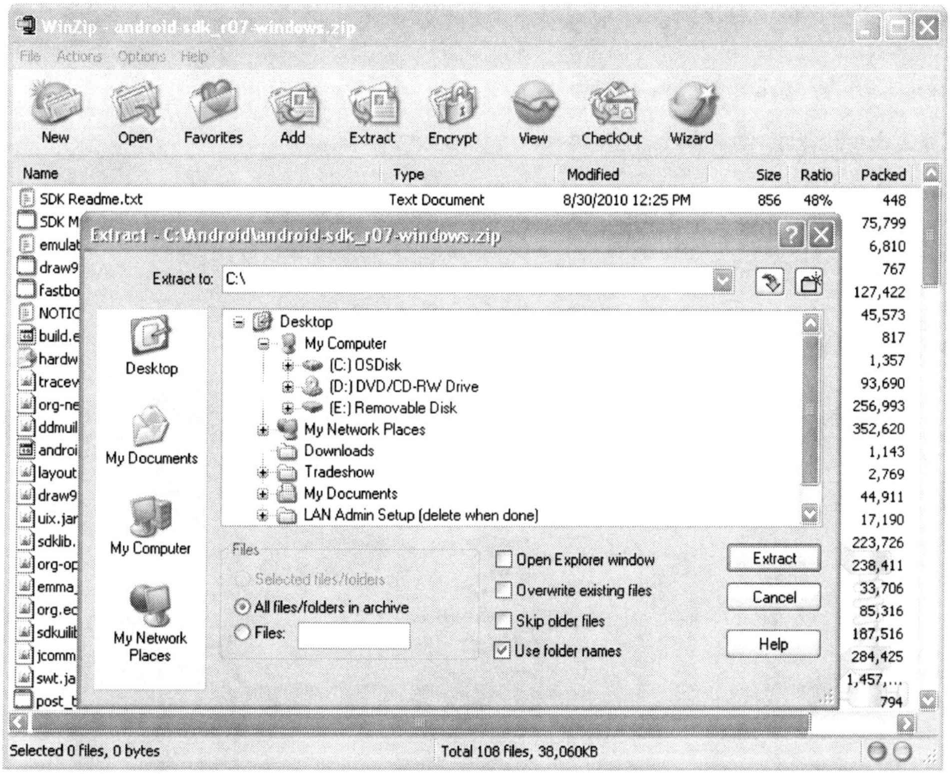

Figure 3–6. *Unzipping the Android SDK onto your hard disk drive*

Notice that the software installs into a folder called *C:\android-sdk-windows*. Because this is the folder where other software, like Eclipse, will look for the Android SDK, it is best to use the folder name Google already set for it in the *.zip* file.

The Android SDK is now installed on your system. Since it will run inside the Eclipse IDE (becomes a part of Eclipse), you don't need to create a shortcut for it—you already have one for Eclipse.

What you need to do now is show Eclipse where the Android SDK is located so that Eclipse can make the Android SDK functionality an integrated part of the Eclipse IDE. This is done by installing the Android Development Tool plug-in for Eclipse, which we will do in the next section.

Android Development Tool: Android Tools for Eclipse

It's time to fire up Eclipse and add the Android Development Tool (ADT) plug-in to the IDE.

> **NOTE:** To perform the rest of the configuration and updates described in this chapter, you need to be connected to the Internet.

Follow these steps to perform the installation:

1. Click the Eclipse Quick Launch bar icon to start Eclipse.

2. Accept the default workspace location (it will be under your *Documents* folder). If a graphic with some circular buttons comes up, select Workspace to enter the programming workspace environment.

3. From the main Eclipse menu, select **Help ➤ Install New Software...**, as shown in Figure 3–7.

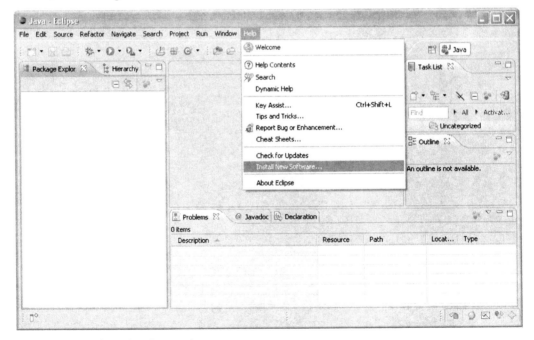

Figure 3–7. *Selecting to install new software*

4. In the Install dialog that appears, click the Add button at the upper right, as shown in Figure 3–8.

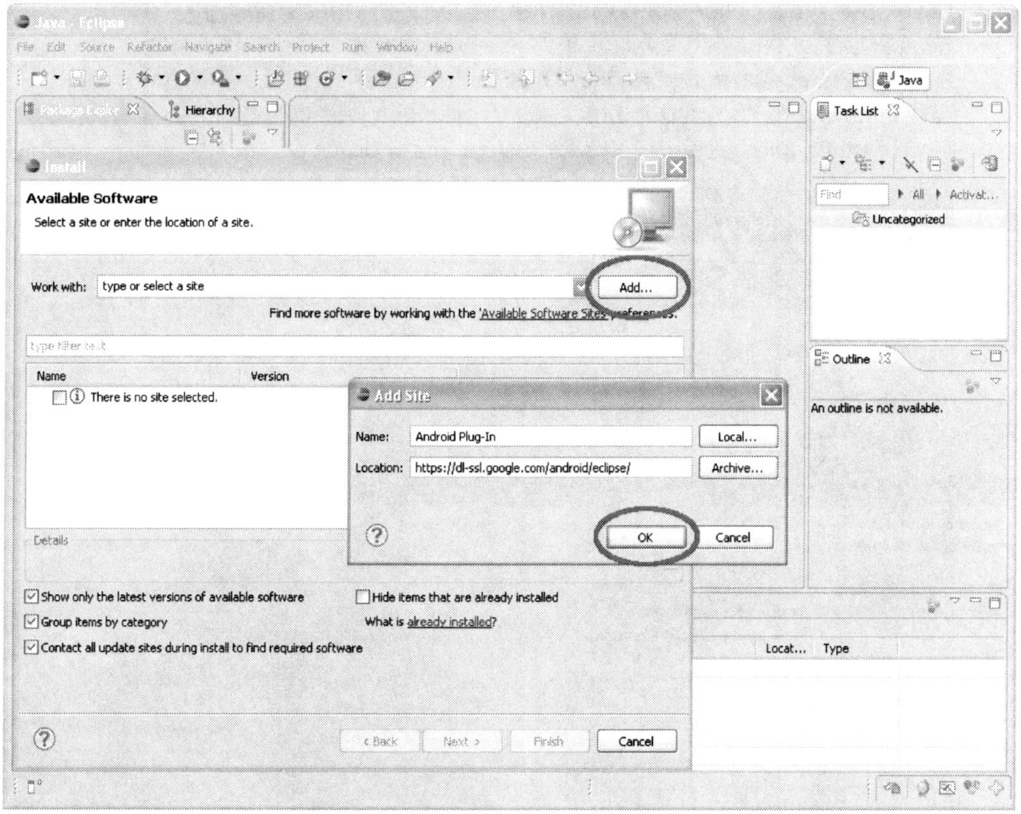

Figure 3–8. *Adding the Android plug-in site to Eclipse*

5. In the Add Site dialog that appears, enter the name **Android Plug-In** in the Name field. In the Location field, enter one of the following:

    ▪ For the secure site, `https://dl-ssl.google.com/android/eclipse/`

    ▪ For the nonsecure site, `http://dl-ssl.google.com/android/eclipse/`

    Figure 3–8 shows the secure HTTPS site selected. Click OK to add the site.

6. Once you've added the new Android plug-in option, its name appears at the top of the Install dialog, and after a few moments, a hierarchy of Developer Tools options populates the center of the Install dialog. Select the first (highest) level, called Developer Tools (which will select them all), as shown in Figure 3–9. Then click Next to continue with the ADT installation. The plug-in proceeds to calculate installation requirements and dependencies for several seconds.

NOTE: When you select Android Plug-In as the add-in, Google provides a URL, which appears next to its name in the Install dialog.

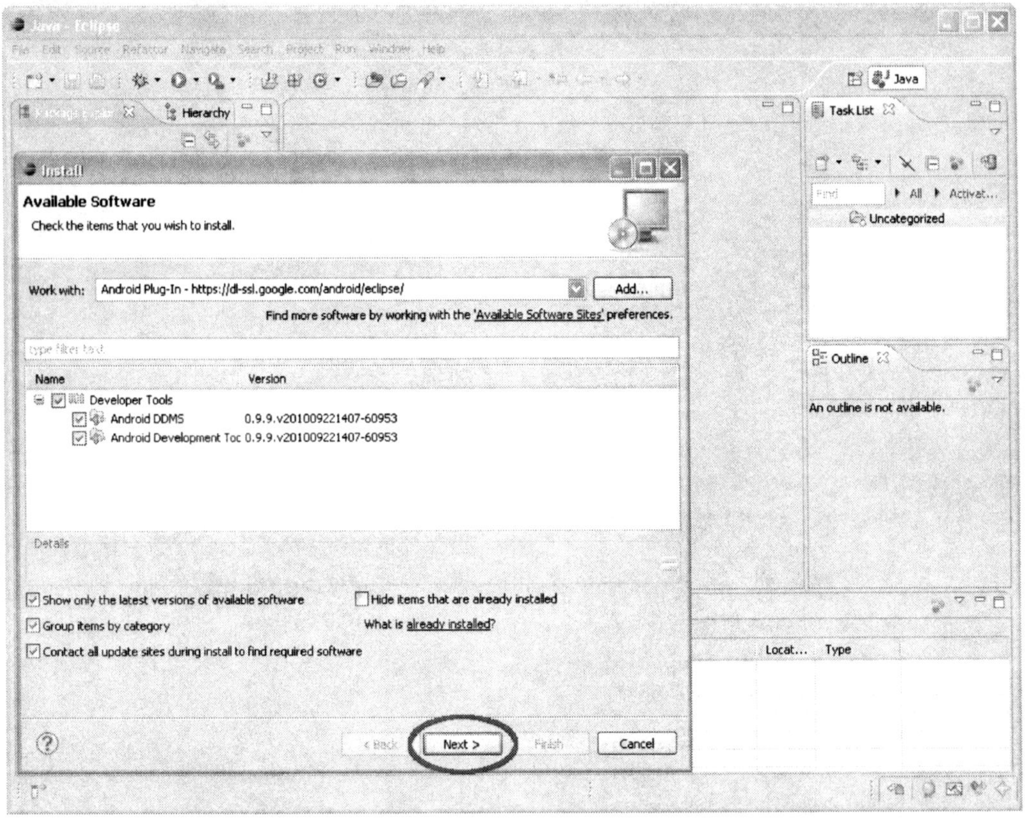

Figure 3–9. *Installing the ADT plug-in in Eclipse*

7. The next screen lists the Android Development Tools and Android Dalvik Debug Monitor Server (DDMS, which is a debugging tool). Click Next to accept these items.

8. Select the Accept Terms of License Agreement radio button, and then click Finish. The Android development environment will be installed and updated from the Google Android web site. If a message comes up that asks you to approve an unsigned certificate, click OK to continue the installation, which will leave you with a screen like the one shown in Figure 3–10.

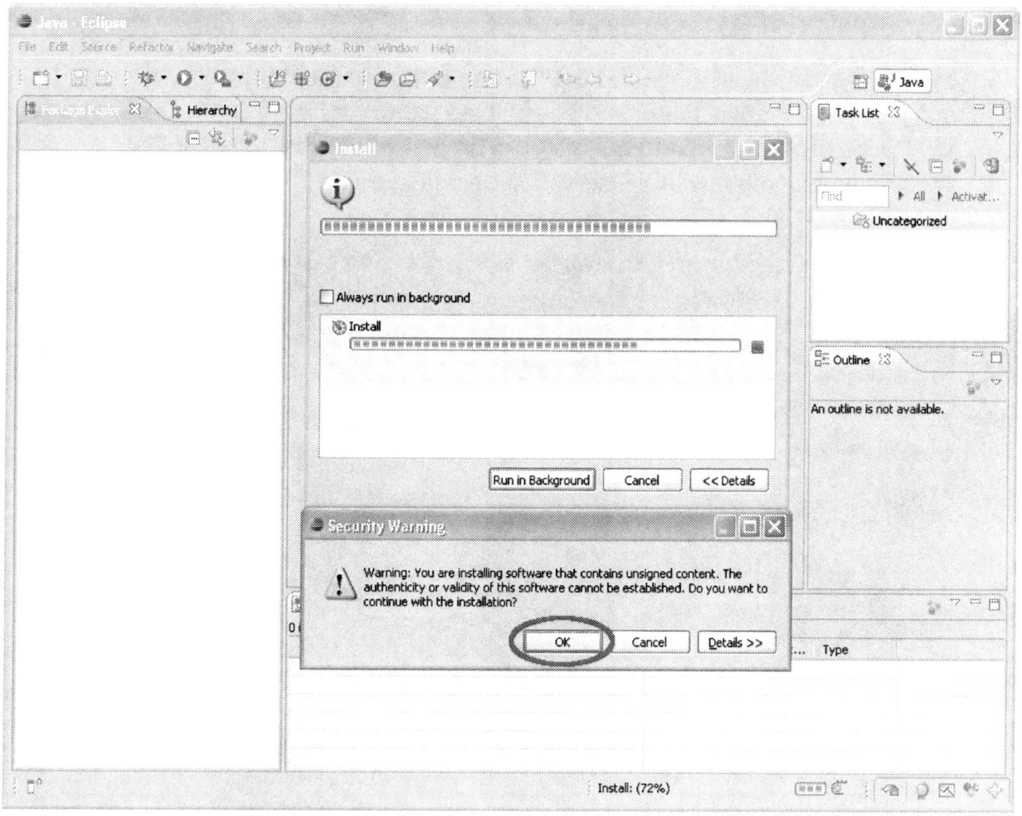

Figure 3–10. *Approving the unsigned content*

9. Select the check box next to the Eclipse Trust Certificate and select OK.

10. A dialog appears, asking you to restart Eclipse to allow the changes to be installed into memory and take effect in the IDE. Select Yes.

The Android Environment Within Eclipse

Once Eclipse restarts, the final step is to configure the ADT plug-in to point to your Android SDK installation. Follow these steps:

1. In Eclipse, select **Window ➤ Preferences**. Click the Android node on the left to select the Android Preferences option.

2. In the Preferences window, use the Browse button to locate the *android-sdk-windows* folder and select it, as shown in Figure 3–11. Click the OK button, and the Android SDK will be part of Eclipse, meaning the Android environment within Eclipse will be configured.

> **NOTE:** You do not need to restart Eclipse for the Android SDK to become a part of it, because the SDK just needs to be referenced in Eclipse in case any of the SDK tools need to be called by Eclipse.

3. Select **Help ➤ Check for Updates** to make sure you have the latest versions of everything.

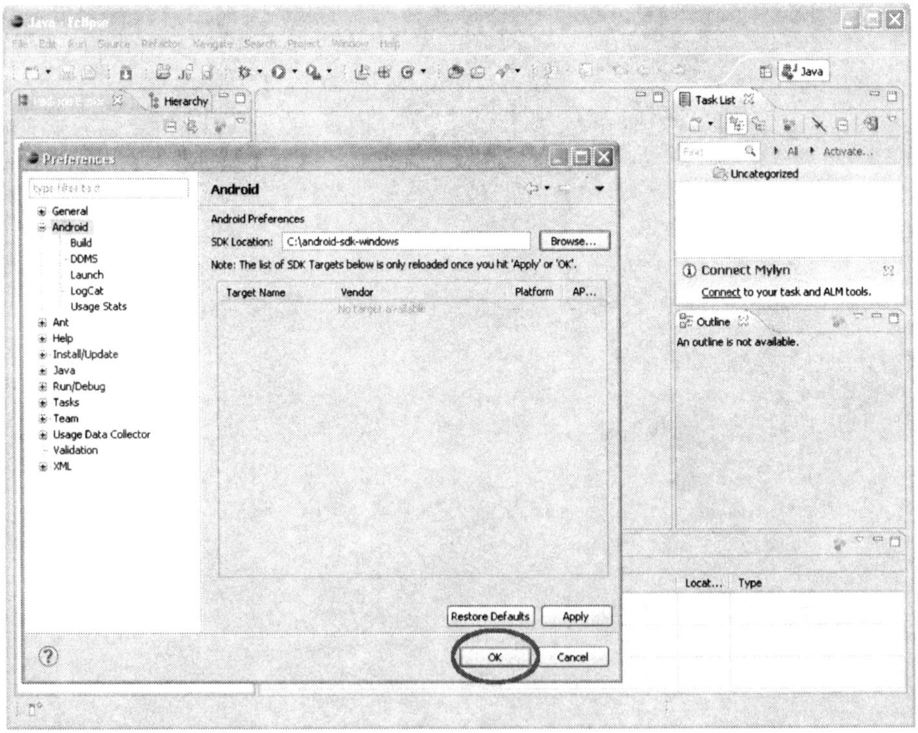

Figure 3–11. *Showing Eclipse the location of the Android IDE*

Your Android development environment is now installed. Next, you will update the software to make sure that you have the most recent releases available.

Updating the Android SDK

SDK updates often offer new elements that have been added since the SDK was originally released, so this step brings you up to the most current status, in real-time relative to today. Eclipse makes it easy to perform these updates though the Android SDK and AVD Manager window. Follow these steps to open the window and get updates:

1. Click the Android SDK and AVD Manager icon (it's the one with the cute green Android robot peeking over the edge of a down arrow, located at the top left of the Eclipse toolbar) or select **Window ➤ Android SDK and AVD Manager** from the Eclipse main menu.

2. In the Android SDK and AVD Manager window, click Available Packages to display the updated packages available to you for download, as shown in Figure 3–12.

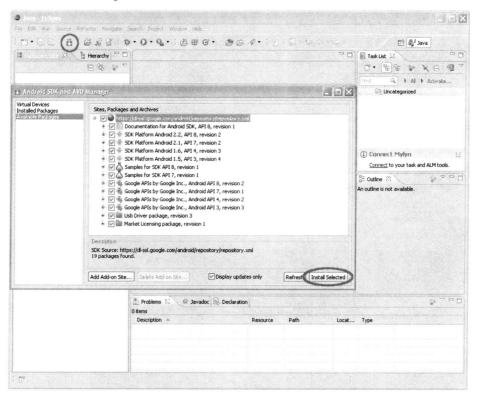

Figure 3–12. *Installing available packages via the Android SDK and AVD Manager window*

3. Click the top check box in the Sites, Packages and Archives panel. This selects all of the listed packages for installation. Then click the Install Selected button.

> **NOTE:** You are installing a whole lot of development power here. In the example shown in Figure 3–12, this includes every SDK and API from 1.5 through 3.0, as well as documentation and even the USB Driver package, revision 4, which you'll use in an upcoming section. The reason we also install the older versions of Android is that we usually want to develop our application with the earliest version of Android to obtain the most backward-compatibility and the widest user base possible.

4. On the next screen, make sure all packages, documentation, and APIs, as well as the USB drivers, are selected with a green check mark. If any of the entries have a black question mark next to them, click to select those entries, and then select the Accept radio button option (circled in Figure 3–13) to replace the black question mark with a green check mark.

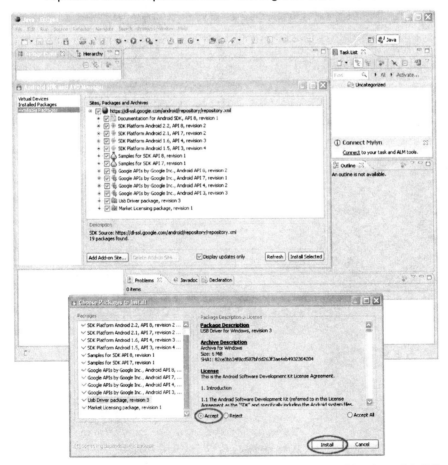

Figure 3–13. *Accepting the Android license and installing the latest Android packages into Eclipse*

5. When the all the packages are selected, click Install. The installation process may take some time, even on a fast Internet connection. My updates took about 50 minutes at 200 Kbps. Yes, this is a significant amount of data you are getting to update your Android development environment.

6. At the end of the installation, the installer may ask you if it is OK to restart the Android Debug Bridge (ADB). Reply Yes, and you are finished updating everything Android. Now when you select Installed Packages in the Android SDK and AVD Manager window, all of the packages you just installed will be listed there.

At this point, you have downloaded, configured, and updated hundreds of megabytes of Android-related development software for Java and Eclipse. You now have a finely tuned, up-to-date, open source, professional Android software development environment on your system and ready for use.

We have made significant progress at this point. Let's finish up by installing some emulators for our testing, as well as USB drivers for connecting to a physical Android handset.

Setting Up AVDs and Smartphone Connections

The Android development environment ships with AVDs, which let you run your applications on a graphical representation of an Android handset, otherwise known as an *emulator*. You'll want to install one now, before you begin to write code, so that you can test your apps.

AVDs: Smartphone Emulators

To install an AVD, you use the same Android SDK and AVD Manager window you used in the previous section. Here are the steps:

1. To open the Android SDK and AVD Manager window, click the icon located at the top left of the Eclipse toolbar (see Figure 3–12, shown earlier) or select **Window ➤ Android SDK and AVD Manager**.

2. In the Android SDK and AVD Manager window, select Virtual Devices, the first entry in the list in the left pane. Then click the New button (see Figure 3–14).

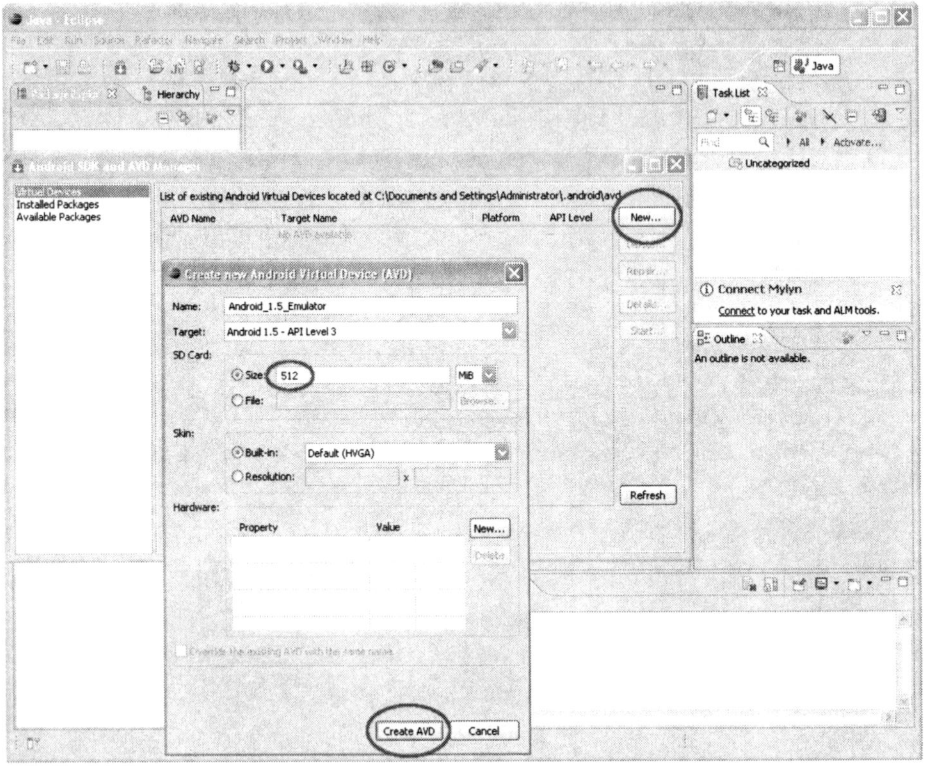

Figure 3–14. *Creating a new AVD to test Android 1.5 compatibility in an Android 1.5 emulator*

3. Fill in the Create new Android Virtual Device (AVD) dialog as follows:

▪ Enter a name for the emulator in the Name text box. I used the name `Android_1.5_Emulator`.

▪ From the Target drop-down menu, select an API. I chose the Android 1.5 API.

▪ In the SD Card section, set a memory card size for the SD card. I selected a size of 512MB (for the widest phone support).

▪ In the Skin section, choose a screen resolution for the device skin. I selected the default HVGA screen setting because my Android phone has a 320 × 480 resolution display. Most Androids out there use HVGA resolution, so by choosing this option, you'll obtain the widest phone handset compatibility.

Figure 3–14 shows the dialog I completed to create an Android 1.5 smartphone emulator. Click the Create AVD button after you've filled in the dialog.

As you can in Figure 3–15, the new virtual device is now listed in the Virtual Devices section of the Android SDK and AVD Manager window. Also note the message in the bottom console area of the IDE telling of the successful emulator creation.

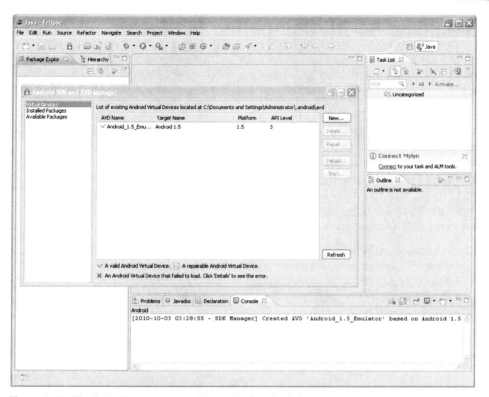

Figure 3–15. *The Android 1.5 emulator added to the list of existing AVDs*

USB Smartphone Drivers: External Devices

Since the latest USB driver for Android was installed as part of your environment upgrade in a previous section, you've already taken care of installing the most up-to-date USB drivers to interface the Eclipse IDE with your Android smartphone.

It is important to note that this driver is only for Windows. Using the external Android smartphone on Mac and Linux does not require this driver download.

The driver is not intended to make your Android phone visible to Windows. You can simply plug your Android in via USB, and it will be visible on your Windows desktop. However, the driver is necessary to have the development interface to and from Eclipse.

Note that the USB driver you installed earlier went into the ADT plug-in for Eclipse, *not* into the Windows driver registry. Possibly the term *driver* is misleading in this instance, as this driver provides the ability for Eclipse to talk with your Android smartphone during development, so that Android packages (*.apk* files) can be transferred to the smartphone for testing and development purposes.

Developing on 64-Bit Computing Platforms

Since Android development does not require a 64-bit computer like other advanced development types such as 3D and audio synthesis do, most of us are going to use a standard 32-bit operating system (possibly on a 64-bit capable computer) to run and develop with Eclipse.

The primary advantage of running a 64-bit operating system, such as Windows 7 64-bit, is that you can address more than the 3.3GB physical memory limit imposed (mathematically) by a 32-bit operating system environment. Why mathematically? Because a 32-bit system allows 3.3 billion as its largest number, and cannot count any higher, and that includes memory addressing. Fortunately, the Android Eclipse development environment does not need gigabytes of memory in order to function, so you do not need a 64-bit system or operating system to develop for Android.

If you have a computer with 6GB or 8GB of memory, you are probably running a 64-bit operating system. Therefore, you will need to download 64-bit (compatible) versions of Java and Eclipse and substitute these packages for the 32-bit versions used in the examples in this chapter. Other than the version you are installing or extracting, there should be no difference from the process described in this chapter to install and configure the Android environment. (I have Android development environments working on both 64-bit Windows 7 and 32-bit Vista systems, so I know the process works as far as JDK 6u24 and Eclipse Galileo or Helios are concerned.)

To download the 64-bit version of the Java SE JDK, go to the following URL:

```
https://cds.sun.com/is-bin/INTERSHOP.enfinity/WFS/CDS-CDS_Developer-
Site/en_US/-/USD/ViewProductDetail-Start?ProductRef=jdk-6u24-oth-JPR@CDS-
CDS_Developer
```

Click the Download button, which will take you to the downloads page shown in Figure 3–16. From the Platform drop-down menu, select Windows x64 as your operating system version, and then click Continue to download the 64-bit version of the JDK.

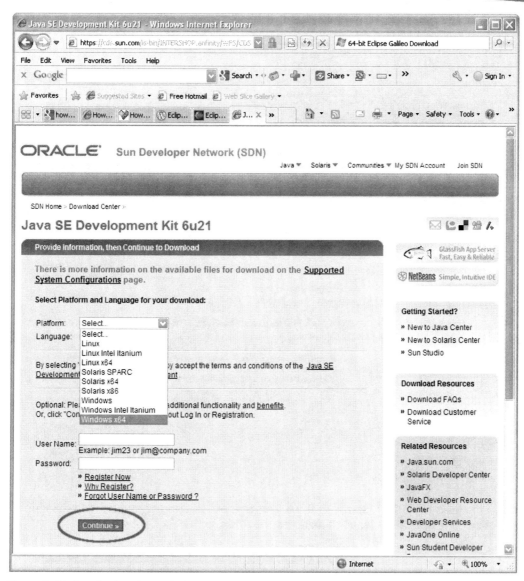

Figure 3–16. *Downloading the 64-bit JDK*

There is currently no 64-bit version of Eclipse Galileo 3.5.2—only of Galileo 3.5.1. If that's still true when you visit the Eclipse web site, you can use that version for your 64-bit Android Eclipse development environment.

The 64-bit version of Galileo SR2 Eclipse download page is at the following URL:

`http://phoenix.eclipse.org/packages/release/galileo/sr2`

Click the Windows 64-bit link, shown in Figure 3–17, to download the file *eclipse-SDK-3.5.2-win32-x86_64.zip*.

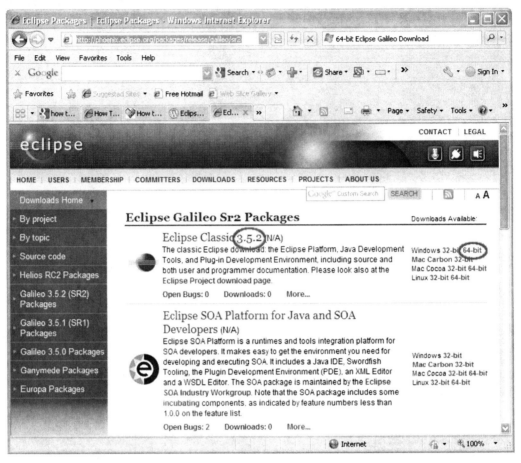

Figure 3–17. *Downloading 64-bit Eclipse Galileo*

Install the 64-bit JDK first, and then the 64-bit Eclipse IDE, and configure them exactly as outlined for the 32-bit versions as far as the Android SDK is concerned.

Whew! We're finished! Now we can get to the business of Android development!

Summary

To set up your Android development environment, you begin by installing the Oracle Java SE JDK, which is required to run both the Java programming language and the Eclipse IDE (and is proof that Java can be used to develop large-scale, enterprise-quality applications).

With the JDK installed, the next logical step is to install the Eclipse IDE, which the Android development environment uses as a "host," or platform, to support its ADT plug-in.

Your next major step is to install the Android SDK, which contains all of the tools and utilities that you need to develop Android applications. Once the SDK is installed on the hard drive, you go into Eclipse and point Eclipse to the Android SDK installation directory, so that Eclipse and Android's SDK can work seamlessly hand in hand.

After installation, you can use Eclipse to check on the Internet for the very latest versions of the Android SDK tools. You can install those you've found (which takes a while even on a fast connection). Finally, you want to add an AVD on which to test your applications.

You also can include 64-bit software addresses, on the off chance you are using a 64-bit development system. To do this, just download and install the 64-bit versions of the software.

In the next chapter, we'll examine the Android platform and its components, to prepare for writing Android applications.

Introducing the Android Software Development Platform

The Android platform is a collection of software that includes an operating system and a number of higher-level libraries that simplify the task of communicating with the operating system. It also includes several applications that smartphone users have come to expect, such as a phone (obviously), e-mail client, contact manager, Google Maps, a web browser, a calendar, and so on.

Everything in the Android development environment, as well as all of the included applications, can be programmed with a combination of Java and XML thanks to the so-called *runtime* that is included with the Android SDK. The runtime translates the Java and XML code that you write into a language that the operating system and the device understand.

The foundation on which Android is built is carefully coded and painstakingly tested Linux 2.6, an operating system that rarely crashes. Linux and its core services manage the physical phone and give Android applications access to its features: touchscreen, memory, data, security, various network receivers and transmitters, camera, and more.

Linux doesn't do it all alone. Android has a number of libraries that provide higher-level customized functions and services for 2D graphics, 3D graphics, and the audio and video file formats in widest use today. In other words, Android supports all of the media formats you could possibly want to use (for more information see http://developer.android.com/guide/appendix/media-formats.html).

This chapter introduces the Android environment and shows you how to write your first Android app.

NOTE: In this book, you'll build apps using a combination of XML and Java, which sit in a layer on top of the operating system (with the runtime as the component that translates Java and XML into instructions for the operating system). However, you could, if you wished, access the operating system and its services directly using lower-level languages such as C or C++. You might consider this approach for an application that needs the utmost speed, such as a 3D game or a real-time heart-monitoring program.

Understanding Java SE and the Dalvik Virtual Machine

The Android runtime environment provides a core set of operating system libraries that can be accessed via Java and XML. These give you access to device features and lower-level Android operating system functions so that you don't have to do any of that hard programming yourself. You simply include the appropriate components from the libraries you need in your program—something called *importing*—and then employ their capabilities. You'll learn how to put a number of these little engines to work in later chapters.

To run Java SE code, Android uses a tool called the Dalvik Virtual Machine (DVM). The DVM is an optimization mechanism and technology that allows application code and resources to be highly optimized for use in mobile and embedded environments.

The good news is that the DVM is *not* something that a developer needs to worry about. I describe it here only to give you a sense of what's going on under the hood with Android.

When you launch an Android application, it creates a process that allocates memory and CPU processing resources (processor time slices) to the application, so that it has the resources needed to function. Each time an application is launched and a process is spawned, an instance or copy of the DVM is launched into your Android smartphone's memory. The DVM actually takes the Java language instructions and application's design guidelines in an XML format, along with any external resources (images, audio files, and so on), and translates them into optimized low-level binary code that goes into the smartphone's memory and eventually into the processor for processing.

So, what is the advantage of this DVM? The use of the DVM allows many more applications to run within the somewhat limited memory resources (1GB) and processing power of consumer electronic devices, and it also protects all of the other spawned processes from each other. In this way, the crash of one application will *not* bring down the entire operating system (as happened in the olden days of DOS and Macintosh). That's huge.

The Directory Structure of an Android Project

Android does its best to externalize all application assets that do not absolutely need to be in your Java code. It does this by using the simpler XML markup language to define UI and data structures that would otherwise need to be declared and coded in Java. This modularization is aided by having a clearly defined project hierarchy folder structure, which holds logical types of application assets together in an orderly fashion.

Since Android is very particular about where the *assets* of your project are stored within the project directory, you need to learn where each belongs early in the game. When it comes time to generate your application—a process called *compilation*—Android looks into these standardized folders to locate each type of asset it needs, and expects to find like assets logically grouped together.

The assets of a project include its Java code, XML layouts, XML animation definitions, and the rich media files that your Java code and XML markup reference. As shown in Figure 4–1, default folders are created in an Android project to hold menus, images, layouts, colors, fixed data values, raw (uncompressed) media, XML constructs, and animation.

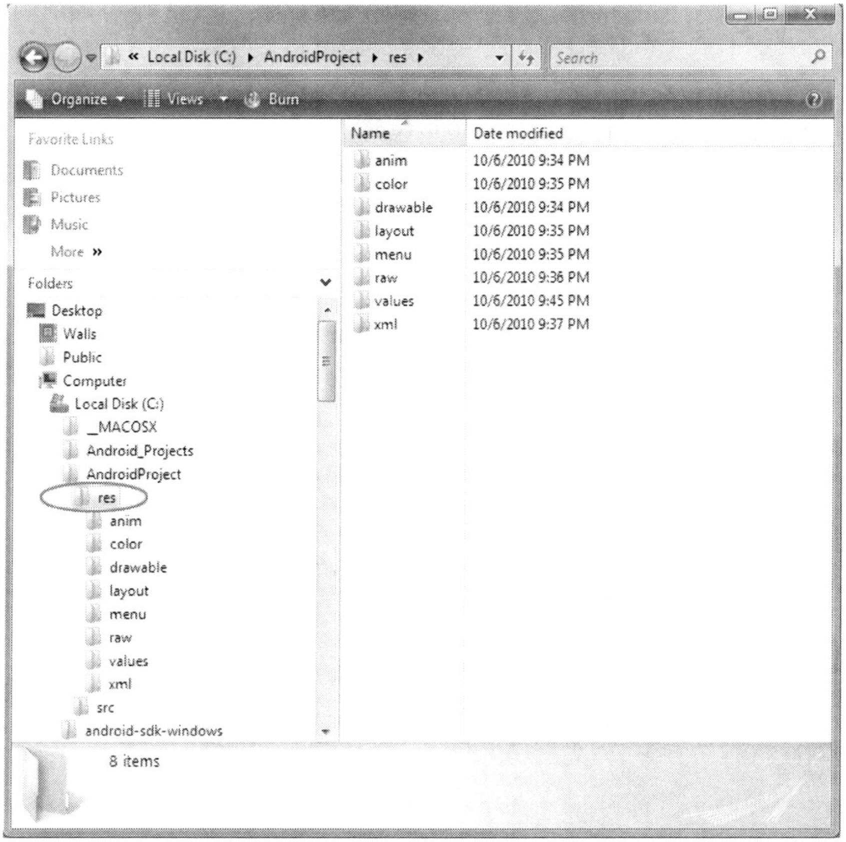

Figure 4–1. *Android's file structure, showing the res (resources) folder and its subfolders*

The Java code that drives an application is located in the /src (source code) folder and in any subfolders that are defined by your Java code.

You'll find other assets used by your application in logical subfolders of the /res (resources) folder as needed. It is very important that *only folders* go in the /res folder. If the Android compiler sees any files in this folder, it will generate a compiler error.

> **NOTE:** The name of the game is to avoid compiler errors at all costs, because if Eclipse sees compiler errors in your code, it does not even bother generating your application. And if your application is not generated, you certainly cannot test it to see how it works.

If you don't have any resources of a certain type (say animation), you do not need to have an empty folder for it. This means that you do not need to create folders that you will not use.

Common Default Resources Folders

The most common of the default resources (/res) subfolders are shown in the Figure 4–1. The following are the eight provided when you create a project in Eclipse:

- **layout**: UI screen layouts go in the /res/layout folder, which holds XML files containing UI layout definitions written in XML.

- **anim**: XML files that define animation go in the /res/anim folder.

- **drawable**: Images in PNG format (which Google prefers) or the JPEG format (acceptable but not favored by Google) go into the /res/drawable (screen-drawable imagery) folder.

- **values**: XML files that define constant values are in the res/values folder.

- **color**: XML files that specify related color values for your application's UI go in the /res/color folder. For example, if your app has complicated color bundles for different states of a button (a different color for when it is pressed, focused, or unused), they will be logically arranged in this folder.

- **xml**: XML files that define custom data constructs are in the res/xml folder.

- **menu**: XML files defining menu layouts are in the res/menu folder.

- **raw**: Video files that are precompressed go in the res/raw folder, so Android knows not to process them further.

The Values Folder

Let's examine the *res/values* folder in more detail. This is where you place predefined application values in the form of XML files that define the variable names (x or y, for instance) and their values that are later referenced in your Java code. For example, these values might be strings (collections of text characters) or constants (hard-coded values that your Java code uses in its program logic and can't change).

Think of the *values* folder as holding all of your constant values for your application in one place. This way, if you need to adjust them during application development and testing, you make the changes in a single location.

Figure 4–2 shows examples of files that can be placed in this folder:

- *colors.xml*: An XML file that will define the color values to be used in the app. These allow you to standardize the UI. For example, you would define your background color. Then, if you decide to tweak it later, you need to do the tweak in only one place.

- *dimens.xml*: An XML file that defines dimension values, such as standard heights and font sizes for your UI. You can then use these values across your app to ensure it is consistent.

- *arrays.xml*: An XML file that defines a series of values to be used together (known as an *array*). For example, this could be a list of icon files or a list of options to display to the user.

- *strings.xml*: An XML file that defines text strings to be used in the application. For example, you can place any screen titles or the app's name here and reference them in your code. If you need to change these items, you simply do it here rather than in your code.

- *styles.xml*: An XML file that defines styles to be used in the application. These styles are then applied to the UI elements that require them, so you separate the look of your app from the layout and functionality. This makes your app easier to maintain.

Notice the Android file name conventions for the different types of XML files in the *values* folder, adding another level of complexity.

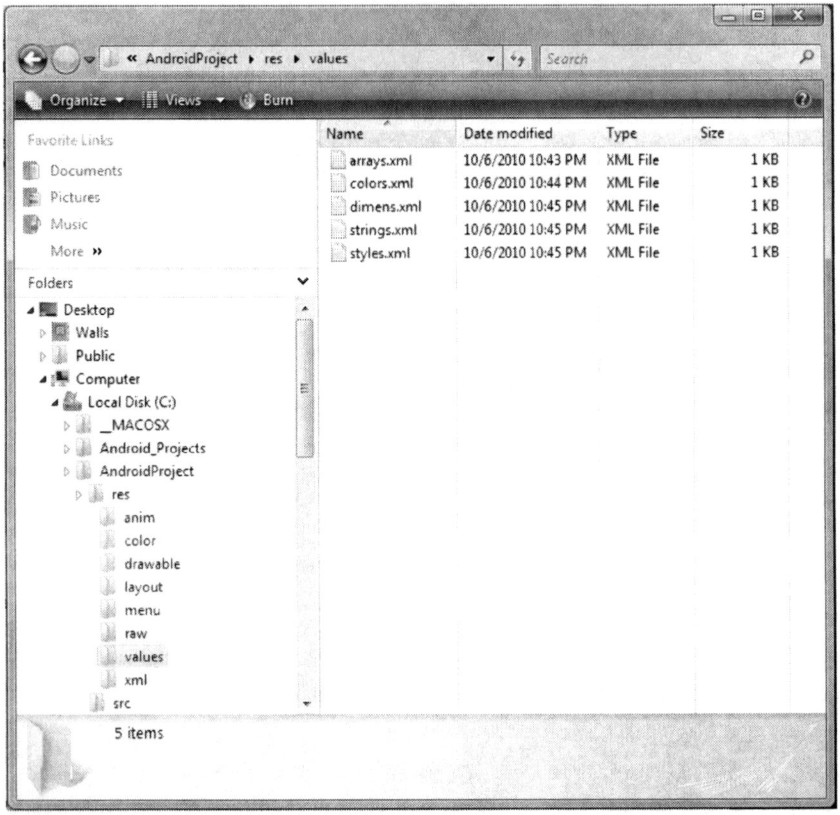

Figure 4–2. *Files in the res/values folder. These files contain constants for an Android application.*

Leveraging Android XML (Your Secret Weapon)

One of the most useful features of Android as a development environment is its use of XML to define a great number of attributes within your application's infrastructure. Because you don't need to work inside the Java programming language to handle these attributes, you save hundreds of lines of Java code. Everything within the application— from your UI layouts, to your text strings, to animation, to interprocess communication with Android's operating system services (like vibrating the phone or playing a ringtone)—can be defined via XML.

What makes XML ideal for Android development, and especially for beginners, is its ease of use. It is no more complicated than HTML markup. So, if you know how to use tags to boldface text or insert an image in your web site, you already understand how to use XML.

You will be learning how this works in the next chapters of the book. Suffice it to say that you will become familiar with XML in your Android development. XML brings one heck of a lot of flexibility to Android development.

Android's use of XML for application design is very similar to the way HTML, Cascading Style Sheets (CSS), and JavaScript are used in today's popular Internet browsers. CSS is used to separate the layout and look of a web page from its content and behavior, which are specified by HTML markup and JavaScript code, respectively. This approach leads to more modular and logically structured web pages. Designers can work on the look of a web site using CSS, while search engine optimization (SEO) professionals optimize its findability with HTML, leaving user interaction to programmers who know how to use JavaScript. The same approach applies to Android. Designers can create the UI for an application with XML, while programmers can call and access its elements using Java without affecting screen formatting, animation, or graphics. Genius.

XML gives us amazing flexibility to accommodate variations within our apps, such as different screen sizes, languages, and UI designs. Here, we'll look at a couple of brief examples to give you an idea of XML's power.

Screen Sizes

Because UI designs can be defined precisely by an XML file, it's easy to deal with the variety of screen sizes available on Android devices today. Let's say that you want to do a custom layout for each of the three primary screen sizes used in Android phones:

- Quarter VGA (QVGA), 240 × 320 pixels
- Half VGA (HVGA), 320 × 480 pixels (the "sweet spot" for most Android phones)
- Wide VGA (WVGA), 800 × 480 pixels (found on the newest phones)

How does XML provide a solution? Simply create a UI design in XML for each size and use Java to determine the screen resolution of the phone.

Desktop Clocks

As another example of how XML can be leveraged, let's take a look at a few lines of code that define an important utility: Android's popular desktop clock. (In Chapter 6, you'll learn how to create your own custom desktop clocks.)

The XML tag for an Android program function usually has the same name as its Java counterpart, so you can access the power of the programming language from simple XML. For example, here is the XML tag that corresponds to Java's `AnalogClock`:

```
<AnalogClock />
```

Android's XML tags start with a left-angle bracket (<), followed immediately (no space) by a class name, a space, a slash mark, and a right-angle bracket (/>).

To customize an `AnalogClock`, you must add *attributes* to the `AnalogClock` tag, inserting them before the closing part of the tag (/>). Suppose you want to add an ID to reference the utility from other parts of the application. Here's how:

```
<AnalogClock android:id="@+id/AnalogClock />
```

This adds an ID to your `AnalogClock` with the name `AnalogClock`, which you can use to reference it elsewhere in your application.

For each XML tag in Android, there are dozens of parameters that allow you to control the tag's appearance and implementation, including its positioning, naming (used in the Java code), and other options.

In real-life, for readability, programmers usually write this code with each configuration parameter indented on a separate line, like this:

```
<AnalogClock
        android:id="@+id/AnalogClock
        android:layout_width="fill_parent"
        android:layout_height="wrap_content"
/>
```

The Android compiler considers everything inside the `AnalogClock` tag to be a parameter, or a customization option, until it reaches a closing tag (`/>`). The `fill_parent` parameter stretches content to fill a container, and the `wrap_content` parameter tiles the content. We'll cover these and other view and layout concepts in Chapter 6.

Using Your Android Application Resources

In addition to Java code and XML markup, the resources your application draws on consist primarily of media elements and other file types that contribute to its functionality in one way or another. These may include XML files that contain animation parameters or text strings, bitmap image files, and even audio and video streams.

One of the primary reasons for externalizing resources is that you can have sets of resources for variations, such as different screen sizes or language versions. *Language localization* localizes the application to any given country. These language localizations can be easily referenced in the Java code and switched when necessary by pointing to different external file names or folders.

Bitmap Images

Let's look at an example of a common application resource: the bitmap image. Your PNG or JPEG bitmap image goes into the */res/drawable* folder. It can then be referenced by its file name only (*excluding* its extension) in the Java code as well as in the XML. For this reason, be sure not to give a PNG file and a JPG file the same name.

Also, contrary to normal file-naming conventions, image file names can contain only numbers and lowercase letters, so make sure to remember this rule (one of the many anomalies of Android programming).

In summary, to set up bitmap images to be used in your application, do the following:

- Name them correctly.
- Use PNG or JPG format.
- Make sure they are in the */res/drawable* folder so that Android can find them.

Alternate Resource Folders

Another great example of resource usage is supplying different UI screen layouts for portrait and landscape orientations. Usually, we will set our default screen UI for phones to portrait mode, as most people use their phone in this way (turning it sideways only to view video).

Android provides support for alternate resources. If you set these up correctly, Android will determine the current settings and use the correct resource configurations automatically. In other words, you provide resources for each orientation, and Android uses the correct resources as the user changes from one orientation to another.

Each set of alternative resources is in its own folder, where it can be referenced and located later on in your Java code. We can provide resources for different screen orientations and resolutions in this fashion, and have Android decide which folders to look in for our application resources based on each user's smartphone model.

Android offers three screen resolutions: low resolution (320 × 240), medium resolution (320 × 480), and high resolution (800 × 480).

To add an alternate resource folder, create a directory under */res* with the form *<resource_name>-<config_qualifier>*. For instance, create */res/drawable-hdpi*.

This creates an alternate resource folder for high-density dots per inch (hdpi) images. The alternate folder will be used automatically if the Android smartphone screen uses a WVGA (800 × 480) screen high-end model. Otherwise, it will use the normal HVGA (320 × 480) screen images, located in the default */res/drawable* folder.

If you want to also support low-end screens, you can use the low-density dots per inch qualifier, ldpi. There is a medium dots per inch qualifier, mdpi, as well.

So, to have images for QVGA, HVGA, and WVGA screens arranged in folders in a way that allows Android to automatically recognize the folder hierarchy, set up your folder structure as follows:

- */res*, with only folders
- */res/drawable-ldpi*, with the following low-density DPI screen images (QVGA):
    - *icon.png* (application icon file), 32 × 32 pixels
    - *background.png* (application background), 320 × 240 pixels
- */res/drawable-mdpi*, with the following medium-density DPI screen images (HVGA):
    - *icon.png*, 48 × 48 pixels
    - *background.png*, 320 × 480 pixels
- */res/drawable-hdpi*, with the following high-density DPI screen images (WVGA):

- *icon.png*, 72 × 72 pixels

- *background.png*, 800 × 480 pixels

You're well on your way to correctly setting up your Android application's resources. One more file we need to examine is *AndroidManifest.xml*.

Launching Your Application: The AndroidManifest.xml File

When Android launches your application, the first file it seeks out is the application *manifest* file. This file is *always* located in the root of your project folder and directory structure, and is *always* called *AndroidManifest.xml* so that it can be located easily on startup.

The Android manifest declares some very high-level definitions and settings for your application using (surprise!) the XML markup language. The following are some of the key items *AndroidManifest.xml* includes:

- References to the Java code you will write for your application, so that your code can be found and run

- Definitions of the components of your Android application, including when they can be launched

- Definitions of permissions for application security and for talking with other Android applications

- Declaration of the a minimum level of Android operating system version support, which amounts to defining which version(s) of Android your application is going to support

All of the apps that we will write in this book will support Android versions 1.5, 1.6, 2.0, 2.1, 2.2, 2.3, and 3.0. We call this "Android 1.5 compatibility," because it supports every version of Android all the way back to version 1.5.

> **TIP:** I try to develop for the 1.5 API level 3 so that my applications run on API versions 1.5, 1.6, 2.0, 2.1, 2.2, 2.3, and 3.0. Later versions are obviously backward-compatible, so the further back you develop your minimum version level support, the more people will be able to use your application. If you want to make money selling Android apps, this concept translates directly into dollars, as there are millions of 1.5 and 1.6 phones still out there.

Creating Your First Android Application

By now, you're probably aching to fire up Eclipse and create an application to see how all this works. A tradition in all programming languages for new users is the crafting of the "Hello World" application, so let's create our own Hello World application right here and now.

First, we'll launch Eclipse and create the application. Then we'll take a look at the files and Java and XML code that Eclipse generates to get your app up and running. Finally, we'll give the app an icon to display on the Android main menu.

Launching Eclipse

The first step is to launch Eclipse. From there, you'll create a project to house the application.

To launch Eclipse, find and click the Eclipse shortcut launch icon on your workstation. If a security warning dialog like the one shown in Figure 4–3 appears, click Run. If you don't want to see this dialog every time you start Eclipse, uncheck the box that reads "Always ask before opening this file."

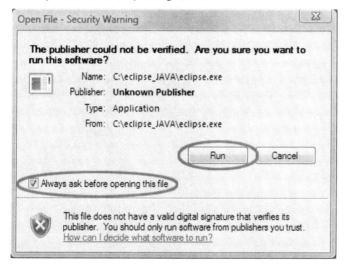

Figure 4–3. *The Windows Security Warning dialog*

Next you will see the Eclipse startup screen. Then, in a few more seconds, a dialog will appear, allowing you to tell Eclipse where your projects folder is kept on your hard disk drive. Mine is kept on my *C:* drive and is called *\Projects,* so the entry is *C:\Projects*, as shown in Figure 4–4. If you don't want to specify this each time you start Eclipse, you can check the "Use this as the default and do not ask again" option. Once you click the OK button, Eclipse will start, and the IDE will appear.

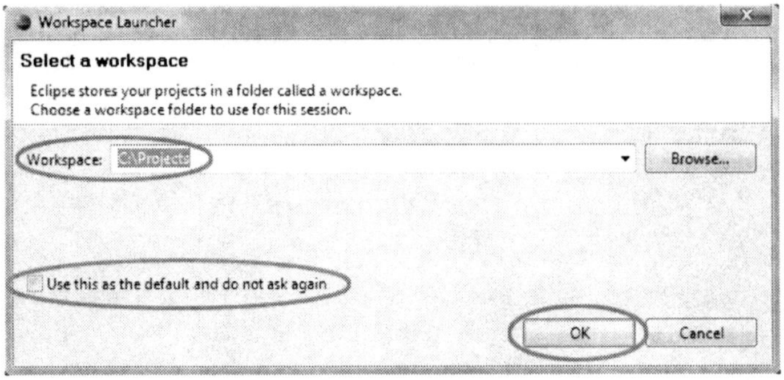

Figure 4–4. *The Eclipse Workspace Launcher dialog*

Creating an Android Project

Once the IDE has launched, select File ➤ New ➤ Project in the Eclipse main menu to create a new project. In the New Project dialog, select Android Project from the list of wizards to tell Eclipse the type of project you wish to create, as shown in Figure 4–5. Click the Next button to continue.

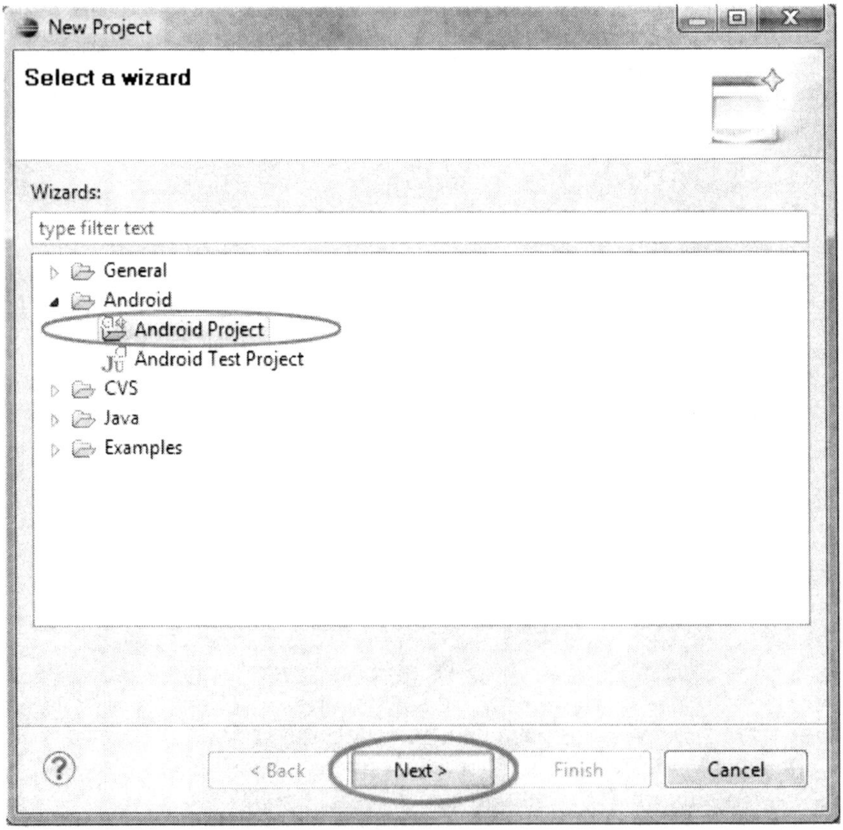

Figure 4–5. *The Eclipse New Project dialog*

You'll see the New Android Project dialog, which allows you to specify all sorts of important variables for your applications. Let's address them one by one.

- **Project name**: This is the name of the folder in your *C:/Projects* folder that holds your Hello World application folders and files. Let's give this folder the same name as our application: *HelloWorldAndroid*.

CAUTION: We have omitted spaces from the folder name because spaces are not supported in Java names. It is not advisable to use spaces in names of folders that you use for software development.

- **Create new project in workspace**: We'll keep this radio button selected so that Eclipse will create the new project within its IDE working area for us automatically.

- **Use default location**: You can see what folder structure Eclipse will use for your project folder by keeping this option checked.

- **Build Target**: This panel allows you to specify the versions of Android your application will support. The more you support, the more users will be able to use your application, so let's use a build target of Android 1.5. That version has everything that we will need to build most applications that work across all current Android smartphones. You do not need to select the Google APIs for 1.5—just pick the 1.5 Android open source package, which includes everything.

- **Application name**: The Properties section lets you specify where you want Eclipse to set up the framework for your application, which is where some of the basic Java and XML code will be written by the IDE to get you started (a really a nice feature of Eclipse). The first field in this section is for the application name, which is the name that will appear in the application's title bar when it runs. Let's set that name to **Hello Great Big Android World Out There!**

- **Package name**: This is the name you want to use for your Java *package*. For now, we will simply define this as the name of the container that will hold all of the Java code our application uses. Let's name this package Hello.World. (Java package names are separated by periods, much like file pathnames are separated by forward slashes).

- **Create Activity**: Leave this box selected and let's name our Java activity class MyHelloWorld. A Java *activity class* is a collection of code that controls your UI (you will learn more about activities in the next chapter).

- **Min SDK Version**: Set this value to **3**. This matches up with your Android 1.5 build target selection, since version 1.5 of Android uses the level 3 SDK.

Figure 4–6 shows the completed New Android Project dialog for this example. When you are finished filling it out, click the Finish button. Eclipse will create your first Android project for you.

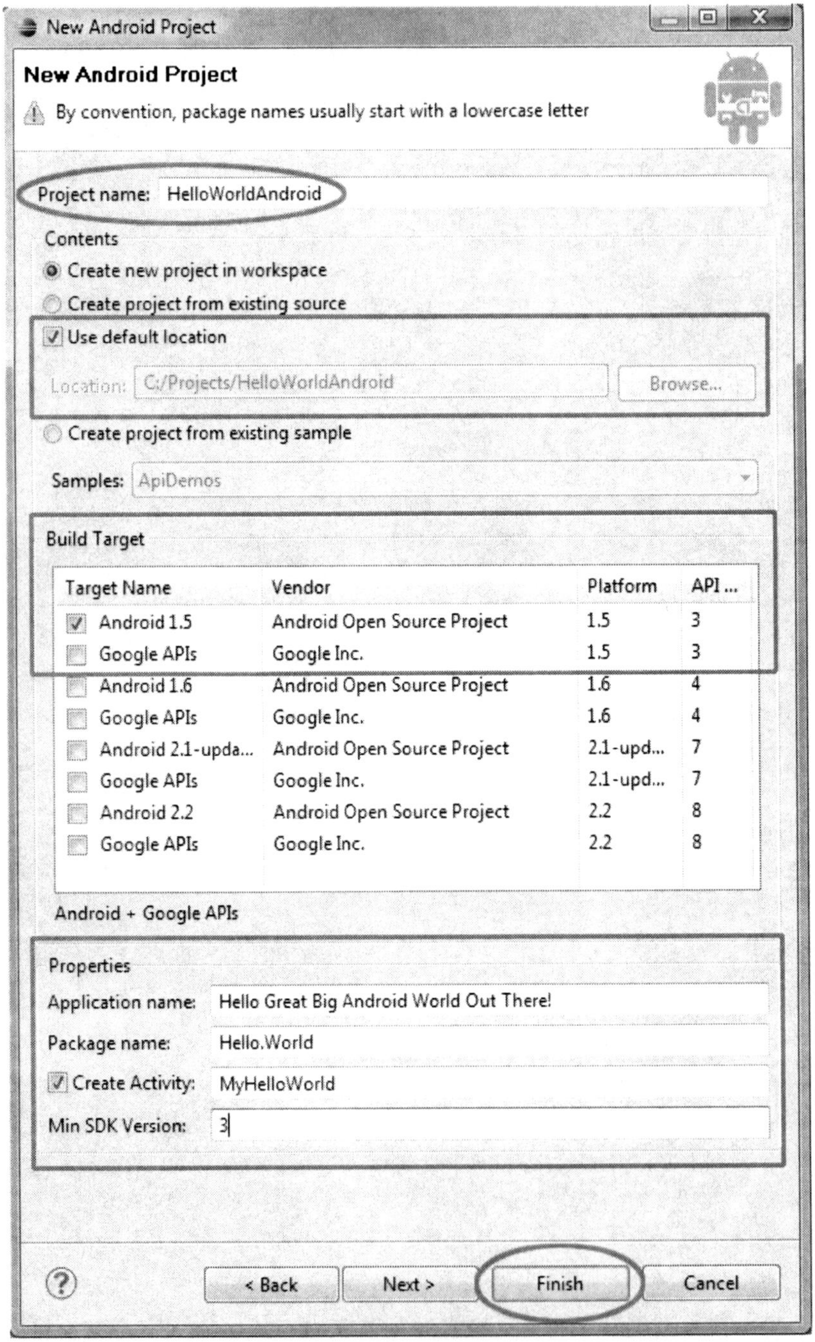

Figure 4–6. *The New Android Project dialog for your first Android app*

Inspecting and Editing the Application Files

After you click Finish in the New Android Project dialog, you are returned to Eclipse. In the IDE, you can navigate through the project using the Package Explorer pane.

Let's look at the folder hierarchy that Eclipse has automatically created for our project. Click the arrow icons next to the *HelloWorldAndroid* folder, and then click the arrow icons next to the *src* and *res* folders under it.

Going further, click the open folder arrows next to the *Hello.World*, *drawable*, *layout*, and *values* folders, so you can see the Java and XML files that Eclipse has so kindly created for us. Figure 4–7 shows the Package Explorer pane at this point.

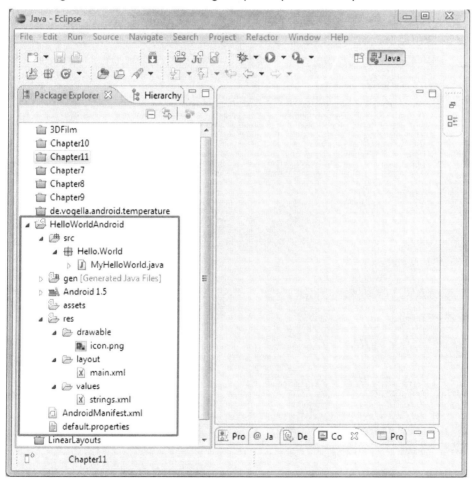

Figure 4–7. *The Eclipse Package Explorer pane*

Now let's open some of these files and see just how much coding Eclipse has done for this project.

To open any of the files listed in the Package Explorer, select the file by clicking once on it (the icon will turn blue), and then press F3. Alternatively, right-click the file name to get a context-sensitive menu, and then select the **Open** option.

Opening the MyHelloWorld Activity

The *MyHelloWorld.java* file holds our activity class. Right-click it and select **Open** to explore it now. As shown in Figure 4–8, Eclipse has already written the code to create a UI screen for the application and set its content to the UI defined in the *main.xml* file (with the R.layout.main text), which we will look at next.

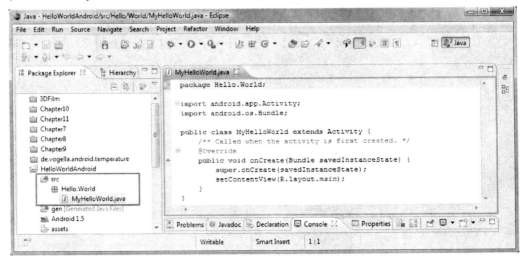

Figure 4–8. *Our MyHelloWorld activity*

Let's examine this in a little more detail:

```
package Hello.World;

import android.app.Activity;
import android.os.Bundle;

public class MyHelloWorld extends Activity {
    /** Called when the activity is first created. */
    @Override
    public void onCreate(Bundle savedInstanceState) {
        super.onCreate(savedInstanceState);
        setContentView(R.layout.main);
    }
}
```

As you can see, Eclipse used the information in our New Android Project dialog to create a usable Java file, which includes a Hello.World package declaration, import statements, a MyHelloWorld activity class, and an onCreate() method.

Opening the UI Definition

Next, let's take a look at our UI interface markup code in the *main.xml* file in the *layout* folder, as shown in Figure 4–9. The XML code in the *main.xml* file is quite a bit different from the Java code.

```xml
<?xml version="1.0" encoding="utf-8"?>
<LinearLayout xmlns:android="http://schemas.android.com/apk/res/android"
    android:orientation="vertical"
    android:layout_width="fill_parent"
    android:layout_height="fill_parent"
    >
<TextView
    android:layout_width="fill_parent"
    android:layout_height="wrap_content"
    android:text="@string/hello"
    />
</LinearLayout>
```

It uses tags like those in HTML to define structures that you will be using in your applications. In this case, it is a UI structure that contains a LinearLayout tag, which keeps our UI elements in a straight line, and a TextView tag, which allows us to put our text message on the application screen.

> **NOTE:** If you don't see something like Figure 4–9, to view the file, click its icon in the *layout* folder, select **Open**, and then choose *main.xml* at the bottom of the window.

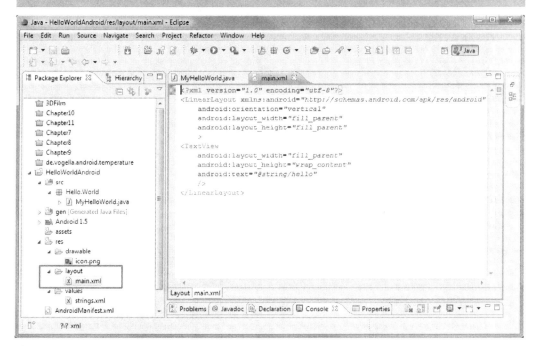

Figure 4–9. *The XML UI layout for our activity*

Notice that the TextView tag uses an attribute called android:text, which is set equal to @string/hello. This is a reference to the *strings.xml* file, which we are going to look at next.

Opening the Strings Resource File

So far, we have looked at the Java code, which points to the *main.xml* file, which in turn points to the *strings.xml* file. Open that file now (right-click the file's icon in the Package Explorer and select **Open**). The file will open in a third tab within the Eclipse IDE, as shown in Figure 4–10.

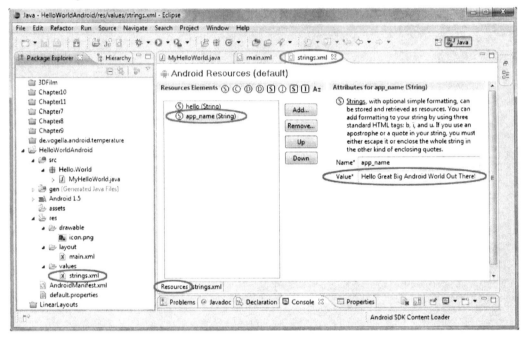

Figure 4–10. *The strings.xml file when it first opens*

When you open the *strings.xml* file, you will see that Eclipse has already added two variables: hello and app_name. The string variable named hello is to hold the text that we want our application to display. The app_name variable is to hold the string data that will appear in the title bar at the top of the application. We already specified it in the New Android Project dialog as Hello Great Big Android World Out There!.

Notice the tabs at the bottom of the editing pane labeled Resources and strings.xml. These tabs allow you to switch between the actual XML code and the more user-friendly interface that you see in Figure 4–10, which makes editing Android resources a bit easier than coding straight XML.

Since the app_name value is already specified thanks to our New Android Project dialog, let's leave it alone and set the value of hello.

Setting a Variable Value in strings.xml

To set the value of hello, all you need to do is to click its name in the left pane of the Resources view and edit its text. Once you click hello, two fields will appear. One contains the string variable name (hello), and the other has its value. In the Value field, type **Hello Android World, Here I Come!**, as shown in Figure 4–11.

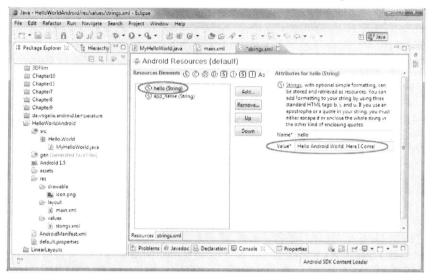

Figure 4–11. *Editing the value of hello*

Once you have entered a string for the hello variable, click the strings.xml tab at the bottom of the editing pane and take a look at the XML code that Eclipse has generated, as shown in Figure 4–12.

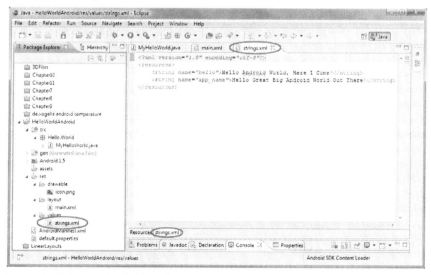

Figure 4–12. *The updated XML code*

In this view, you can see the actual XML code for the string tags, which are nested inside the <resources> tags that allow us to define resources for our Android application.

```
<?xml version="1.0" encoding="utf-8"?>
<resources>
    <string name="hello">Hello Android World, Here I Come!</string>
    <string name="app_name">Hello Great Big Android World Out There!</string>
</resources>
```

Each <string> tag has a variable name attribute so we can refer to it by name in our Java code. Tags are ended by the same tag that started them with the addition of a forward slash, like this: *<string>XXX</string>*.

As you can see in the XML code, Eclipse has created the correct XML code for us to use to write our Hello World message to the smartphone screen. The code reads as follows:

```
<string name="hello">Hello Android World, Here I Come!</string>
```

Now it's time to compile and run the application.

Running the App

To compile and run the application, right-click the *HelloWorldAndroid* folder icon in the Eclipse Package Explorer and select **Run As ➤ Android Application**.

Eclipse will compile your app, and then open a version 1.5 emulator window to display a virtual phone on which to run it. When the emulator first starts up, it will display the standard smartphone screen, simulating a background image and standard Android icons for system time, signal strength, and so on.

To actually run the app in the emulator, you need to click the Menu button in the middle-bottom area of the screen, or use the Home button to display your application icons and then select an icon to run. So, your application will not just run in the emulator automatically. You must use the phone interface, finding and running the app as you would in real life. Give it a shot now. Figure 4–13 shows Hello World running in the emulator.

Figure 4–13. *Running Hello World in the emulator*

Congratulations, you have created your first application. Next, we'll customize its Android icon.

Adding an Application Icon

The final thing that we are going to do in this chapter is give our application an icon that will show up on users' Android devices and can be used by them to launch the application. We'll use what you have learned about defining alternate resources by creating an icon that works on small, medium, and large screens. We'll add the appropriate icon files into the correct alternate folders so that Android automatically finds and uses the correct icon for each type of Android screen:

- */res/drawable-ldpi* for small screens (*/res/drawable-small* is another option that is based more on size than density)

- */res/drawable-mdpi* for medium screens (or */res/drawable-normal*)

- */res/drawable-hdpi* for large screens (or */res/drawable-large*)

Not surprisingly, this is done by giving your icon an exact name and file format, and putting it into an exact directory. When Android finds an icon file there, it automatically puts it into play as your application's icon. The file must follow these rules:

- Be placed in the correct /res/drawable-dpi folder, which holds all of the drawable resources for that screen resolution

- Be named icon.png

- Be a 24–bit PNG file with an alpha channel (transparency), so that the icon overlays any system background wallpaper seamlessly

Here, I'll use my 3D company logo, but you can use any image you like. Also, I use Photoshop for this type of image editing, but you can use any image-editing program you prefer.

Adding Transparency

The first thing we need to do is to put the logo onto a transparency. Here are the steps to remove the white background from the logo (illustrated in Figure 4–14):

1. Open the logo file. It is 200 × 200 pixels.

2. Select the Magic Wand tool (in the toolbar) and set the tolerance at 12 (top toolbar). Click the white areas to select them.

3. Choose **Invert the Selection** to grab only the logo and select **Edit ➤ Copy** to copy this image data to the clipboard.

4. Create a new file of 200 × 200 pixels and paste the logo pixels on top of the transparency.

5. Save the file as Mylcon.

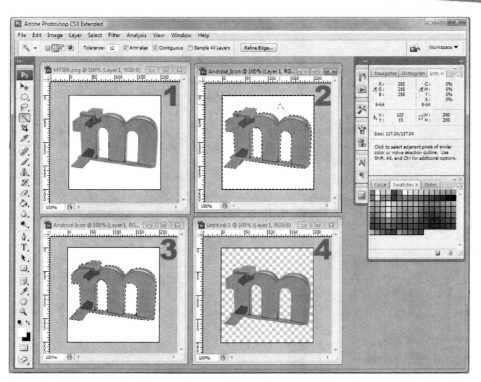

Figure 4–14. *Steps to extracting artwork on a solid color background into a transparency mask (alpha channel)*

Creating the Icons

Now, we'll create three standard Android-sized icons by using the **Image ➤ Resize** command, as follows:

- **High-resolution icon**: Resize the image from 200 × 200 to 72 × 72 pixels, as shown in Figure 4–15. Then use **Save For Web** to save it as a 24–bit PNG file with the transparency option checked in your project folder: *C:/Android_Project/res/drawable-hdpi*. Name it *icon.png*.

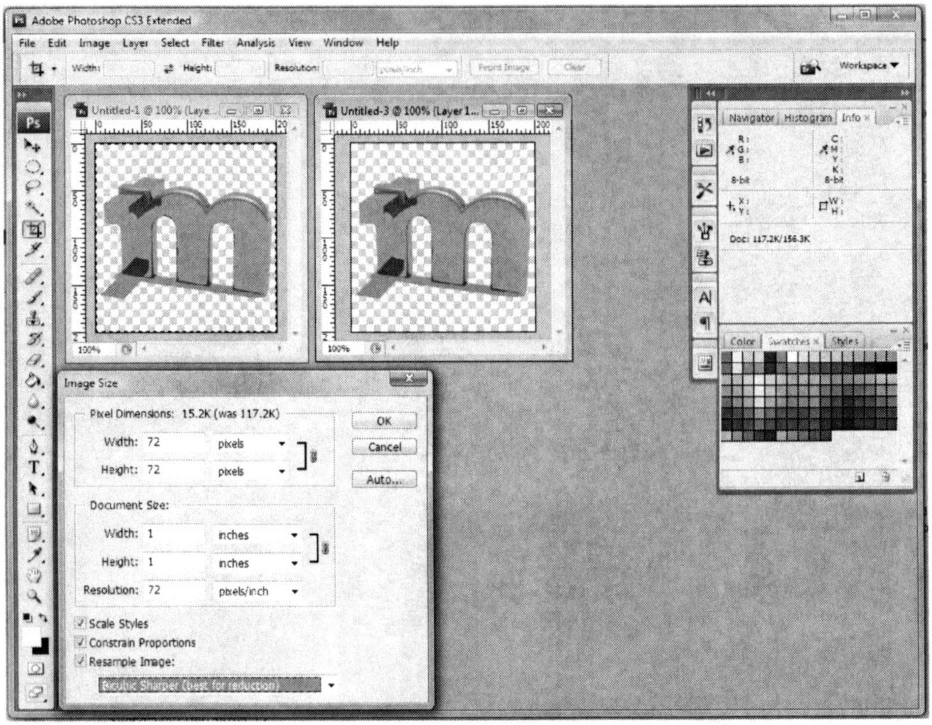

Figure 4–15. *Using the Image Size command to create a high-resolution, 72-pixel square application icon*

- **Medium-resolution icon**: Repeat the same process for the medium-resolution icon. First, select **Edit ➤ Step Backwards**, which will undo the resizing to restore the image to 200 pixels. Then choose **Image ➤ Resize** to set the image to 48 pixels this time. Save the file in the same format with the same options in the medium folder: *C:/Android_Project/res/drawable-mdpi*. Name it *icon.png*.

- **Low-resolution icon**: Go back and resize the image to 32 pixels, and save it to the low-density image folder: *C:/Android_Project/res/drawable-ldpi*. Name it *icon.png*.

Figure 4–16 shows the three different *icon.png* files, illustrating their relative sizes to the original. Android will now pick the appropriate icon when your application is run.

> **NOTE:** Don't delete the *drawable* folder, because Android will use the icon in it if none of your resources matches the characteristics of the device running your app.

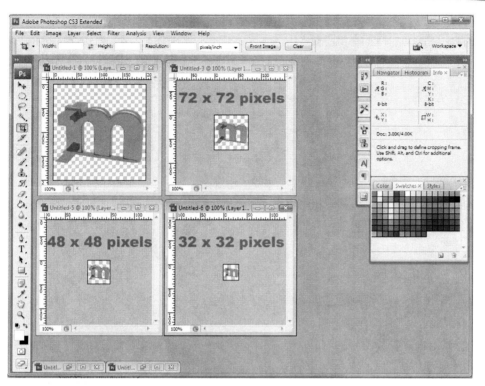

Figure 4–16. *High-, medium-, and low-resolution icons in Photoshop, with transparency (checkerboard)*

Summary

Android is very particular about which types of files you use and where you put them within your project folder. We will be looking at the particulars of how things need to be set up in order to work properly in Android throughout this book.

In this chapter, you created and compiled your first project for Android inside Eclipse using the Android application development environment you installed in Chapter 3. You saw that the Android environment in Eclipse gives you a lot of development assistance, and as a beginner, you'll want to take advantage of every bit of help you can get. The proof is in the pudding, as they say. You just developed an Android Hello World application and needed to change only one line of code in the Eclipse IDE. You saw how Android sets up a basic application, and which Java and XML files are needed in order to create a UI and a basic application.

Your Android application icon is very important to the branding of the application, as it represents your application on the users' desktop, which is usually crowded with all of the other installed application icons. Customizing an app icon is as simple as putting the icon file into the correct folder. You just must make sure that the icon is saved in the correct file type, is the correct resolution, uses an alpha channel, and has the correct file name: *icon.png*.

The next chapter provides an overview of Java and how Android compartmentalizes things having to do with an application. In the remaining chapters, we will get down to actually coding in Java and creating XML markup that delivers your application's UI and functionality.

Chapter 5

Android Framework Overview

The primary programming language used in developing your Android applications is Java SE, from Oracle (formerly Sun Microsystems). As noted in Chapter 1, Java SE stands for Java Standard Edition, and many people shorten this to just Java to refer to the programming language. Two other editions of the Java programming language are called Java EE, short for Java Enterprise Edition, and Java ME, for Java Micro Edition.

Java EE is designed for massive computer networks, such as vast collections of blade computers that are used to run large enterprises or corporations with thousands of active users. Thus, Java EE has more multiuser scalable features than Java SE, which is more for a single user on a single computer system, say a home PC or a handheld PC, like Android.

Java ME is designed for embedded systems to create highly portable computers such as mobile phones. It has fewer features than Java SE, so that it can fit onto a phone without using too much memory and resources to run it. Most mobile phones run Java ME, but Android phones run the more powerful Java SE. Android phones can run Java SE because they have a full gigabyte of memory and a 1GHz or faster CPU, so essentially today's Android smartphones are tiny Linux computers.

Java is an object-oriented programming (OOP) language. It is based on the concepts of developing modular, self-contained constructs called *objects*, which contain their own attributes and characteristics. In this chapter, you will learn about the OOP characteristics of Java, and the logic behind using these modular programming techniques to build applications that are easier to share and debug due to this OOP approach.

After you've had a taste of the power of Java, we'll quickly cover XML, because it's the way you define UIs and configurations in your Android apps. Without it, you would need to rely solely on Java code, which would make developing apps a lot more complicated.

Finally, we'll cover the main parts of the Android framework, and you will be able to see the OO underpinning it has. We'll briefly cover each component and explain which chapter covers it in more detail.

The Foundation of OOP: The Object

The foundation of an OOP is the object itself. Objects in OOP languages are similar to objects that you see around you, except they are virtual, and not tangible. Like tangible real-world objects, objects have characteristics, called *states*, and things that they can do, called *behaviors*. One way to think about it is that objects are nouns, or things that exist in and of themselves, and behaviors are like verbs.

As an example, consider a very popular object in all of our lives: the automobile. Some characteristics, or states, of a car might be as follows:

- Color (red)
- Direction (N, S, E, or W)
- Speed (15 miles per hour)
- Engine type (gas, diesel, hydrogen, propane, or electric)
- Gear setting (1, 2, 3, 4, or 5)
- Drivetrain type (2WD or 4WD)

The following are some things that a car can do, or behaviors:

- Accelerate
- Shift gears
- Apply the brake
- Turn the wheels
- Turn on the stereo
- Use the headlights
- Use the turn signals

You get the idea.

Figure 5–1 is a simple diagram of the object structure using the car example. It shows the characteristics, or attributes, of the car that are central to defining the car object, and the behaviors that can be used. These attributes and behaviors define the car to the outside world.

ANATOMY OF A CAR OBJECT

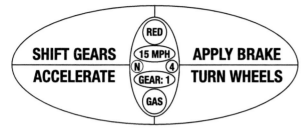

Figure 5–1. *Car object showing car characteristics (inner oval) and car behaviors (outer oval)*

Objects can be as complicated as you want them to be, and can nest or contain other objects within their structure, or *object hierarchy*. A hierarchy is like a tree structure, with a main trunk and branches and subbranches as you move up (or down) its structure. A good example of a hierarchy is the directory or folder structure on your hard disk drive.

Directories or folders on your hard disk drive can contain other directories or folders, which can in turn contain yet other directories and folders, allowing complex hierarchies of organization to be created. You can do the same thing with objects, which can contain subobjects, which can themselves contain further subobjects as needed to create your structure. You'll see plenty of nested objects when working with Android, because nested objects are useful for grouping objects that are used in only one place. In other words, some types of objects are useful only to one other type of object in an Android app, so they are provided in a nested hierarchy.

You should practice identifying objects in the room around you, and then break their definition down into states (characteristics) and behaviors (things that they can do), as this is how you will need to think to become more successful in your OOP endeavors.

You'll notice that in real life, objects can be made up of other objects. For example, a car engine object is made up of hundreds of discrete objects that function together to make the engine object work as a whole. This same construction of more complicated objects out of simpler objects can be done in OOP languages, where complex hierarchies of objects can contain other objects that have been created in previous Java code.

Some OOP Terminology

Now let's cover some of the technical terminology used for Java objects. First, objects have fields and methods, as follows:

- *Fields*, called *variables*, hold the object's states.

- *Methods* are programming routines that operate on the object's internal states. If object characteristics can be thought of as nouns, then methods can be thought of as verbs using this analogy. Methods also allow other objects external to the object itself to communicate with the object.

One of the key concepts of OOP is *data encapsulation*, where the object's fields are allowed to be modified directly only through that same object's methods. This allows the object to be self-sufficient. For example, to turn the car, you use the steering method, which positions the wheels in the desired direction.

With data encapsulation, each object that is part of a larger construct can be built and tested individually, without requiring accessing data from other objects or modules of the application (which can translate into bugs). Without data encapsulation, people could simply access any part of your object's data and use it however they pleased. This could introduce bugs, affecting the methods you have perfected to manipulate your object and provide your solution.

Data encapsulation promotes the core concept in OOP of *modularity*. Once an object is created and tested, it can be used by other objects without worrying about its integrity. Data encapsulation thus allows code reuse, so programmers can develop libraries of useful objects that do not need to be rewritten or retested by other programmers. You can see how this can save developers money by structuring only the work that needs to be done and avoiding redundant work processes.

Data encapsulation also allows developers to hide the data and the internal workings of the object if desired.

Finally, objects make debugging easier because they can be removed modularly during testing to ascertain where bugs are located in the overall code. In our car object example, the attributes of our car are encapsulated inside the car object, and can be changed only via the methods that surround them in the diagram. For instance, use the Shift Gears method to change the Gears=1 attribute to Gears=2.

The Blueprint for an Object: The Class

In real life, there is seldom just a single kind of object. Usually, there are a number of different types and variations. For instance, for a car object, there are many different manufacturers, sizes, shapes, seating capacity, engine types, fuel types, transmission types, and so on.

In Java SE, we write something called a *class* to define what an object can do (its methods) and the fields it has. Once this class has been coded in Java, we can then create an *instance* of each object that we wish to use by referencing the class definition. In architectural terms, the class is a kind of blueprint as to what the object is, what states it contains, and what it can do (what methods it has).

> **NOTE:** An instance is a concrete object created from the blueprint of the class, with its own states or unique data attributes. For example, you might have a (second) blue car instance that is traveling south in third gear. (In the example, our first car instance is red and traveling north in first gear.)

To illustrate this further, let's construct a basic class for our car object example. To create a car class, you use the Java keyword class, followed by your name for the new class that you are writing, and then curly brackets to hold your code definition, like so:

```
class Car {Code definition for a car class goes in here. We will do this next}
```

The first thing that we usually put inside our class (inside the curly {} brackets) is the data fields (*variables*) that will hold the states, or attributes, of our car. In this case, we have six fields that define the car's gear, speed, direction, fuel type, color, and drivetrain (two- or four-wheel drive), as specified in the basic diagram shown earlier in Figure 5–1.

To define a variable in Java, you first declare its data type (int means a whole number, and string means text), followed by your variable name. You can also (optionally) set a default, or starting, value by using an equal sign and a data value. The variable definition ends with a semicolon.

> **NOTE:** Semicolons are used in programming languages to separate each code construct or definition from the other ones in the same body of code.

So, with our six variables from our anatomy of an object diagram in place, our class definition looks like this:

```
class Car {
    int speed = 15;
    int gear = 1;
    int drivetrain = 4;
    String direction = "N";
    String color = "Red";
    String fuel = "Gas";
}
```

Remember that these are all the default values—the ones each object instance will have when we create it.

Notice how the example spaces out the curly braces ({}) on their own lines and indents lines, so that you can see what is contained within those braces more easily.

The next part of the class file will contain the methods that define how the car object will operate on the variables that define its current state of operation. Methods can also return a value to the calling entity, such as values that have been successfully changed or even answers to an equation. For instance, there could be a method to calculate distance that multiplies speed by time and returns a distance value.

To declare a method that does not return any value to the calling entity, you use the void keyword. A good example of using void is a method that triggers something—the method is used to invoke a change in the object, but does not need to send a value back to the calling function.

If your method or function returns a value, instead of using the void keyword, you use the data type of the data that is to be returned, say int or string. For example, an addition method would return a number after finishing its calculation, so you would use int.

After the void keyword comes a name for the method (say, shiftGears). This is followed by the type of data (in this case, an int) and variable name (newGear) in parentheses.

```
void shiftGears (int newGear) {
```

The variable contains a data parameter that will be passed to the method, so the method now has this variable to work with.

> **NOTE:** The normal method-naming convention is to start a method name with a lowercase letter, and to use uppercase letters to begin words embedded within the method name, like this: methodNameExample().

Some methods are called without variables, as follows:

```
methodSample();
```

To call the shiftGears() method, you would use the following format:

```
shiftGears(4);
```

This passes 4 into the shiftGears() method's newGear variable, which sets its value. This value then is passed into the interior of the shiftGears() method logic (the part inside the curly braces), where it is finally used to set the object's gear (internal) field to the new gear shift value of 4, or fourth gear.

A common reason to use a method without any parameters is to trigger a change in an object that does not depend on any data being passed in. So, we could code an upShift() method and a downShift() method that would upshift and downshift by one gear level each time they were called, rather than change to a gear selected by the driver. We then would not need a parameter to shift gears on our car; we would just call upShift() or downShift() whenever gear shifting was needed.

> **NOTE:** Notice the empty parentheses after the method names in the text. These are used when writing about the method, so that the reader knows that the author is talking about a method. You will see this convention used throughout the rest of this book.

After the method declaration, the method's code procedures are contained inside the curly braces. In this example, we have four methods:

- The shiftGears() method sets the car's gear to the gear that was passed into the shiftGears() method.

```
void shiftGears (int newGear) {
        gear = newGear;
}
```

- The accelerateSpeed() method takes the object's speed state variable and adds an acceleration factor to the speed, which causes the object to accelerate. This is done by taking the object's current speed setting, or state, and adding an acceleration factor to it, and then setting the result of the addition back to the original speed variable, so that the object's speed state now contains the new (accelerated) speed value.

```
void accelerateSpeed (int acceleration) {
      speed = speed + acceleration;
}
```

- The applyBrake() method takes the object's speed state variable and subtracts a braking factor from the current speed, which causes the object to decelerate, or to brake. This is done by taking the object's current speed setting and subtracting a braking factor from it, and then setting the result of the subtraction back to the original speed variable, so that the object's speed state now contains the updated (decelerated) braking value.

```
void applyBrake (int brakingFactor) {
      speed = speed - brakingFactor;
}
```

- The turnWheel() method is straightforward, much like the shiftGears() method, except that it uses a string value of N, S, E, or W to control the direction that the car turns. When turnWheel("W") is used, the car will turn left.

```
void turnWheel (String newDirection) {
      direction = newDirection;
}
```

The methods go inside the class and after the variable declarations, as follows:

```
class Car {
    int speed = 15;
    int gear = 1;
    int drivetrain = 4;
    String direction = "N";
    String color = "Red";
    String fuel = "Gas";

    void shiftGears (int newGear) {
        gear = newGear;
    }

    void accelerateSpeed (int acceleration) {
        speed = speed + acceleration;
    }

    void applyBrake (int brakingFactor) {
        speed = speed - brakingFactor;
    }

    void turnWheel (String newDirection) {
```

```
        direction = newDirection;
    }
}
```

This Car class allows us to define a car object, but it can't do anything until we use it to instantiate an object. In other words, it does not do anything until it is called.

To create an instance of an object, we instantiate it. Here's the onCreate() method of an Android application, where we instantiate two cars and use them (refer to the example in Chapter 4 to see how to create an onCreate() method in an Android app):

```
public void onCreate(Bundle savedInstanceState) {
    super.onCreate(savedInstanceState);
    setContentView(R.layout.main);

    Car carOne = new Car();          // Create Car Objects
    Car carTwo = new Car();

    carOne.shiftGears(3);
    carOne.accelerateSpeed(15);                 // Invoke Methods on Car 1
    carOne.turnWheel("E");

    carTwo.shiftGears(2);                       // Invoke Methods on Car 2
    carTwo.applyBrake(10);
    carTwo.turnWheel("W");
}
```

Upon launch or creation of our Android application, we now have two empty car objects. We have done this using the Car() *class constructor*, along with the new keyword, which creates a new object for us, like so:

```
Car carOne = new Car();
```

The syntax for doing this is very similar to what we used to declare our variables:

- Define the object type Car.

- Give a name to our object (carOne).

- Set the carOne object equal to a new Car object definition, which has all the default variable values set.

To invoke our methods using our new car objects requires the use of something called *dot notation*. Once an object has been created and named, you can call methods by using the following code construct:

```
 objectName.methodName(variable);
```

So, to shift into third gear on car object number one, we would use this:

```
carOne.shiftGears(3);
```

So, as you can see in the final six lines of code in the onCreate() method , we set carOne to third gear, accelerate it from 15 to 30 mph by accelerating by a value of 15, and turn east by using the turnWheel() method with a value of "E" (the default direction is north, or "N"). Car two we shift into second, applyBrake() to slow it down from 15 to 5 mph, and turn the car west by using the turnWheel("W") method via our dot notation.

Providing Structure for Your Classes: Inheritance

There is also support in Java for developing different types of car objects by using a technique called *inheritance*, where more specific car classes (and thus more uniquely defined objects) can be subclassed from a more generic car class. Once a class is used for inheritance by a subclass, it becomes the *super class*. There can be only one super class and an unlimited number of subclasses. All the subclasses inherit the methods and fields from the super class.

For instance, from our Car class, we could subclass an Suv class that extended the Car class to include those attributes that would apply only to an SUV type of car, in addition to the methods and states that apply to all types of cars. An SUV car class could have onStarCall() and turnTowLightOn() methods, in addition to the usual car operation methods. Similarly, we could generate a subclass for sports cars that includes an activateOverdrive() method to provide faster gearing and an openTop() method to put down the convertible roof. You can see these subclasses in the extension of our car object diagram shown in Figure 5–2.

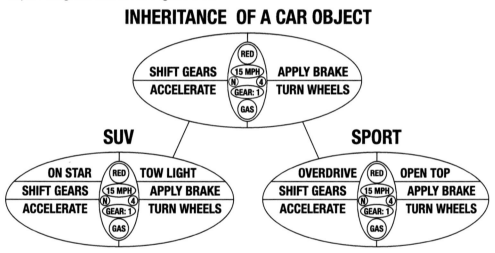

Figure 5–2. *Inheritance of a Car object*

To create a subclass from a super class, you extend the subclass from the super class using the extends keyword in the class declaration, like this:

```
class Suv extends Car { New Fields and Methods Go Here }
```

This extends to Suv all of the fields and methods that Car features, so that the developer can focus on just the new or different fields and methods that relate to the differentiation of the SUV from the regular car definition. Since the original core fields and methods come from the Car class, it becomes the super class, and the Suv class becomes the subclass. Suv is said to be *subclassed* from the Car super class.

To refer to one of the super class methods from within the subclass you are writing, you can use the super keyword. For example, in the Suv class, we may want to use a generic car's `applyBrake()` method, and then apply some other factor to the brakes that is specific to SUVs. The following code does this:

```
class Suv extends Car {
    void applyBrake (int brakingFactor) {
        super.applyBrake(brakingFactor);
        speed = speed - brakingFactor;
    }
}
```

This means the SUV's brakes are twice as powerful as a generic car's brakes.

Be sure to use good programming practices and document the super class fields and methods within each subclass. This documentation lets the users know that the super class's fields and methods are available, since they do not explicitly appear in the code for the subclass.

Defining an Interface

In many Java applications, the classes conform to a certain pattern, so that the rest of the application knows what to expect of those classes when they are instantiated as objects. This is especially common when using a framework like Android.

The *public interface* that the classes present to the rest of the application makes using them more predictable and allows you to use them in places where any class of that pattern is suitable. In other words, the public interface is a label that tells the application what this class can do, without the application needing to test its capabilities.

In Java terms, making a class conform to a pattern is done by implementing an interface. The following is an `ICar` interface that forces all cars to have the methods defined in the interface. This also means that the rest of the application knows that each car can do all of these actions, because the `ICar` interface defines the public interface of all cars.

```
public interface ICar {
    void shiftGears (int newGear);
    void accelerateSpeed (int acceleration);
    void applyBrake (int brakingFactor);
    void turnWheel (String newDirection);
}
```

So, a car is not a car unless it contains these particular methods.

To implement an interface, use the `implements` keyword as follows, and then define all the methods as before, except they must be `public`.

```
class Car implements ICar {
    int speed = 15;
    int gear = 1;
    int drivetrain = 4;
    String direction = "N";
    String color = "Red";
    String fuel = "Gas  ";
```

```
    public void shiftGears (int newGear) {
        gear = newGear;
    }

    public void accelerateSpeed (int acceleration) {
        speed = speed + acceleration;
    }

    public void applyBrake (int brakingFactor) {
        speed = speed - brakingFactor;
    }

    public void turnWheel (String newDirection) {
        direction = newDirection;
    }
}
```

The public keyword allows other classes to call these methods, even if those classes are in a different package (packages are discussed in the next section). After all, this is a public interface, and anyone should be able to use it.

Bundling Classes in a Logical Way: The Package

Each time you start a new project in Android, the Eclipse IDE will create a package to contain your own custom classes that you define to implement your application's functionality. In the Hello World application we created in the previous chapter, our package was named Hello.World. In fact, the New Android Project dialog asked us for this package name.

The package declaration is the first line of code in any Android application, or in any Java application for that matter. The package declaration tells Java how to package your application. Recall the first line of code in our Hello World application:

```
package hello.world;
```

After the package keyword and declaration come import statements, which import existing Java classes and packages into your declared package. So, a package is not only for your own code that you write yourself, but also for all code that your application uses, even if it is open source code written by another programmer or company.

Basically, the package concept is similar to the folder hierarchy on your computer. A package is just a way of organizing your code by its functionality. Android organizes its classes into logical packages, which we will routinely import and use throughout this book.

In our Hello World application in the previous chapter, we needed two import statements in our *MyHelloWorld.java* file to support class functions in our application:

```
import android.app.Activity;
import android.os.Bundle;
```

These are basically addresses to where the code for each import statement is located. Here is a generalization of how an import statement follows a path to the class:

```
import platform.functionality.classname;
```

This applies to our two statements as follows:

- ▪ android says this is an Android package.

- ▪ app and os refer to the broad functionality of the package in question.

- ▪ Activity and Bundle refer to the classes we are importing.

Thus, the Activity class, which is the super class for any activity that you create, is found within the android.app package. This app part says that this package logically contains classes that are necessary for the creation of Android applications, and one of these is the Activity class, which allows us to define UIs.

The android.os package we referenced in our import statement contains classes that are operating system utilities. One of these is Bundle, which allows us to create bundles of variables for convenience and organization.

You might be wondering if the package is the highest level of organization in Java. The answer is no, there is one higher level. This level is sometimes called a *platform* or *application programming interface* (API). This is a collection of all the core packages for a given language, such as Java SE or Java ME, or all the packages of a specialized product, such as Android.

An Overview of XML

There are actually two types of languages used in Android development: Java and XML. XML stands for eXtensible Markup Language. Developed in 1996, XML is similar to HTML (for Hyper-Text Markup Language), which is used for web site design.

The primary use of XML is to structure data for items that require a predefined data structure, such as address books or computer-aided design (CAD). Like Java, XML is very modular, which allows complicated data definition constructs to be created.

XML uses structures called *tags*, just as HTML does. And as in HTML, these tags use tag keywords bracketed by the ‹ and › characters. For example, in Android, the ‹resources› tag contains resource definitions, and the ‹string› tag contains string resource definitions. The ‹string› tag also features *attributes* (which I think of more as parameters of sorts); for instance, a ‹string› tag has a name attribute that allows it to be named.

> **NOTE:** A *parameter* is a choice of data options that can be set, telling some code what you want it to do—sort of a way you can configure it exactly to your liking. So, you could set a background color of red by specifying a red parameter to a method or as an attribute to an HTML element.

In our Hello World application in Chapter 4, we defined two string resources with the following XML in the *strings.xml* file:

```
<resources>
        <string name="hello">Hello Android World, Here I Come!</string>
        <string name="app_name">Hello Great Big Android World</string>
</resources>
```

You can readily see the modularity via the nesting of tags. The `<resources>` tag contains the two `<string>` tags and their attributes, putting them into one resources group. Nesting can be as many levels deep as required for more complicated data definition constructs.

XML is used in Android to define constructs so that you do not need to create them in more complicated Java code. It is easier to write definitions in XML than it is to write them in Java. This is because XML has the simpler markup format used in HTML, rather than the more complicated block code structure used in Java. This makes it easier for nonprogrammers to help write applications.

Because XML is easier to use than Java, and because this is a book for beginners, we will do everything that we can using XML instead of Java. Android allows this, and the XML works as well as Java code to achieve exactly the same results.

The Anatomy of an Android Application: The APK File

The cornerstone of Android application development is the application package file format, or the APK file format. When you compile and output an application for distribution to your Android users, the Eclipse IDE and Android SDK output your application file name with an *.apk* extension. There is only one *.apk* file, and it includes all of your application code (in the form of a DVM executable *.dex* file format), as well as any new media resources or assets and the *AndroidManifest.xml* file (which we'll discuss in detail in the final section of this chapter). Interestingly, the Android Market increased file size limits for *.apk* files from 25MB to 50MB, which is great news for developers.

So, if your application is called Zoomerza, for instance, the file that you get upon final publishing will be called *Zoomerza.apk*, and it will run on any Android phone. This file format is closely related to the standard Java *.jar* format, and uses the familiar ZIP type compression. The *.apk* file is specifically set up so that it can be run in place without going through the unpacking process.

You can look at the *.apk* file using the familiar file packing and unpacking software packages, such as PKZIP, WinZip, WinRAR, Ark, and 7-Zip. If you are interested in looking inside your application's *.apk* file to see its folders, it will not hurt the *.apk* file to do so.

If you have Windows Vista or Windows 7, the ZIP functionality is built into the operating system. An easy way to see your *.apk* file is to rename it to a *.zip* extension and open it inside the Windows Explorer file management utility. Another clever way to do this without renaming the file is to right-click the *.apk* file and use the **Open with** option to select a ZIP extraction utility. Let's do that here, so you can see what I'm talking about.

1. Rename *HelloWorldAndroid.apk* to *HelloWorldAndroid.zip*.

2. When you're warned about renaming the file, choose to do so anyway.

3. Click *HelloWorldAndroid.zip*. You will be able to see the internal file structure, as shown in Figure 5–3.

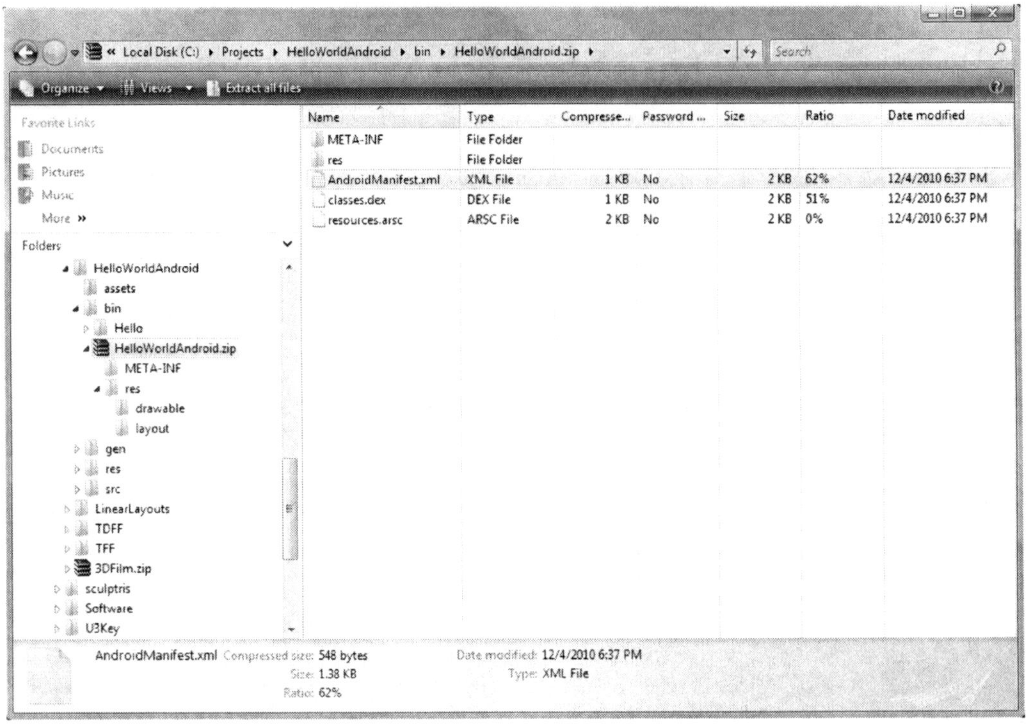

Figure 5–3. *Viewing the structure of HelloWorldAndroid.zip*

As shown in Figure 5–3, the application includes an *AndroidManifest.xml* file and a *classes.dex* file. It also contains the */res* folder with the */drawable* and */layout* subfolders, which hold the assets we used to develop the app.

Android Application Components

Android is designed with the maximum amount of modularity in mind. This modularity makes it easy for developers to exchange functionality between their applications, which is a central concept of the open source paradigm upon which Android is based. For instance, if you have coded a cool animated UI element, and you make this available to other applications, they can implement your class and use that element. And you do not need to have that code inside those other applications. As long as the application that contains the element's code is running (or can be launched) on the Android smartphone, you can call the method via the Android operating system.

There are four main types of components that can be (but do not need to be) used within an Android application:

- Activities handle the UI to the smartphone screen.

- Services handle background processing.

- Broadcast receivers handle communication in your apps.

- Content providers handle data and database management issues.

Let's take a closer at each of these components, to prepare for the hands-on use of them in the rest of this book. Here, you'll get an overview of what Android is made up of, before we get into the details about class creation and such in later chapters.

Android Activities: Defining the UI

An Android *activity* contains a UI construct that accomplishes a given user-input task via the smartphone display screen.

Android applications can have more than one activity. In fact, more complex applications usually have one activity for each UI screen implementation. For example, if you are programming a game, you might have the following activities:

- The introductory splash screen with the Continue to Play Game OR Press Button to Play Game

- The instructions screen, with a scrolling text UI

- The high-score screen, with UI elements that allow the user to manage high-score entries

- A player groups screen, where users choose who will play the game with them

- The actual core gameplay screen itself

If an application has more than one activity, one is marked as the activity that is presented when the application is launched. In our game example, that is the splash screen (although it could be the instructions screen). This activity has an onCreate() method that calls the *main.xml* file, as you saw in the Hello World application we created in the previous chapter.

Here is the code for the onCreate() method from the Activity base, or super, class (note the super keyword) and sets the content View to the *main.xml* UI definition:

```
public class MyHelloWorld extends Activity {
    /** Called when the activity is first created. */
    @Override
    public void onCreate(Bundle savedInstanceState) {
        super.onCreate(savedInstanceState);
        setContentView(R.layout.main);
    }
}
```

An activity can be full screen, or it can be part of a screen, allowing for floating windows on top of other windows. An activity can also make use of other windows. For instance, an activity might show a pop-up dialog requesting that the user enter information, or it could display a product information window when a user clicks a product name or SKU.

We will get into Activity class creation in all of the following chapters, and cover it specifically in Chapters 6 and 7,

Android Services: Processing in the Background

Unlike activities, services do not have any visual UI (that's what an activity is for). Services handle the processing or heavy lifting for your application. They are often used for doing things that need to be done in the background or back end of the application, while the user works with your UI in the foreground or front end of your application.

Here are some examples of what service components can do:

- Calculate numeric values
- Process game logic
- Play media elements such as video and audio streams
- Pull data from remote network locations
- Transfer data between devices via Bluetooth

Services handle calculations or processing that needs to be done in the background while the user is busy looking at the results of this processing on the activity-generated UI screen elements.

Not surprisingly, you create your own services in Android by subclassing the Android Service class. Services can run in the background, even after an activity UI screen is no longer visible, such as when a user picks an MP3 audio file to play, and then does something else with the phone while listening to the music. We will take a look at using services in Chapter 11. There, you'll learn how to use a MediaPlayer to play audio and video streams in the background of your applications.

Broadcast Receivers: Announcements and Notifications

Broadcast receivers are communication components that receive messages that are sent between the Android operating system and other application components, or between Android application components themselves.

The Android operating system often sends out messages regarding the status of what is going on in real time with the Android phone itself. These are statuses that any Android application may want or even need to know about in order to protect the application integrity, such as if the phone is about to lose power and your app needs to save files.

The following are some examples of Android operating system-initiated broadcast messages:

- A low battery life warning

- A time zone change notice

- A language preference change notice

- A message that the camera has been used to snap a picture

And here are a couple examples of application-to-application broadcast messages:

- An alert that data has finished downloading

- A message that streaming video media has arrived, is cached, and is ready for the start of playback

Your application can implement as many broadcast receivers as you like, in order to intercept any of the types of messages that need to be monitored for your application's operation.

Like Android services, broadcast receivers operate in the background, and thus do not have any associated UI elements. However, this does not mean that the broadcast receivers cannot trigger or invoke a UI activity in response to the messages that they carry. In fact, it is common practice to have broadcast receivers trigger UI elements that alert the user as to what is going on within the application.

Broadcast receivers can also use the Android `NotificationManager` class to alert the user via built-in phone notification methods, such as flashing the screen backlight, playing a sound, triggering phone vibrations, and placing a persistent alert icon on the smartphone status bar.

Broadcast receivers are created by extending the Android `BroadcastReceiver` class. We will look at using them in Chapter 11.

Content Providers: Data Management

Content providers in Android provide a way to make data available to your application and to other applications, if that is desired. This can be data that is created in and for your own application, or it can be data that can be accessed by your application, but that is created by other applications, or even by the Android phone utilities themselves. It can also be data that is created by your application and is made accessible to other applications. The content provider component is both powerful and flexible.

For example, an Android phone utility uses a content provider to access the phone number database that is kept within your smartphone. Android comes with a number of built-in content provider databases, including contacts, images, audio, and video. These can be accessed via phone system utilities, as well as by your applications through coding.

Content data can be stored in a file system on your SD card in your smartphone, off-phone in a remote HTTP server, or in a proper database. The latter is the preferred method for storing and accessing data within Android, and you'll see that in action in Chapter 10, which covers using content providers.

To create your own content provider, you extend the ContentProvider base class, which implements a standard set of methods that are used to store and retrieve data. Applications access the methods defined by your ContentProvider class with a ContentResolver object, which is used to talk to any content provider, in order to navigate the data that is needed by the application.

A content provider is activated when it receives a request for data from a content resolver. The other three components—activities, services, and broadcast receivers—are activated via asynchronous messages called *intents*, which we'll look at next.

Android Intent Objects: Messaging for Components

An Intent object in Android holds the contents of a message that is sent between modules, typically to launch them or to send them new task instructions. For activities and services, an Intent object provides an action to be taken, the data that the action needs to operate on, and optionally, some details or additional information that may be required for more complicated operations.

You communicate with each type of Android component (activity, service, and broadcast receiver) using a different set of methods to receive the Intent object that is passed to it. For this reason, Intent objects are easy to keep separate and well defined, as they will be different for each type of Android component.

The components use the Intent object methods as follows:

- An activity is started up, or if it's already started, given a new task, by passing an Intent object to the Context.startActivity() method. The Activity class can look at the contents of the Intent object via the getIntent() method, and at subsequent intent objects via the onNewIntent() method.

- An Android service component is started by passing an Intent object to the Context.startService() method, which then calls the service class onStart() method, and passes it the Intent object that contains the actions for the service to perform and the data on which to perform them.

- If the service is already running and the Intent object contains new instructions, then the intent is passed to the Context.bindService() method in order to establish an open connection between the calling component and the service that is being used. This always open, real-time connection between code modules is commonly called *binding* in programming.

- An Android broadcast receiver component is started by passing an Intent object to the Context.sendBroadcast() method, or optionally to the Context.sendOrderedBroadcast() method or Context.sendStickyBroadcast() method. The Intent object in this case contains the message action to be taken and the data (the message) on which that action needs to be taken.

We will look closely at using Intent objects with activities in Chapter 11.

Android Manifest XML: Declaring Your Components

You have seen that Android needs to have a single XML file in your root project folder: *AndroidManifest.xml*, which is the file that Android uses to launch your application. The only other file in your project root folder is *default.properties*, which is generated by Eclipse and should never be modified. So, the only file in your project root folder that you ever need to worry about is *AndroidManifest.xml*.

The Android manifest uses XML for several good reasons:

- It is easy to code.

- It allows you to define a logical data structure that is easy for Android to parse (break down into logical data definition components) and understand.

- It can exist outside your Java code, so that Android can access it before it starts looking at your Java code and asset resources.

The Android manifest XML file is essentially a road map for the Android operating system, telling it what your application is going to do, which components are needed, and what Android assets it needs permission to use within the Android smartphone operating environment.

When your application is launched initially, the *AndroidManifest.xml* data definitions are used by Android to set up areas of system resources and memory for application components that need to be supported. They also are used to define secure access permissions for the more sensitive areas of Android (such as private, internal smartphone databases) that you need to access with your application.

Let's take a look at the *AndroidManifest.xml* file for our Hello World app.

```xml
<?xml version="1.0" encoding="utf-8"?>

<manifest        xmlns:android="http://schemas.android.com/apk/res/android"
        package="Hello.World"
        android:versionCode="1"
        android:versionName="1.0">

    <application        android:icon="@drawable/icon"
                        android:label="@string/app_name">
        <activity android:name=".MyHelloWorld"
                android:label="@string/app_name">
```

```
        <intent-filter>
          <action android:name="android.intent.action.MAIN" />
          <category android:name="android.intent.category.LAUNCHER" />
        </intent-filter>
      </activity>
    </application>

    <uses-sdk android:minSdkVersion="3" />
</manifest>
```

The opening line is the XML version and encoding declaration—standard fare inserted for us by Eclipse (as are other manifest entries). This is followed by the following tags:

- **<manifest>**: This tag has four standard attributes, including the Hello.World package name that we entered in our New Android Project dialog. The xmlns:android attribute points to the online definition of the Android XML schema and is also standard fare in all XML files. The other two attributes are the Android XML version code and name, which are version 1 and 1.0, respectively.

> **NOTE:** An XML schema definition is a road map as to what is allowed in a given XML file—that is, the structure that it must follow and the tags or attributes it may contain. Think of it as defining all of the rules that you need to follow for any given class of XML file, where the Android manifest is a certain class of XML that needs to conform to a set format.

- **<application>**: This tag's android:icon attribute points to our *icon.png* file in our */drawable* folder. The android:label attribute points to our application name (the name that goes in the application title bar at the top of the smartphone screen) in the *strings.xml* file. Note that the <application> tag is nested inside the <manifest> tag. You can see nesting by looking at the order of the closing tags at the end of the manifest file structure.

- **<activity>**: Here, we declare our application's activity class by specifying its name via the android:name attribute as .MyHelloWorld, which we also specified in our New Android Project dialog. Note that if we had a service class or broadcast receiver class, we would also declare them in this area of the manifest, along with their related <service> and <receiver> tags, as you will see in Chapter 11.

- **<intent-filter>**: This tag specifies the action and category of the Intent object that launches our application. The action is android.intent.action.MAIN, which launches *main.xml*. The category is android.intent.category.LAUNCHER, which specifies that MyHelloWorld is the activity that launches the application (because it is the activity that contains this <intent-filter> tag).

- **<uses-sdk>**: This tag specifies our minimum SDK support level of Android 1.5 SDK 3 via the attribute named android:minSdkVersion, which we also specified in our New Android Project dialog. This comes after the closing tags for the <application>, <activity>, and <intent-filter> tags.

After that, we close our <manifest> tag, and we are finished declaring our Hello World application manifest XML file.

We will look at Android manifest files in later chapters that cover more advanced Android features, so you will be learning more about these tags before you are finished with this book.

Summary

This chapter gave you an overview of the Java and XML languages, as well as the various components of the Android operating system. We also looked at the *AndroidManifest.xml* file, which ties everything together when Android launches your application.

The main component of Java is the object, which contains fields, or states, and methods that operate on those states in order to change the attributes of the objects, just as in real life. This approach allows objects to mimic real-world objects and also to exhibit data encapsulation, which allows objects to be secure and self-contained. This modularization helps in testing and debugging, because problems can be localized more precisely.

Objects can be created using classes, which are programming code constructs that are used to define the object fields and methods, and thus their architecture. These classes define the initial, or default, fields for the objects that are created from them, as well as the programming code that defines methods for changing these default states as the program executes. We used a car example to demonstrate the different attributes and methods that would define a car object, such as acceleration, braking, steering, and gear shifting.

Classes can be used to create more detailed classes through a process called *inheritance*. Through inheritance, the original base class becomes a super class, and new, more finely detailed classes are subclassed from the base class to form different types of class definitions. In our car example, we created SUV and sports car classes, which allowed us to create SUV and sports car objects.

Once you have finished coding all of your classes, you can bundle them logically together in a package, which allows you to group your classes and even your application together as one logical, well, package. You use the import statement to load Android packages and classes. The format import *platform.package.classname* allows you to precisely specify which packages and classes you wish to include and use in your own applications.

We also took a look at XML, which uses tags to allow users to structure data. Tags can be nested to become subsets of other tags, and thus complicated and precise data structures can be created. Android uses XML so that some of the programming can be done in an easier language than Java. This allows nonprogrammers to become involved in the application design process.

The Android APK (*.apk*) file holds our application code binaries and resources in a compressed *.zip* file format. This includes the *classes.dex* Dalvik executable file and the Android manifest and application resources. Renaming the *.apk* file to *.zip* allows you to look inside the file and see its assets. Recently, file size limits for *.apk* files were increased from 25MB to 50MB.

Then we looked at Android application components. Android activity components hold your UI elements and are the front end of your applications to your end users. Android services define your processing routines and are the back ends of your applications. Android broadcast receivers send messages between your application components and are your intercomponent application messengers. Android content providers store and distribute your application data within your application to other applications and to the Android operating system itself.

We next looked at Android Intent objects. These are our task managers. They send instructions between our application components as to which actions to perform and on which data to perform them.

Finally, we covered the Android manifest file, *AndroidManifest.xml*. This file defines to the Android operating system how to start up your application, including which components will be used and which permissions and SDK levels your application will support on various model smartphones.

All of the concepts in this chapter will be covered in detail in the remaining chapters of this book.

Chapter 6

Screen Layout Design: Views and Layouts

One of the most important parts of any application's design and development is the graphical user interface (GUI) and screen layout design. Many of the most widely circulated Android applications are popular because of their visual design, animated graphics, and easy- or fun-to-use interfaces. We will explore the Java classes that provide the core foundation for all of these front-end capabilities in this chapter.

Android View Hierarchies

In Google Android, in order to interface with the smartphone screen, you use two core Java classes. These are two of the most important and often used classes in Android development:

- The `View` class
- The `ViewGroup` class

`View` and `ViewGroup` are core, high-level classes, created or subclassed from the Java `Object` class, as are all Java classes. `View` objects are created using the `View` class. The `View` class can also be used to create many lower-level, or more customized, Java classes. Those classes that are subclassed from the `View` class inherit the characteristics of their superclass.

So, the basic screen layout in Android is controlled by a `View` object, which contains a complex data structure that represents the content and layout parameters for a given rectangular section of the smartphone's display screen.

Using the View Class

There may be one or more View objects that make up the entire display screen, depending on how you use the View and ViewGroup classes to create the UI structure for your Android application's screen.

Each View object controls and references its own rectangular view parameters, allowing you to control many attributes. Here are just some examples of the many attributes controlled by the View class parameters available to programmers:

- Bounds (measurements)
- Layout on the screen
- Order in which its layers are drawn
- Scrolling
- Focus
- Keystroke interactions
- Gesture interactions

Finally, Views have the ability to receive events—interaction events between your application's end user and the View object itself. For this reason, the View class is the logical Java construct to subclass to build more detailed and specific UI elements, such as buttons, check boxes, radio buttons, and text fields.

> **NOTE:** The View class serves as the foundation for UI elements that are subclasses of the View class. Recall that in Java, a *subclass* is a more specific or detailed implementation of the class from which it is subclassed. For instance, the Button class is subclassed from the TextView class, which is subclassed from the View class, which is subclassed from the Object class. The Button class is subclassed from the TextView class because the Button has a TextView label and is thus a more specialized version of a TextView; that is, it is a clickable TextView with a button background appearance.

So many UI classes have been subclassed from the View class that there is a name for them: *widgets*. All of these widgets are contained in a package (a collection of classes) called android.widget. For example, you can access a Button class via this package using android.widget.button.

Nesting Views: Using the ViewGroup Class

One of the most useful classes subclassed from the View class is the ViewGroup class. The ViewGroup class is used to subclass layout container classes, which allow groups of View objects to be logically grouped, arranged, and cascaded onto the screen.

ViewGroups are layout containers, usually collections of UI elements. In the diagram in Figure 6–1, View could mean a button, a text field, a check box, and so on. This applies to any other type of UI element.

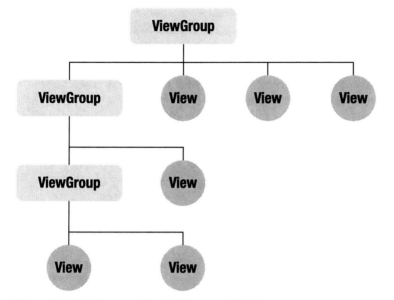

Figure 6–1. *ViewGroups and nested Views and ViewGroups*

The remainder of this chapter explores the different types of ViewGroup subclasses. These are the foundation that Android developers use to organize and group their View objects (UI elements) on the smartphone display screen.

Direct subclasses of the ViewGroup class include AbsoluteLayout, RelativeLayout, FrameLayout, LinearLayout, and SlidingDrawer. We'll look at the two most often used ViewGroup subclasses: LinearLayout and RelativeLayout. We'll also explore one of the coolest ViewGroup subclasses: SlidingDrawer. This subclass can be used to greatly expand your Android screen real estate by 200%.

In the diagram in Figure 6–1, the top level ViewGroup object is the *parent* of the View objects and ViewGroup objects underneath it, which are called its *children*. The ViewGroup object in the second row is both a child as well as a parent, and the same goes for the ViewGroup object in the third row.

As you can see, ViewGroup objects can contain other ViewGroup objects (a concept called *nesting*; it's all so familial, isn't it?), but View objects cannot contain other objects. They are the end object, so to speak, and are simply UI components for which you can set via a plethora of configuration parameters.

Defining Screen Layouts: Using XML

The primary way of defining screen layouts (I will stop calling them ViewGroup objects now, assuming that you are now classifying them as such when you see the term) is via XML. This XML goes inside a file called *main.xml*, placed inside a folder called */res/layout* within your project folder.

Once this *main.xml* file is in place, with your XML screen layout (UI) definition inside it, you can use the Java onCreate() method to push it onto your screen on the startup of your application activity, as discussed in Chapter 5.

We'll first take a look at the onCreate() code and how it works, and then we'll use it for real in the next sections, where we will create three vastly different types of screen layouts.

Setting Up for Your Screen Layout

Just three lines of Java code inside an onCreate() method set your content view to the *main.xml* screen layout XML definition:

```
public void onCreate(Bundle savedInstanceState) {
        super.onCreate(savedInstanceState);
        setContentView(R.layout.main);
}
```

The words before the method name determine who can access its methods and data. A public method is one that is open to any part of your Android application.

The words that follow the method name (always enclosed in parentheses) are the parameters that an application can pass to the method for its use. *Parameters* are chunks of data the method needs to do its job.

The savedInstanceState object is a Bundle object, which is a collection of all of the states for your activity screen UI elements. It exists so that the screen UI elements can be restored if the screen is replaced by navigation to other screens during the use of your application. As you learned in Chapter 5, the state of a UI screen consists of its attributes and their values, including the UI elements it uses, which one has the focus, the colors, and similar attributes that define its appearance.

> **NOTE:** The Activity class saves your state for you, so you don't need to worry. Simply extend it, and it does the work for you.

The super keyword calls the superclass (the class containing the onCreate() method that was subclassed from android.app.Activity), so it is basically referencing the onCreate() method of the android.app.Activity class from which our activity class was subclassed. It's just a shortcut for android.app.Activity.onCreate(savedInstanceState). Since it is called from this activity class, it affects this activity locally and applies to this activity only. This `savedInstanceState` object is the one Android kindly saves for us when it deals with saving state.

> **TIP:** If you ever want to save some state that is out of the ordinary, write your own method called `onSaveInstanceState(Bundle savedInstanceState)`. Then save your custom state to the `savedInstanceState` object, remembering to call `super.onSaveInstanceState(savedInstanceState)`.

The `onCreate()` method will always be called by the Android operating system when any activity (remember that these are defined in the *AndroidManifest.xml* file) is started. This part of your code is where all of your initializations and UI definitions will be performed, so it must be present—at least if you need your users to interact with the smartphone screen area.

The way that layouts contain other nested layouts in XML code (as shown in Figure 6–1) is by nesting them inside each other. The closing tags are nested at the bottom of these structures, and they must be nested in the correct order to show Android which layouts are inside of which other layouts. Layouts underneath or inside of another layout conform to, and are controlled by, their parent layout container. The code examples in this chapter indent the nested code structures to show the nested layout hierarchy.

You are about to see all of this in action in the next section, where we'll work with the most commonly used layout container in Android: the linear layout. We'll talk about the `LinearLayout` class, which has been subclassed from the `ViewGroup` class, which is subclassed from the `View` class, which is subclassed from the `Object` class.

> **NOTE:** Java implements subclasses so there is no redundancy in the construction of your code. Once a method has been written, it is available to every subclass (and its subclasses) that inherits from its base class.

Using Linear Layouts

In a layout, usually buttons are placed across the top of the screen, or sometimes down the side of the screen, in a line. This is exactly what the `LinearLayout` class does. It is designed to contain and arrange UI elements placed inside it across the screen (using the horizontal orientation parameter) or up and down the screen (using the vertical orientation parameter).

> **NOTE:** The `LinearLayout` container should not contain any scrolling views. (I think that's common sense, but some folks will try anything once.)

In Java code, to set the LinearLayout object's orientation, use the setOrientation(integer) method, with either the constant HORIZONTAL for horizontal or VERTICAL for vertical:

```
myLinearLayout.setOrientation(HORIZONTAL);
```

After the LinearLayout has been set up in your XML, it's possible to change its orientation on the fly inside your Java code.

> **NOTE:** Recall that *constants* are hard-coded values that your Java code uses in its program logic and can't change. In this case, Android provides easy-to-remember names so that you don't need to use fiddly numbers. You use the name HORIZONTAL, rather than the value it is set to, which is 0. This also helps if the value of HORIZONTAL ever changes. You're protected because the name does not change, even if the value inside Android does.

Here's the attribute for orientation in the LinearLayout tag for XML:

```
android:orientation="vertical"
```

Thus, the entire LinearLayout tag looks like this:

```
<LinearLayout android:orientation="vertical">
```

However, we should really have a few more key parameters in the LinearLayout tag to make it more useful and standardized, so here's how it's normally coded:

```
<LinearLayout xmlns:android="http://schemas.android.com/apk/res/android"
        android:layout_width="fill_parent"
        android:layout_height="fill_parent"
        android:orientation="horizontal">
```

The first parameter of the LinearLayout XML tag is the path to the Android XML schema definition. This parameter sets the variable android used in the rest of the tag to http://schemas.android.com/apk/res/android, so that you don't need to write the other parameters like this:

```
http://schemas.android.com/apk/res/android:layout_width="fill_parent"
```

The value for the layout width and height parameters, fill_parent, simply tells the LinearLayout to expand to fill its parent container. Since this is the top level LinearLayout container, that would mean to fill the smartphone display screen. We already know what the orientation does, so now we have our LinearLayout defined. Anything we place inside this container will display across the screen from left to right.

As discussed earlier in the chapter, the Java onCreate() method is used to load the *main.xml* layout parameters for the application.

Well, it's time to fire up Eclipse again, and create an application to see how all of this cool stuff works together.

Creating the LinearLayouts Project in Eclipse

We'll build a simple UI that stacks some TextView elements along the left side of the screen, just to see how LinearLayout works. Let's fire up Eclipse and get started!

After you launch Eclipse, you will be presented with a Workspace Launcher dialog, where Eclipse will present you with a suggested workspace folder. Alternatively, you can select your own folder. I created a *C:\Projects* folder for my Android projects, and I used the Browse button to find this folder and select it, as shown in Figure 6–2.

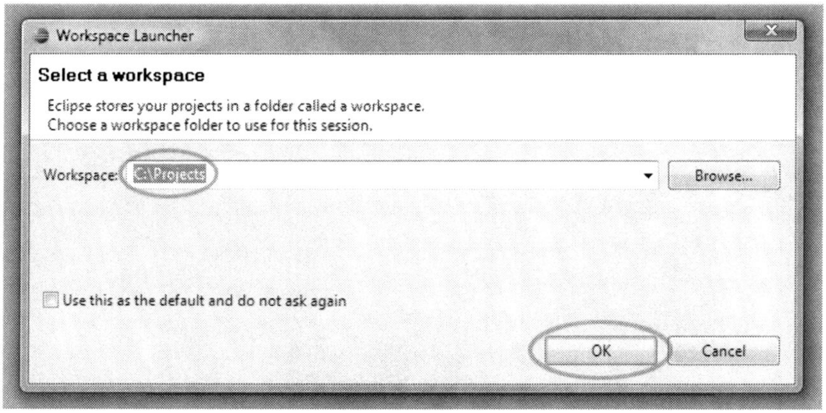

Figure 6–2. *Selecting the project workspace in Eclipse*

After you have set your project folder, and Eclipse has launched its development environment, select **File ➤ New ➤ Project**, as shown in Figure 6–3. Then select the Android Project wizard from the *Android* folder, as shown in Figure 6–4.

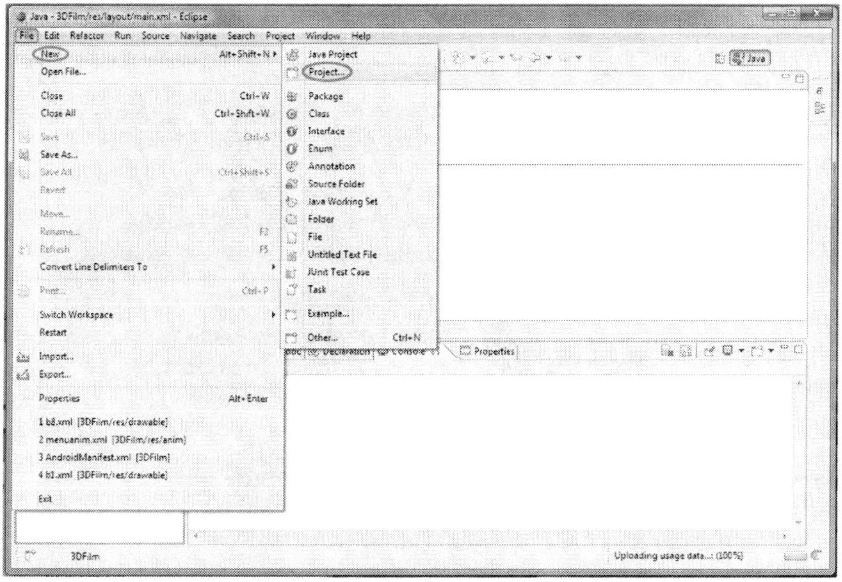

Figure 6–3. *Choosing to create a new project in Eclipse*

NOTE: Once you have created an Android project, there will also be other options, such as an Android XML File option and an Android Test Project option.

Figure 6–4. *Creating a new Android project in Eclipse*

Now we need to create a new project resource, so hit the Next button. This takes you to the New Android Project dialog, where you need to fill out six important elements:

- **Project name**: In this field, enter **LinearLayouts**. This is the Eclipse project name, as well as the name of the folder that will hold all of the project files. We'll set the name of our application in this dialog as well.

- **Build Target**: For our build target, we want as much platform compatibility as possible, so we choose support all the way back to Android 1.5. This way, our app will also work on Android versions 1.6, 2.0, 2.1, 2.2, 2.3, and 3.0. Version 1.5 equated to package release 3, as you can see in the middle area of this dialog.

- **Application name**: In the Application name field in the Properties section, enter **LinearLayout_Example**. This is the name that will appear under our icon and in the title bar of our application.

- **Package name**: In the Package name field in the Properties section, enter `linear.layout`. (Remember that the package name is at least two names separated by a period.)

- **Create Activity**: Make sure the Create Activity check box is checked, and type `LinearLayoutActivity` in that field.

- **Min SDK Version**: Enter **3**, which matches the table in the middle of the dialog.

Figure 6–5 shows the completed dialog. Click the Finish button after you've filled out the fields.

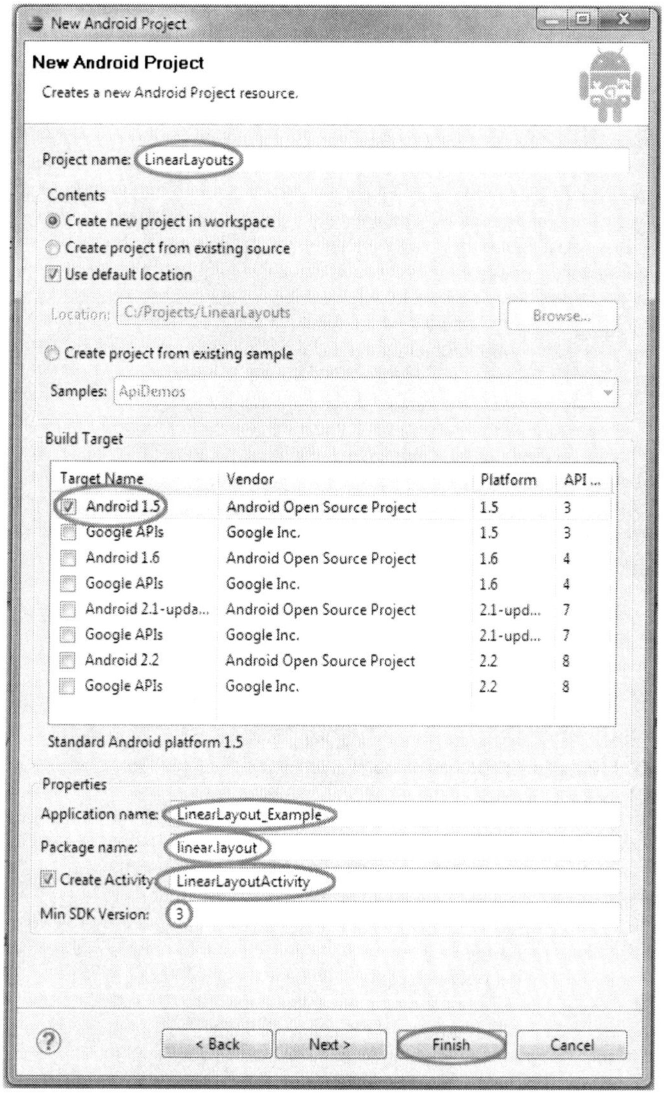

Figure 6–5. *The settings for our new LinearLayout project*

Note that Eclipse Galileo has a bug where the compiler thinks the /gen folder is not created. But as you can see with a look at the expanded Package Explorer pane shown in Figure 6–6, the /gen folder is in fact present, and contains both files and data.

CAUTION: /gen is the compiler-generated folder, and not to be touched in any way during development.

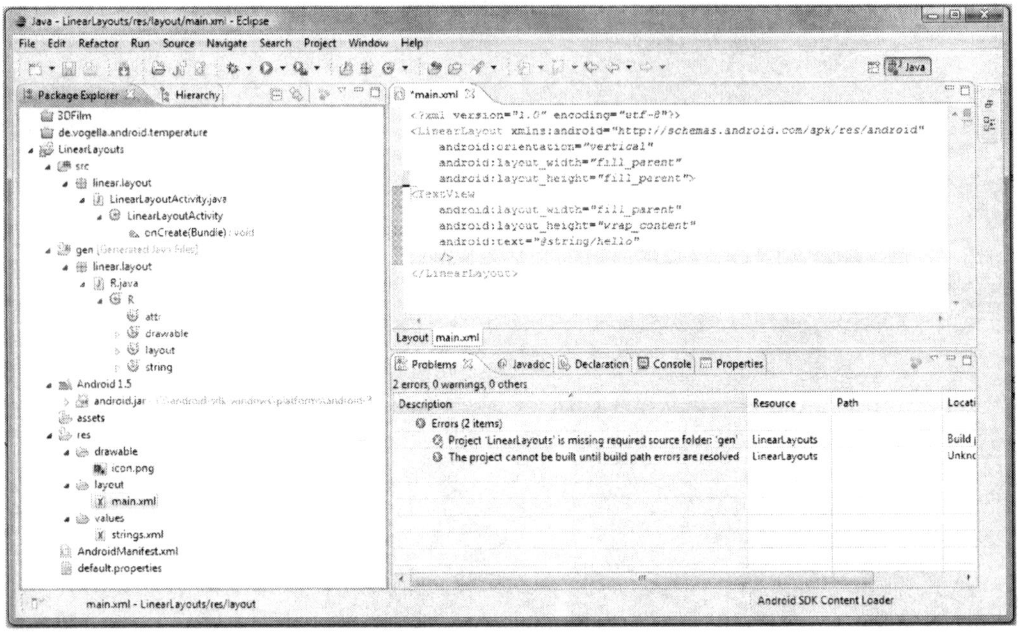

Figure 6–6. View of the Eclipse main.xml and Problems tab with errors

Editing the main.xml File

Now it's time to work on main.xml. Right-click main.xml (if it is not open in a tab already) and select Open. You will see some default XML code setting up a linear layout with vertical orientation and a text field. Here is the code, which also appears in the main.xml tab shown in Figure 6–6:

```
<?xml version="1.0" encoding="utf-8"?>
    <LinearLayout xmlns:android="http://schemas.android.com/apk/res/android"
android:orientation="vertical"
android:layout_width="fill_parent"
android:layout_height="fill_parent" />
<TextView
    android:layout_width="fill_parent"
    android:layout_height="wrap_content"
    android:text="@string/hello" />
</LinearLayout>
```

In this file, add another TextView object by copy and pasting the <TextView> element.

```
<?xml version="1.0" encoding="utf-8"?>
<LinearLayout xmlns:android="http://schemas.android.com/apk/res/android"
    android:orientation="vertical"
    android:layout_width="fill_parent"
    android:layout_height="fill_parent"
    >
<TextView
    android:layout_width="fill_parent"
    android:layout_height="wrap_content"
    android:text="@string/hello"
    />

<TextView
    android:layout_width="fill_parent"
    android:layout_height="wrap_content"
    android:text="@string/hello"
    />

</LinearLayout>
```

We will edit the text strings to say "Text Area One!" and "Text Area Two!."

Editing the strings.xml File

The text strings are edited in the *strings.xml* file, found in the *values* folder (shown in the Package Explorer). Right-click *strings.xml* and select **Open**, so it opens in its own tab in the editing area.

Change the hello text to Text Area One!. Also add another string variable textareatwo and set it to Text Area Two!. Here's the code:

```
<?xml version="1.0" encoding="utf-8"?>
<resources>
    <string name="textareaone">Text Area One!</string>
    <string name="textareatwo">Text Area Two!</string>
    <string name="app_name">LinearLayout_Example</string>
</resources>
```

Figure 6–7 shows the strings added to the file.

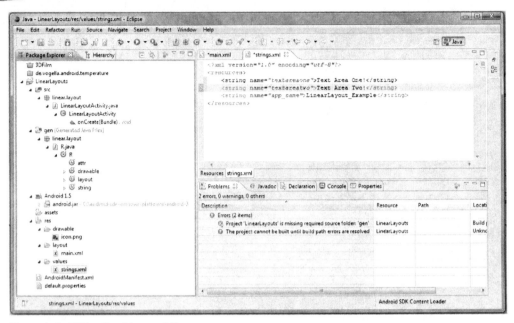

Figure 6–7. *Editing the strings.xml file*

Notice that the app_name string was added from the information you gave in the project-creation dialog, so you don't need to code this (but this is where you change the app_name later, if you want to).

Updating main.xml File

Next, change *main.xml* to reference the textareaone and textareatwo string variables, which we set in the *strings.xml* file in the previous step, as shown in the code and in Figure 6–8.

```xml
<?xml version="1.0" encoding="utf-8"?>
<LinearLayout xmlns:android="http://schemas.android.com/apk/res/android"
    android:orientation="vertical"
    android:layout_width="fill_parent"
    android:layout_height="fill_parent"
    >
<TextView
    android:layout_width="fill_parent"
    android:layout_height="wrap_content"
    android:text="@string/textareaone"
    />

<TextView
    android:layout_width="fill_parent"
    android:layout_height="wrap_content"
    android:text="@string/textareatwo"
    />

</LinearLayout>
```

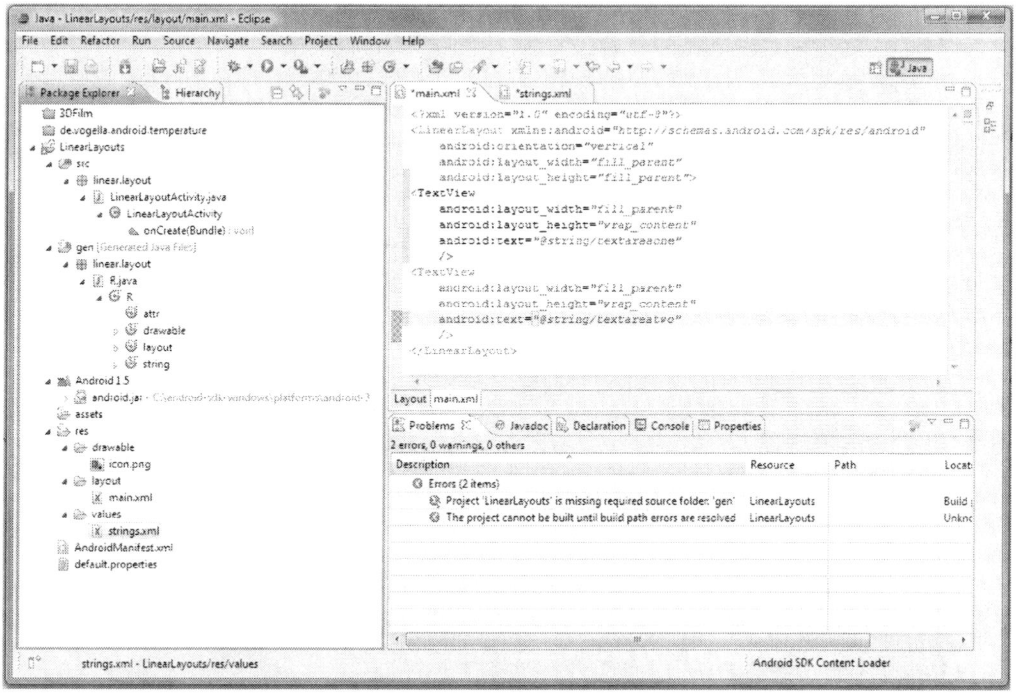

Figure 6–8. *LinearLayout XML code in main.xml*

Viewing LinearLayoutActivity.java

Now it is time to take a look at what our Java code is doing. Right-click the *LinearLayoutActivity.java* file on the left in the Package Explorer and select **Open**.

> **TIP:** REMEMBER there is another way to open a file for editing in its own tab: just select the *.java* or XML file and press the F3 key. A tab will open showing the contents of that file.

The file opens in its own tab next to the main.xml and strings.xml tabs in Eclipse. Here is the code (Figure 6–9 shows what it looks like in Eclipse):

```java
package linear.layout;

import android.app.Activity;
import android.os.Bundle;

public class LinearLayoutActivity extends Activity {
    /** Called when the activity is first created. */
    @Override
    public void onCreate(Bundle savedInstanceState) {
        super.onCreate(savedInstanceState);
        setContentView(R.layout.main);
    }
}
```

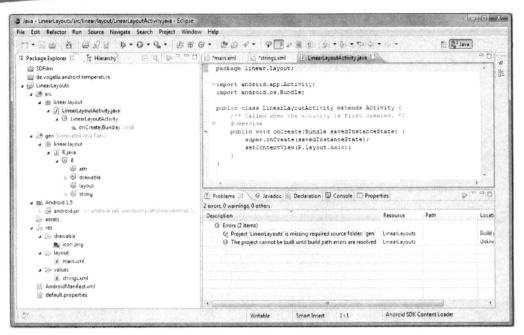

Figure 6–9. *The LinearLayout application Java code and Problems tab*

As you can see, the package name that we defined in the New Android Project dialog is declared at the top of the Java code, as well as two `import` statements that reference the Java classes that are needed (accessed or used) in the Java code: the `Activity` class and the `Bundle` class. Below this is the Java code that loads the XML layout that we created earlier in the other two tabs.

Running the LinearLayout App

Now we are ready to compile and run our Android application. Since we have already set up our 1.5 phone emulator in Chapter 3, all we need to do to compile and run our app is right-click the top-level *LinearLayouts* project folder in the Package Explorer on the left and select **Run As ➤ Android Application**. Then click the Console tab at the bottom of Eclipse to see what is happening in the compilation process.

In Figure 6–10, you can see the process that the Android compiler goes through to compile and launch your app in the 1.5 emulator. After around 30 seconds or so of loading, the emulation environment will launch your app (click the Home and/or Menu buttons on the emulator to see it). Note the name of the project and the name of our activity as they are loaded into the emulator.

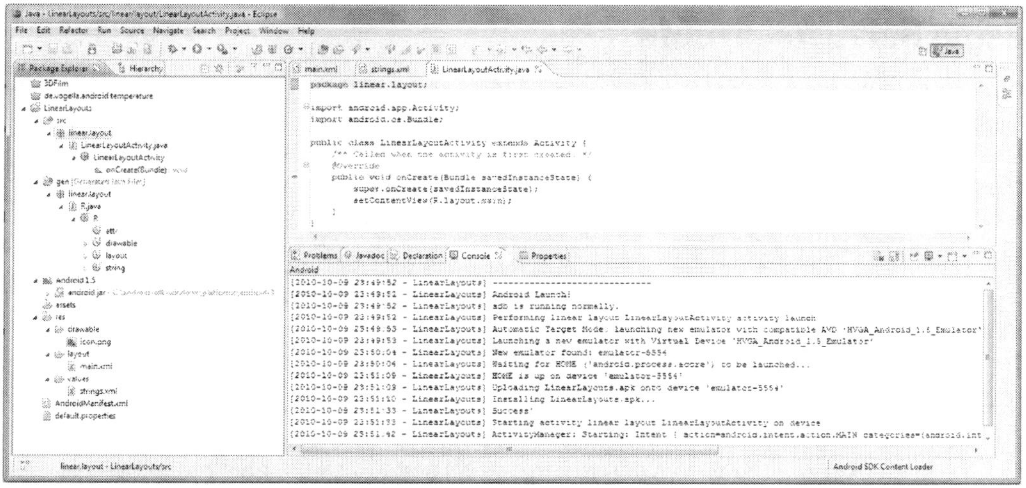

Figure 6–10. *View of Eclipse IDE with LinearLayout Java code and Console Tab Complier Progress Output*

You'll see that the `LinearLayout` vertically stacks our text fields as expected, as shown in Figure 6–11.

Figure 6–11. *Running the LinearLayout_Example application in the emulator*

Using Relative Layouts

Relative layouts are for more complicated UI layouts for which you need to define the UI elements in a not so linear fashion. The RelativeLayout layout class allows you to define how the UI elements (the View objects) are to be placed on the screen *relative* to each other, rather than just laid out linearly. For this reason, the XML definition contains a few more variables, so this example will be a number of lines of markup code longer than the LinearLayout example.

If you start to get into the habit of nesting several LinearLayout containers to achieve a more complex UI layout result, you may want to consider using a single RelativeLayout container to achieve the same results with better control.

Simpler is always better, so if you can write a UI layout using fewer nested ViewGroup containers, it will always use less memory and function more quickly. The RelativeLayout container allows you to arrange all sorts of UI elements together in a single ViewGroup to achieve a complex layout.

Relative layouts are also the optimal type of layout container for using sliding drawers, another direct subclass of the ViewGroup class. Sliding drawers extend the screen real estate of the smartphone by allowing drawers to slide out onto the screen from any of the four sides (top, left, bottom, or right). This is very cool functionality that is built into the Android SDK, as you'll see in the next section.

Since we already have our linear layout application open in Eclipse, let's change it to a relative layout configuration. That way, we won't need to type in all the same code. To change a layout, all you need to do is to change the XML code in your *main.xml* file.

Since our Java code references *main.xml*, we do not need to change anything in the LinearLayoutActivity.java tab to make these changes work, a testimony to the power of modularity via XML in Android. We also do not need to change (or even remove) the content in *strings.xml*, even though it will not be used in the application anymore.

> **NOTE:** If the unused code were lines of code in Java, Eclipse would notice that these variables were not used and warn you about it.

We'll edit *main.xml* now. And while we are at it, we'll also add some other UI elements— an editable text field and a couple buttons—so that you can see how easy it is to create (or in this case, change and/or refine) a UI inside Android.

In the first tag of main.xml, change LinearLayout and its closing tag to RelativeLayout. We will add some UI elements to the inside of the tag (before the closing tag </RelativeLayout> line of markup code).

Let's leave in one <TextView> tag and delete the other. Give the remaining tag an ID and a default, or starting, text value. So, this can be specified not only via a reference to a data declaration in *strings.xml* (as in our previous example), but also directly, right here in the *main.xml* file (just to show you two ways to do it), as follows:

```
<TextView
        android:id="@+id/label"
        android:layout_width="fill_parent"
        android:layout_heightfill_parent"
        android:text="Type here:"/>
```

This is the first UI element, so we don't have any relative layout attributes—there is nothing for this UI element to be relative to yet.

Next, let's add an `<EditText>` element (either by typing it in or by dragging from the visual layout editor tab), as follows:

```
<EditText
        android:id="@+id/entry"
        android:layout_width="fill_parent"
        android:layout_height="wrap_content"
        android:layout_below="@+id/label"/>
```

It will be laid out relative to (below) the `TextView` as shown. The key line of XML is the parameter called `layout_below`, which references the ID of the `TextView`, telling Android to position the `EditText` object below the `TextView` object. This is pretty straightforward logic and also very powerful.

Now let's add an OK button UI element, via the `<Button>` XML tag, as follows:

```
<Button
        android:id="@+id/ok"
        android:layout_width="wrap_content"
        android:layout_height="wrap_content"
        android:layout_below="@+id/entry"
        android:layout_alignParentRight="true"
        android:layout_marginLeft="10dip"
        android:text="OK"/>
```

This `<Button>` tag shows some of the power of relative positioning. The button is below the `EditText` (using the parent's ID parameter), aligned right relative to the parent, and with 10 pixels of margin to the left of the button.

To see this 10 pixels of spacing, let's add a Cancel button to the left of the OK button and aligned with it on the top, using this code:

```
<Button
        android:id="@+id/cancel"
        android:layout_width="wrap_content"
        android:layout_height="wrap_content"
        android:layout_toLeftOf="@+id/ok"
        android:layout_alignTop="@+id/ok"
        android:text="Cancel"/>
```

Here is all of the new `RelativeLayout` code in the *main.xml* file (Figure 6–12 shows it in Eclipse):

```
<?xml version="1.0" encoding="utf-8"?>
<RelativeLayout xmlns:android="http://schemas.android.com/apk/res/android"
    android:orientation="vertical"
    android:layout_width="fill_parent"
    android:layout_height="fill_parent"
    >
```

```
<TextView
    android:id="@+id/label"
    android:layout_width="fill_parent"
    android:layout_height="wrap_content"
    android:text="Type here:"/>
    />

<EditText
        android:id="@+id/entry"
        android:layout_width="fill_parent"
        android:layout_height="wrap_content"
        android:layout_below="@+id/label" />

<Button
        android:id="@+id/ok"
        android:layout_width="wrap_content"
        android:layout_height="wrap_content"
        android:layout_below="@+id/entry"
        android:layout_alignParentRight="true"
        android:layout_marginLeft="10dip"
        android:text="OK"/>

<Button
        android:id="@+id/cancel"
        android:layout_width="wrap_content"
        android:layout_height="wrap_content"
        android:layout_toLeftOf="@+id/ok"
        android:layout_alignTop="@+id/ok"
        android:text="Cancel"/>

</RelativeLayout>
```

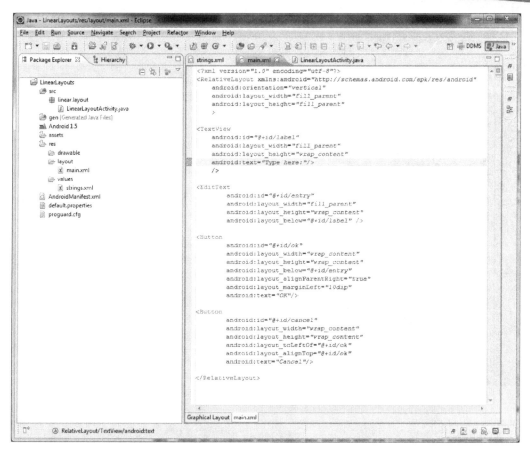

Figure 6–12. *Editing RelativeLayout in the main.xml file*

Now let's compile the project. Right-click the *LinearLayouts* project folder at the top of the Package Explorer pane and select **Run As ➤ Android Application**. Figure 6–13 shows our app running in the emulator. As you can see, the RelativeLayout code works fine and formats the UI perfectly.

Figure 6–13. *Running the relative layout example in the emulator*

Now let's add some animation to our UI by creating sliding drawers for our UI elements.

Sliding Drawers: Expanding Your UI

One of the more advanced layout containers in Android is SlidingDrawer, another direct subclass of the ever so useful ViewGroup class. This layout is not used as often as the others, but it's extremely handy.

Sliding drawers are useful because they give us a way to expand the screen area that can be used by UI components, or even for application content, for that matter.

A SlidingDrawer should be used as an overlay inside either the RelativeLayout container or the FrameLayout container. You cannot use SlidingDrawer as its own container, because it needs to slide out of something.

> **NOTE:** FrameLayout is not as useful as Linear or Realtive Layouts, and as such, is not as frequently used as a layout container type. It can be used to hold a single UI element inside a frame.

How do sliding drawers expand your screen area? By sliding a drawer (vertically or horizontally) onto the display from off the screen, you have another virtual screen available to use. This can be useful if you need the entire screen for your content, because you can keep your UI controls in a drawer that slides on or off the screen whenever it is needed.

Now let's add a sliding drawer to our RelativeLayout of the previous section and see just how cool an application we can create in less than 20 lines of XML code. We'll create an app with an analog clock that slides out inside its own drawer whenever we need to see what time it is.

Leave the RelativeLayout XML tag intact, but delete the text and button elements inside it. Then replace it with the SlidingDrawer tag:

```
<?xml version="1.0" encoding="utf-8"?>
<RelativeLayout
    xmlns:android=http://schemas.android.com/apk/res/android
    android:layout_width="fill_parent"
    android:layout_height="fill_parent">

    <SlidingDrawer
        android:id="@+id/drawer"
        android:layout_width="320dip"
        android:layout_height="440dip"
        android:orientation="vertical"
        android:handle="@+id/handle"
        android:content="@+id/content">

        <ImageView
            android:id="@+id/handle"
            android:layout_width="48dip"
            android:layout_height="48dip"
            android:src="@drawable/icon"  />

        <AnalogClock android:id="@+id/content"
            android:background="#D0A0A0"
            android:layout_width="fill_parent"
            android:layout_height="fill_parent" />
    </SlidingDrawer>
</RelativeLayout>
```

As you can see from the code indenting, the SlidingDrawer tag goes inside the RelativeLayout tag. It has two other XML tags that go inside it: one that defines the graphic that will be used as the handle for opening and closing the drawer (the ImageView tag), and another that defines the content inside the drawer (the AnalogClock tag).

Since Android installed a default *icon.png* graphic (for use as an application icon) in our */res/drawable* folder when we created our project for this chapter, I used that 48×48 pixel (standard size) icon for the handle of the drawer for demonstration purposes. Any size graphic can be used. You'll learn how to replace this with something cooler once we get to using graphics with Android in Chapter 8.

We need to set the layout height and layout width for this handle to match the PNG resolution using a setting of 48 device independent pixels (dip). We also need to point the ImageView tag's file source parameter, android:src, to the *drawable* folder and the *icon* file name, via @drawable/icon. Note that we do not need to specify the resources folder */res/drawable* or the full file name *icon.png*, because Android knows that @ means */res/*, and we just need to specify the first name of the PNG file for a graphic image.

The other XML tag that must be inside any SlidingDrawer layout container is content. Whatever XML tag you want to use for your content must have an ID specified that matches the name that is specified in the SlidingDrawer android:content parameter. In this case, we are using content as the content container's ID, but it could be anything you like.

We are going to use Android's AnalogClock XML tag to give us some impressive working content for this exercise. Note that we are accomplishing this in only four lines of XML code. In fact, this entire "clock in a drawer" Android application is using primarily XML and essentially no Java logic, other than to display the UI design on the smartphone screen.

So that we can see the boundaries of the SlidingDrawer, which we have set in the SlidingDrawer tag layout_width and layout_height parameters, we have placed an android:background parameter in the AnalogClock tag. The content is given a teaberry color background that matches our 1.5 emulator phone. This analog:background parameter will work in virtually any XML tag relating to the screen and uses standard hexadecimal color value representation inside quotes.

Finally, click the strings.xml tab and change LinearLayout_Example to SlidingDrawers_Example.

Figure 6–14 shows the IDE with the new code ready to compile. I have spaced it out so that you can see which XML tags and modules are nested inside each other.

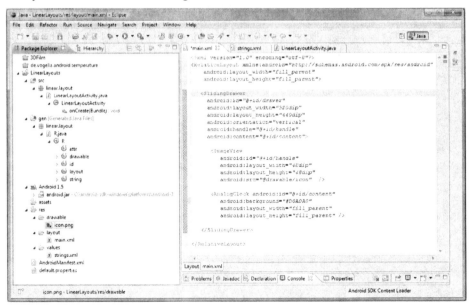

Figure 6–14. *Sliding drawer example XML*

Figure 6–15 shows the sliding drawer example running in the emulator. Some cool things to change so that you can see what this layout container can do are the orientation (horizontal or vertical) and the layout width and height parameters of the SlidingDrawer tag itself. I suggest that you practice compiling and testing Android applications by changing these XML parameters and then choosing **Run As ➤ Android Application** a bunch of times. This will help you to get used to the development work process and more comfortable with Eclipse and how easy it is to use.

Figure 6–15. *Running the sliding drawer example in the emulator*

Using Padding and Margins with Views and Layouts

Padding adds spacing to a view so that a view's content is offset by a certain number of pixels on each of the four sides. This way, the content doesn't touch the edges of the view and look unprofessional. In other words, padding adds space around the outside of a view's content, and you can choose to do so on any of the four sides of the view. When using padding, the padding is considered to be part of the view, which may affect the way Android lays out the view.

Padding values are only available to Views, not to ViewGroups (and thus not available in screen layout containers). ViewGroups instead support margins, which allow the same results as padding to be obtained, except that the margins are not considered part of the ViewGroup. For me, this makes UI design more organized and easy to remember: Views use padding values and ViewGroups use margin values.

Setting Padding in Views

Padding can be set via your Java code using the setPadding() method with four values, for left, top, right, and bottom. Think of going around a clock, starting at 9:00 AM, separated by commas. So, to put a 4-pixel border inside your view, you would use the following (remember that the order of parameters is left, top, right, bottom):

setPadding(4,4,4,4)

You can also separate each side in the Java methods. So, to get the padding for the left side of the view, use getPaddingLeft(). To set just the padding on the top to 8 pixels, write this:

setPaddingTop(8)

Setting Margins in ViewGroups

For ViewGroups, including layout containers (the subject of this chapter), the easiest way to set margins during development is via the XML parameters for any ViewGroup object.

Four layout margin values are available in XML:

- android:layout_marginBottom
- android:layout_marginLeft
- android:layout_marginRight
- android:layout_marginTop

We used one of these in our RelativeLayout example earlier in this chapter.

Be sure to experiment with using these four parameters on your UI elements. You'll see that you can control exactly how your UI elements are spaced around on the screen as you become familiar with what margins can do.

Summary

Android allows us to design screen layouts via XML, which makes it much more simple than it would be via Java code. Nonprogrammers like designers can get involved with the UI design without needing to know Java.

In this chapter, we started to take a look at the foundation for laying out our UI areas on the Android smartphone screen using the View and ViewGroup classes. We use the ViewGroup class and its subclasses to lay out our UI screen elements. Android provides several of these subclasses, including the LinearLayout, SlidingDrawer and RelativeLayout classes we looked at in this chapter.

LinearLayout is the most used layout container in Android programming and the one used in the Android apps that come with the operating system. It arranges UI elements from right to left or top to bottom. It is possible to nest LinearLayout containers within each other to achieve more complicated UIs.

RelativeLayout is the next most used layout container in Android programming. It allows you to arrange UI elements by specifying their placement on the screen relative to each other. This allows for more complicated UI layouts than just the rows or columns supported by the LinearLayout class.

We also took a look at one of the more innovative ViewGroup layout containers called SlidingDrawer. This allows you to slide UI elements on and off the screen, in and out of view. This layout container can be used to greatly increase screen real estate by allowing UI elements to exist off-screen in a "drawer" that slides out only when the user needs it.

In the next chapter, we will look at adding UI elements into our ViewGroup layout containers using View objects called *widgets*. The android.widget package gives us all sorts of precoded UI elements.

UI Design: Buttons, Menus, and Dialogs

The UI design determines the usability of your application, which will ultimately determine its success and even its profitability if you are selling it.

A standard UI is composed of a number of familiar components that can be used by your application's users to control their user experience (often called the UX). These UI elements include items such as buttons, check boxes, menus, text fields, dialog boxes, system alerts, and similar widgets.

This chapter covers how to use several of the most important Android widgets for UI design. First, we'll cover adding image buttons, text, and images to your UI. Then you'll learn about the different types of menus available. Finally, we'll cover displaying dialogs, including alerts, which carry messages to your application user. There's a lot of cool stuff to cover, so let's get started.

Using Common UI Elements

Android has all of the standard UI elements already coded and ready to use in a single package called android.widget. Here, we'll explore how to add an image button, text area, and image to your app's UI.

> **NOTE:** Recall that a *package* in Java is a collection of ready-to-use classes that you can leverage within your application. You just need to tell Java that you are going to use them by importing them via the Java import command.

Adding an Image Button to Your Layout

In Chapter 6, we crafted a UI that included the Button class, which is used to create the standard Android system format buttons, and lets you do so with the greatest of ease. Now, we'll look at the more complex ImageButton class. For professional, customized, high-graphics UIs, this is the class that you will need to use to gain the most control over the user experience.

The android.widget package's ImageButton class allows you to use your own imagery to create custom multistate buttons that are cooler looking than the standard buttons that come with the Android operating environment.

There is a distinct work process to creating a successful multi-state 24-bit PNG image button, which will composite perfectly over background imagery using an 8-bit alpha channel.

Android supports 24 bits of PNG image data, with another 8 bits of anti-aliased image transparency channel (requiring another 8-bit alpha channel). Let's do the math: $24 + 8 = 32$. So, what we really have is a 32-bit PNG image, with 8 bits of data for each of the red, green, and blue image channels, and another 8 bits of data for the alpha (transparency) channel.

In case you're not familiar with some of the terms I used in the previous description, here are some brief definitions:

- **Compositing**: The process of using layers to form a single new image out of more than one component part.

- **Alpha channel**: That part of each layer that is transparent, and thus does not hold any image data passing through visible image data from other layers underneath it.

- **Anti-aliasing**: The edge treatment that is used to make the edges of images within these transparency layers perfectly smooth when these edges are not perfectly square, which they rarely are.

Defining Multistate Image Button Graphics in XML

The XML markup is a bit more complex for multistate image buttons than it is for regular buttons. Your XML file needs to tell Android which image to use for each state of the button:

- Pressed (for touchscreens, the pressed image will be shown when the finger is touching a button image on the screen)

- Released or normal

- Focused (in use or last touched)

Let's look at the code for our *button1.xml* file, which we will reference later when we create our ImageButton XML entry in the *main.xml* file that goes in the *res/layout* folder.

You don't need to create this file now. In fact, when we get to that point in our example, you'll see that Eclipse creates this file for you automatically!

```xml
<?xml version="1.0" encoding="utf-8"?>
<selector xmlns:android="http://schemas.android.com/apk/res/android">
      <item android:state_pressed="true"
            android:drawable="@drawable/button1_pressed" />
      <item android:state_focused="true"
            android:drawable="@drawable/button1_focused" />
      <item android:drawable="@drawable/button1_normal" />
</selector>
```

The first line is the standard first line of every XML file that you code, and it will always say the same thing.

The second line defines a `selector` tag and points to its XML schema, as you have seen in previous chapters. A `selector` tag allows selection between several options. Inside the `selector` tag, we nest three `item` tags to show which drawable (bitmap) images to use for `state_pressed=true`, `state_focused=true`, and the default or normal button state.

For this XML code to work, we must have three 24-bit bitmap PNG images in our project's */res/drawable* folder named *button1_pressed.png*, *button1_focused.png*, and *button1_normal.png*.

NOTE: Recall that each of the image file names must use only lowercase letters and numbers, and can also use the underscore character.

The first `item` tag has an `android:state_pressed` attribute, which is set equal to `true`, and a second `android:drawable` attribute, which is set equal to the location of the file and its name (*sans* the .png extension).

The @ equates to your project's resources folder, */project/res/*, so in this case, `@drawable/button1_pressed` will equate to *c:/projects/imagebuttons/res/drawable/button1_pressed.png* in the Android compiler. The other `item` tags follow the same format as the first one.

Creating the UI Image Button Project in Eclipse

Now that we've reviewed the concepts, let's create the project for real. As you've done in previous chapters, fire up Eclipse and choose select **File ➤ New ➤ Project** to create a new project. In the New Android Project dialog, set the options as follows:

- Project name: Name the folder *Chapter7*.

- Build Target: So our application runs on all of the popular Android operating system versions from 1.5 through 3.0, choose Android 1.5.

- Application name: We'll call this application UI Examples.

■ Package name: Using the proper package name form, enter chapter.seven as the name.

■ Create Activity: Check this box and name the activity UserInterface.

■ Min SDK Version: Enter 3, to complement the build target choice.

Figure 7–1 shows the completed New Android Project dialog for our multistate image button example. Click **Finish** after you've filled it in.

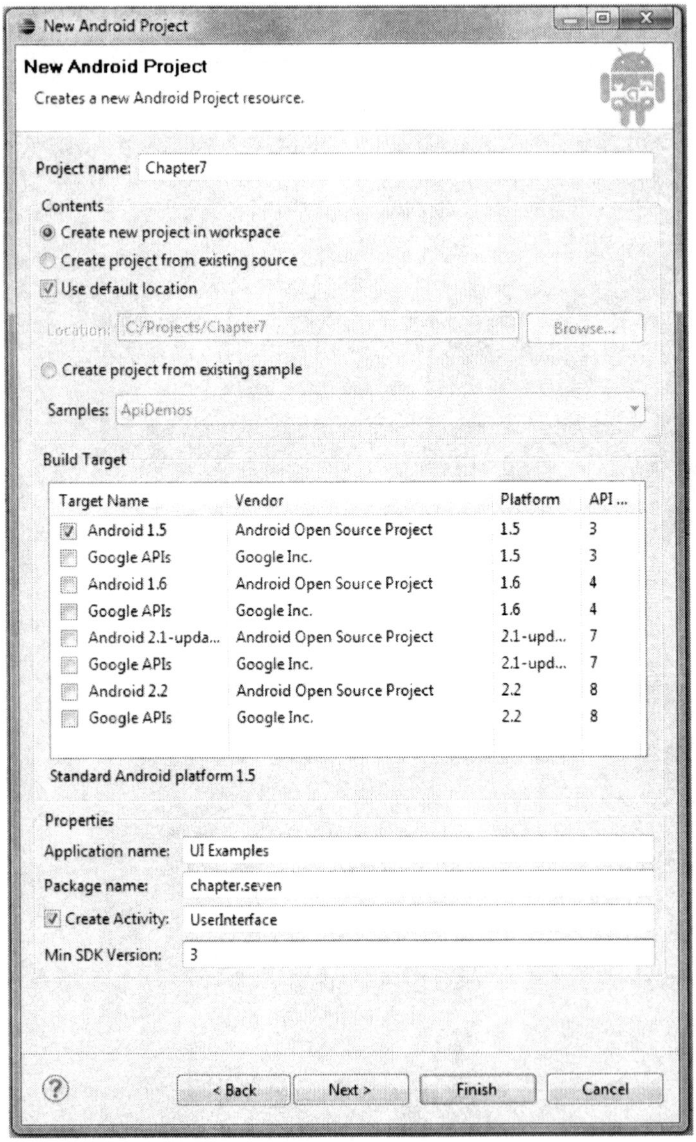

Figure 7–1. *Completed New Android Project dialog for our Chapter7 project*

Creating the button1.xml File

You now have an empty Eclipse project. Next, we'll create the *button1.xml* file so we can add the button state definition XML we created earlier.

Open the project tree on the left Package Explorer tab and expand the *src* folder by clicking the arrow. Then right-click the *drawable* folder and select **New ➤ File**, as shown in Figure 7–2.

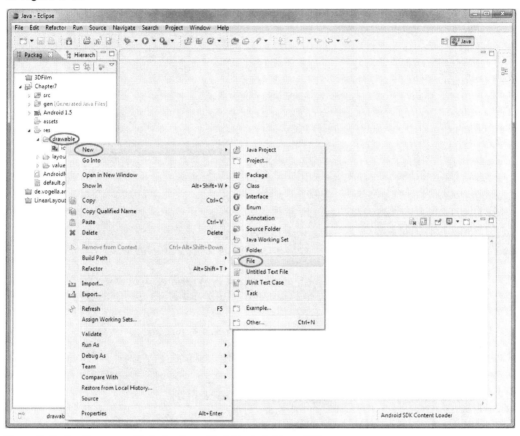

Figure 7–2. *Creating a new file in the drawable folder to hold our XML*

In the New File dialog, ask Eclipse to create the file *button1.xml* in the *Chapter7/res/drawable* folder, as shown in Figure 7–3. Then click Finish to create an empty text file. This is one of the most basic ways that you can have Eclipse create a new, empty text file for you. We will cover other ways of creating new XML files in later chapters.

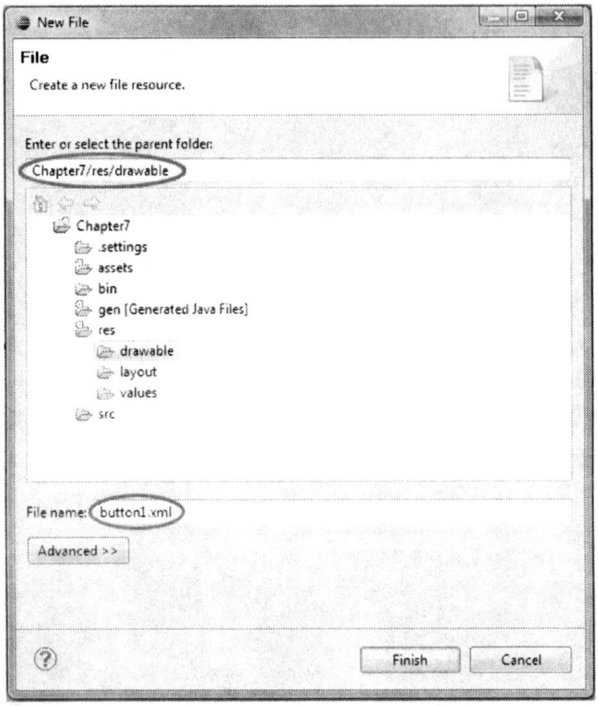

Figure 7–3. *Specifying the drawable folder and button1.xml file name in the New File dialog*

Click the button1.xml tab at the top of your screen, and then type in the XML code that defines the `selector` and `item` tags for setting the three different image button states:

```xml
<?xml version="1.0" encoding="utf-8"?>
<selector xmlns:android="http://schemas.android.com/apk/res/android">
        <item android:state_pressed="true"
                android:drawable="@drawable/button1_pressed" />
        <item android:state_focused="true"
                android:drawable="@drawable/button1_focused" />
        <item android:drawable="@drawable/button1_normal" />
</selector>
```

After you've entered the XML, you'll notice that Eclipse shows that there are three errors in the markup relating to missing file assets. Place your mouse over the red X on the left margin by the markup code. This pops up a diagnostic message regarding why Eclipse thinks this code needs your attention, as shown in Figure 7–4.

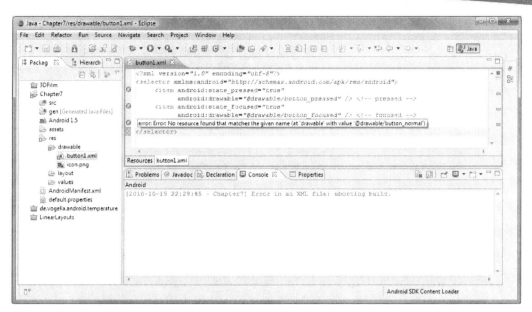

Figure 7–4. *Eclipse shows us that our three image state buttons are missing via error flags in the IDE.*

We have not put the three image button images in the */res/drawable* folder where they belong. Eclipse is telling us that it does not see each file name that is referenced in the markup in the directory where it is supposed to be.

> **NOTE:** Once we add valid XML specifiers and code, the Eclipse error messages will disappear. But this does show how Eclipse is watching out for you in real time, and offering warnings about what might be missing, what might generate compiler errors, and other common problems.

Let's create the three button state files. I'm going to use Photoshop, but other good drawing tools can do the same thing. Also, these PNG images are provided with the book code examples, so you do not need to create them from scratch if you would rather not do that.

Just as in the examples in previous chapters, put the graphics on a transparency layer (indicated in Photoshop by a checkerboard pattern), so that you can overlay the image button on any background color or image you like. Figure 7–5 shows the completed images in Photoshop.

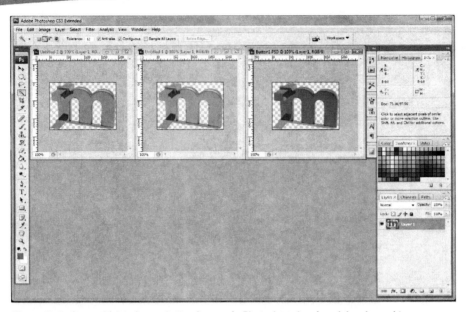

Figure 7–5. *Our multistate image button images in Photoshop showing alpha channel transparency areas*

Whenever you add new images or other assets to Eclipse, you need to tell Eclipse about the new assets. To do this, right-click the top-level project folder and select **Refresh**, as shown in Figure 7–6. You'll notice that the red errors no longer appear in the file.

> **TIP:** There is also a deeper level of refreshing called validating, which will go into even deeper depths in your code and image assets. If the red error marks do not disappear, simply right-click the *Chapter7* top-level folder again and choose the **Validate** option.

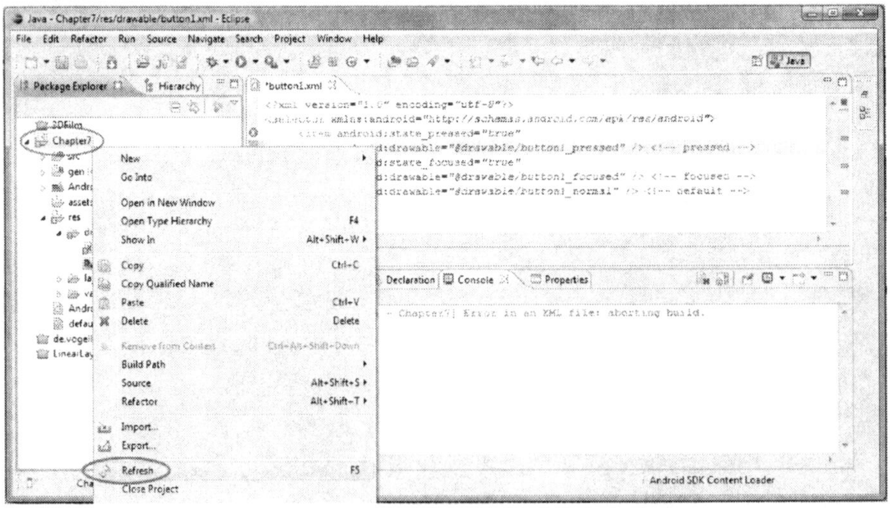

Figure 7–6. *Using the Refresh menu option to tell Eclipse that our images are now in the drawable folder*

Editing the main.xml File

Next, open the *res* folder and right-click the *main.xml* file to open it for editing. Notice that our image button source files now appear in the Package Explorer pane.

We need to replace the default text tag in the *main.xml* file with an ImageButton tag, as follows:

```
<ImageButton android:id="@+id/button_one"
             android:layout_width="wrap_content"
             android:layout_height="wrap_content"
             android:src="@drawable/button1"
             android:paddingTop="5px">
</ImageButton>
```

Figure 7–7 shows the IDE at this point.

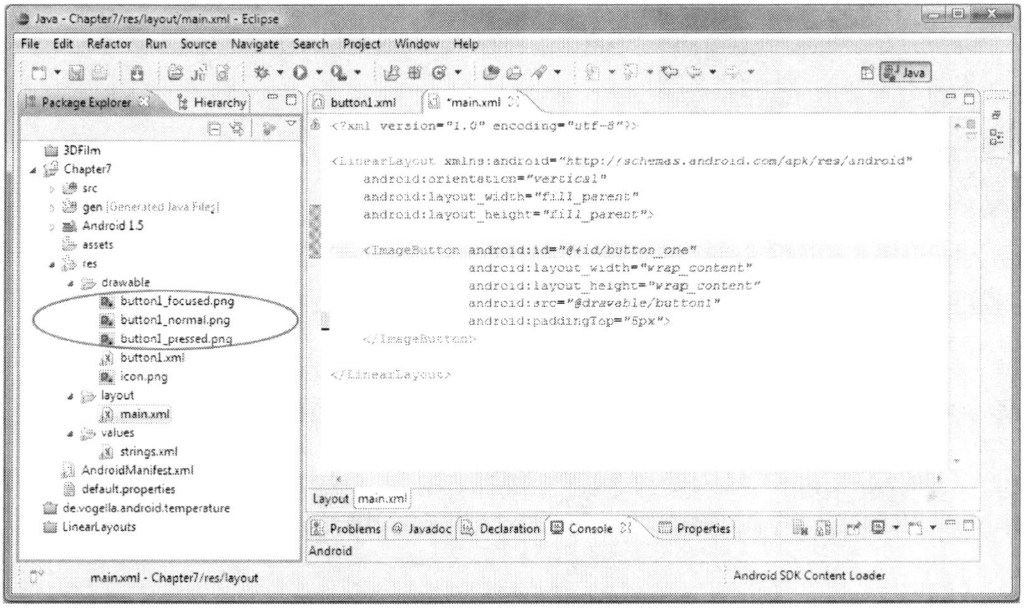

Figure 7–7. *Eclipse with a successful refresh and new ImageButton tag*

The first attribute adds an ID of button_one to the ImageButton so we can access it inside our Java code. The next two lines define the width and height of the image button via the wrap_content attribute—all very standard Android programming fare.

The next line accesses the *button1.xml* file that we have created to reference the various image button states. Notice that you do not need to add the *.xml* extension here, just as you don't need to add *.png* for graphic files. We add 5 pixels of padding to the top of the image, just to practice using padding values.

Figure 7–8 shows how our UI Examples app looks when run in the Android 1.5 emulator (right-click *Chapter7* and select **Run As ➤ Android Application**).

Figure 7–8. *Our multistate image button running in the Android 1.5 emulator*

When you click the image button, it changes color and uses the standard orange background to highlight the button being clicked.

Since we want just the image to be the button (which is why we used transparency and an alpha channel in Photoshop), we will set a background color, or transparency, next.

Replacing the Default Background

We do not want to use the default Android button background. We want the background to be transparent so we can use this ImageButton to put an image on top of a button and its text, as well as being able to make the image itself into a button.

In this example, we are changing the color of the button, rather than changing the size or shape of the button, so the transparent area remains exactly the same, pixel for pixel, between the different image state graphics. Thus, we can either set the background image to our normal button state or set the background color to 100% transparent 32-bit alpha channel with the #00000000 setting (which means zero red, zero green, zero blue, zero alpha). This is similar to setting HTML color with the pattern #RRGGBBAA. That is the most elegant solution, so let's implement that now.

We'll do this in a new way, so that you learn how to use another cool Eclipse function that helps you design your UI widgets and layouts. I think this is a really slick trick, and it was pretty difficult to figure out. As such, this is fairly advanced. Stick with it, though, and you won't be disappointed.

Click the main.xml tab at the top of your screen, and then click the Layout tab at the bottom of the pane that shows your XML for the ImageButton (see Figure 7–9). Eclipse will render your XML markup exactly as it would look in the emulator. Eclipse also provides (on the left) drag-and-drop widgets and layouts, so you can visually design your UI. The normal work process is to switch back and forth between the XML markup coding tab and the visual layout editor tab so you can make sure your XML code is nested properly. This is also a great way to learn XML layout and UI coding in Android.

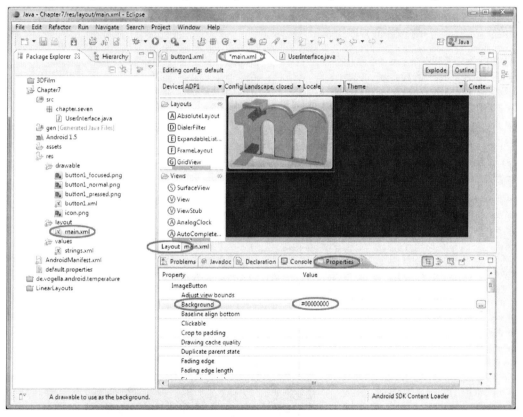

Figure 7–9. *Using the Eclipse visual layout editor and Properties tab to set your image background to transparent*

An even cooler tab is the Properties tab at the bottom of the screen. This tab shows all of the properties assigned or available to the UI element tag that you have selected in the layout view. Click the button element, and a red line will surround the button, showing you what is currently actively selected. In the Properties tab, you will see all of the properties and variables that you can set and customize for the ImageButton class.

Click the Background property in the Properties tab to highlight it. Eclipse then provides a button to search for a file to use as a background image.

Since we are just going to set the background to transparent, we do not need to use this button for the example. Instead, type the transparency value **#00000000** into the field next to Background in the Properties tab, as shown in Figure 7–9. Then click somewhere else in the IDE. The value will be accepted and the results displayed in the Layout tab!

That finishes up our custom image button. Next, let's look at how to add text to your app's UI.

Adding a Text to Your Layout

Besides buttons, another common UI element is text. Android provides the TextView class to implement text in a UI.

Since we are using the visual layout editor in Eclipse, let's continue to explore its functionality. Click the left header bar called Layouts to close the layouts selection view, leaving only the Views (remember widgets are really views) pane open. Clicking these headers will toggle them open and shut at any time (try it now if you don't believe me).

Next, click the scrollbar (gray, with a tiny arrow) until you see the TextView widget. Select and drag (and drop) it into the Layout view window under the ImageButton. Our TextView is now in the UI view and is ready to customize by using the Properties tab at the bottom of the Eclipse IDE. Let's do that now.

Scroll down to the Text properties and set up some custom values, such as **Sample Text**, and a text color of gold to match the ImageButton default image (an RGB value of #CCCC77 will work well; this is a hexadecimal numeric representation of a 24-bit value). Figure 7–10 shows the Eclipse IDE at this point.

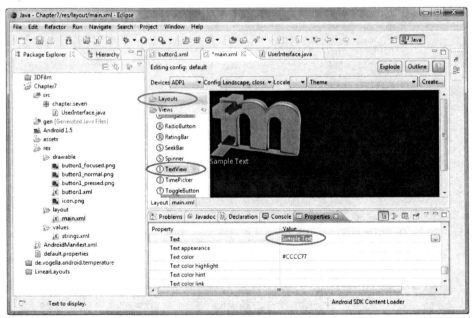

Figure 7–10. *Using the Eclipse visual layout editor to add and configure a TextView widget in the main.xml file*

Finally, we'll set a dpi value for padding, so that there is some space around our TextView. Scroll to the Padding properties in the Properties tab at the bottom of your Eclipse IDE, and type in **12dip**, as shown in Figure 7–11. Then click another field, and you will see the text space itself out.

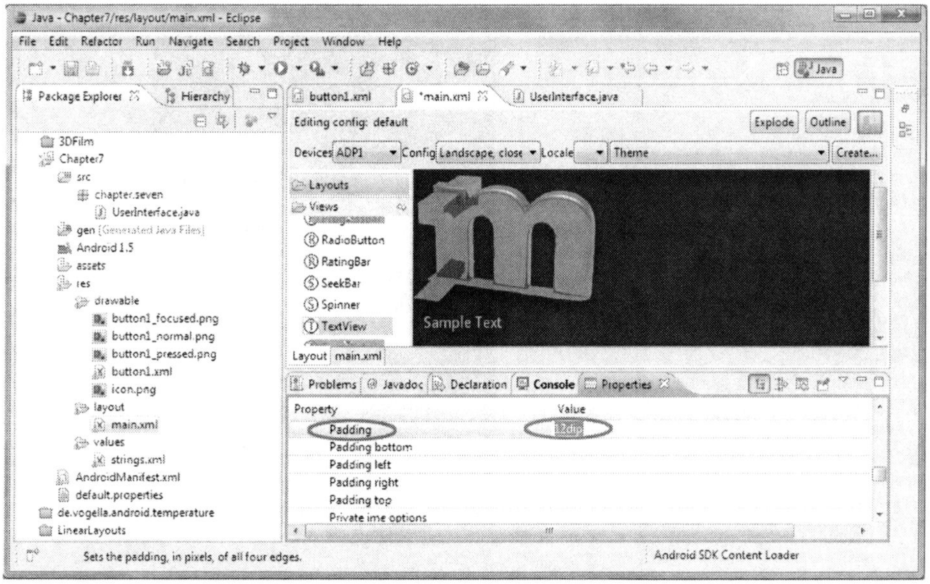

Figure 7–11. *Setting the padding for our TextView via the Properties tab in the Eclipse IDE*

Adding an Image

Finally, let's add another popular type of UI element used for design: the image. Go to the code bundle for this book and copy the two 32-bit image files named *image1.png* and *image2.png* into your *Chapter7/res/drawable* folder.

Right-click the *Chapter7* folder in the Package Explorer pane and refresh the project.

Now, let's add an ImageView tag to our XML. To do this, drag the ImageView from the Views list on the left and drop it under the TextView. This gives us a LinearLayout ViewGroup containing ImageButton, TextView, and ImageView tags.

Next, in the Properties tab below the visual editing window, click the Src (for Source) property, and then click the button on the right with three dots (ellipsis) to open the Reference Chooser dialog. Open the *Drawable* folder and select *image1* for our ImageView source imagery, as shown in Figure 7–12. Click the OK button to close the dialog.

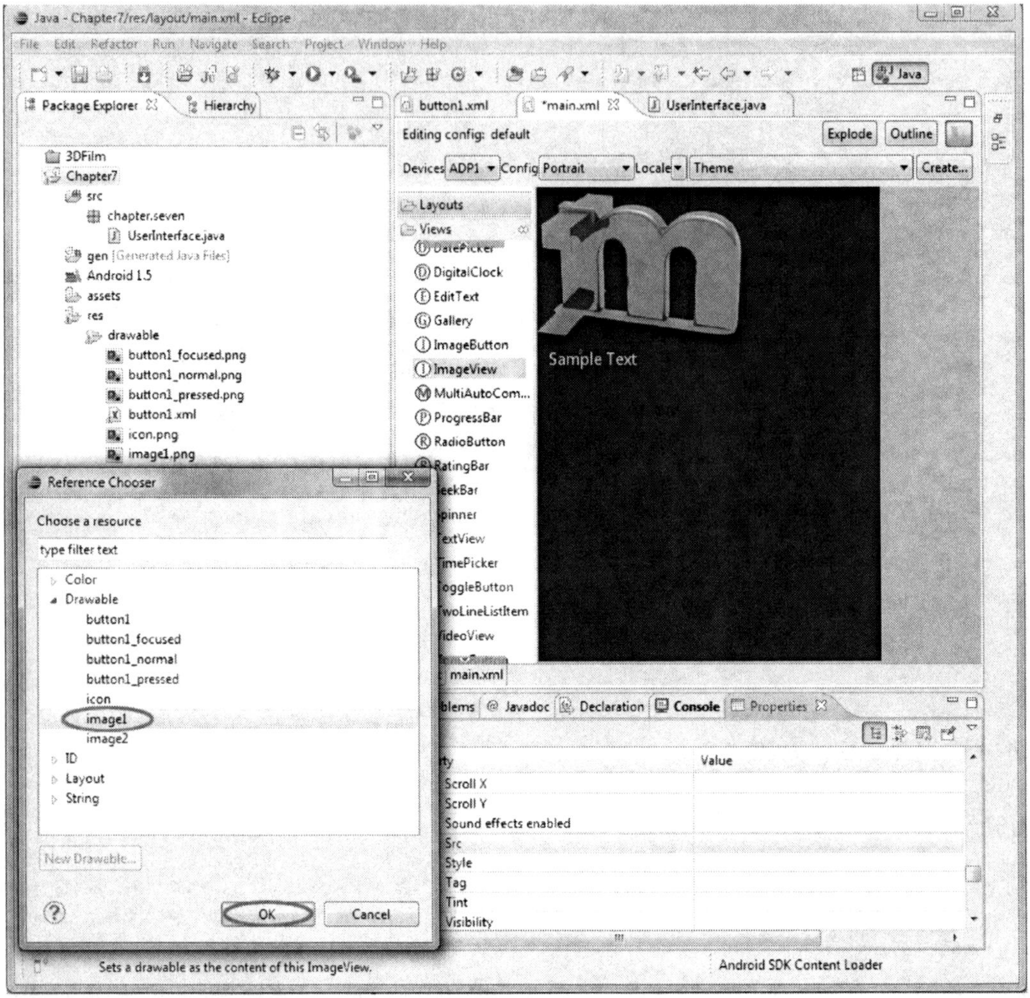

Figure 7-12. *Choosing our image resource via the Reference Chooser dialog, accessed by clicking the ellipsis in the Src field in the Properties tab*

In your visual layout tab, you will now see the image and how its transparency area composites smoothly with the black background color.

Later, when we add a menu to our app, we will change the background color to white to show how this image transparency can help with UI compositing over different background colors or imagery.

So now in the next screen, you will see our ImageButton, TextView, and ImageView with enough screen area to hold a bottom menu of icons. Also note that we used the drop-down at the top to change our orientation to Portrait mode, as shown in Figure 7-13. This orientation fits our application design better. We'll add menus in the next section.

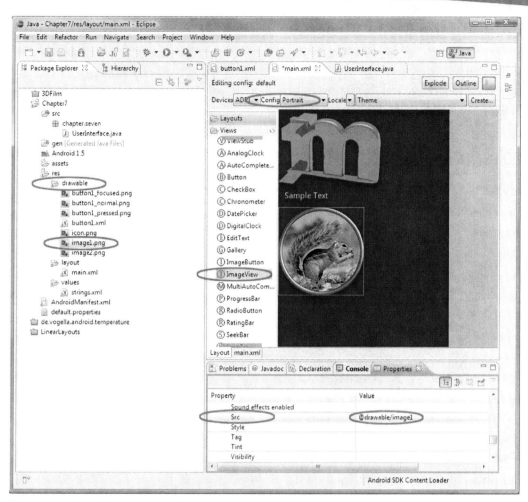

Figure 7–13. *Changing our visual editing environment orientation to portrait*

Using Menus in Android

Menus in Android are quite different from the top-mounted text menus found directly beneath the title bar in PC applications. The menu function on a smartphone is a bit different for ease of use, and is an actual physical button called Menu on Android phones.

Pressing the Menu button calls up a menu, which is—you guessed it—at the bottom of the screen, instead of at the top. To make it even more user-friendly, it is composed of five large square icons that can be easily touched to control application features.

For our application, we will have our menus do things with our ImageView object, background color, and alert dialog (which we'll add later in the chapter), so that everything we cover in this chapter ties together.

Creating the Menu Structure with XML

As you might have guessed, you set up your entire menu structure in an XML file. The menu XML file goes in a /res subfolder named menu, as required by Android. So, first create a folder under the /res folder called menu. Next, right-click the Chapter7 project folder, select **New ▶ File**, and select the Chapter7 folder and its /res/menu subfolder for the file's location. Name the file mainmenu.xml. Then type in the following XML for the menu:

```xml
<?xml version="1.0" encoding="utf-8"?>

<menu xmlns:android="http://schemas.android.com/apk/res/android">

    <item android:id="@+id/buttonone"
          android:icon="@drawable/image1icon"
          android:title="@string/showimage1" />

    <item android:id="@+id/buttontwo"
          android:icon="@drawable/image2icon"
          android:title="@string/showimage2" />

    <item android:id="@+id/buttonthree"
          android:icon="@drawable/menu3icon"
          android:title="@string/showwhite" />

    <item android:id="@+id/buttonfour"
          android:icon="@drawable/menu4icon"
          android:title="@string/showblack" />

    <item android:id="@+id/buttonfive"
          android:icon="@drawable/menu5icon"
          android:title="@string/showalert" />
</menu>
```

The menu XML tag is fairly straightforward. It simply declares the location of its XML schema definition and nested item tags that specify attributes for each menu item to be added. The Android menu holds five items comfortably, and it can hold more than that via a sixth item that drops down a submenu. Most Android applications use five or fewer menu items.

Each of the item tags has the following three attributes:

- The android:id attribute allows the item tag to be given a name and referenced in your Java code.

- The android:icon attribute is the location of the graphic file that will be used for the menu icon. In the first item, it is located in the Chapter7/res/drawable folder and named image1icon.png, shown in Android shorthand as @drawable/image1icon.

- The android:title attribute is the title or label for the menu button. The title is in the strings.xml file, where text constants are defined (we'll do that next).

Figure 7–14 shows the completed *Chapter7/res/menu/menuname.xml* file. The figure also shows the five icon files (*image1icon*, *image2icon*, *menu3icon*, *menu4icon*, and *menu5icon*) placed in the */res/drawable* folder, where Android looks for image files for the application. The images are all 24-bit PNG files with transparency, as you will see when they appear on our menu's buttons.

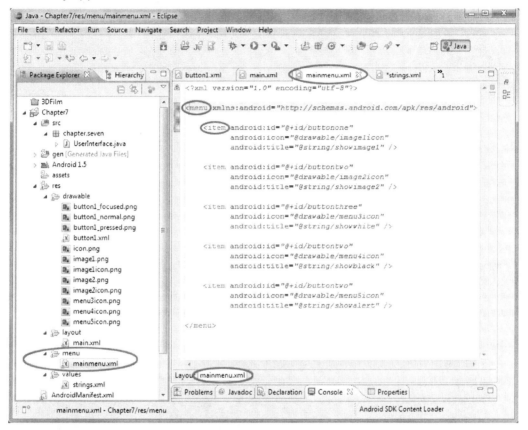

Figure 7–14. *View of the mainmenu.xml file showing menu and item tags. Also note the menu icons in the drawable folder.*

Defining Menu Item Strings

Next, we'll go into the *strings.xml* file in the */res/values* folder (under the *menu* folder in the Package Explorer pane) to edit our application's string constants. We'll add the text for our five menu items. Follow these steps to add the five string values specified in our *mainmenu.xml* file:

1. Right-click the *strings.xml* file and select **Open** to open it in a tab for editing in the Eclipse IDE, as shown in Figure 7–15.

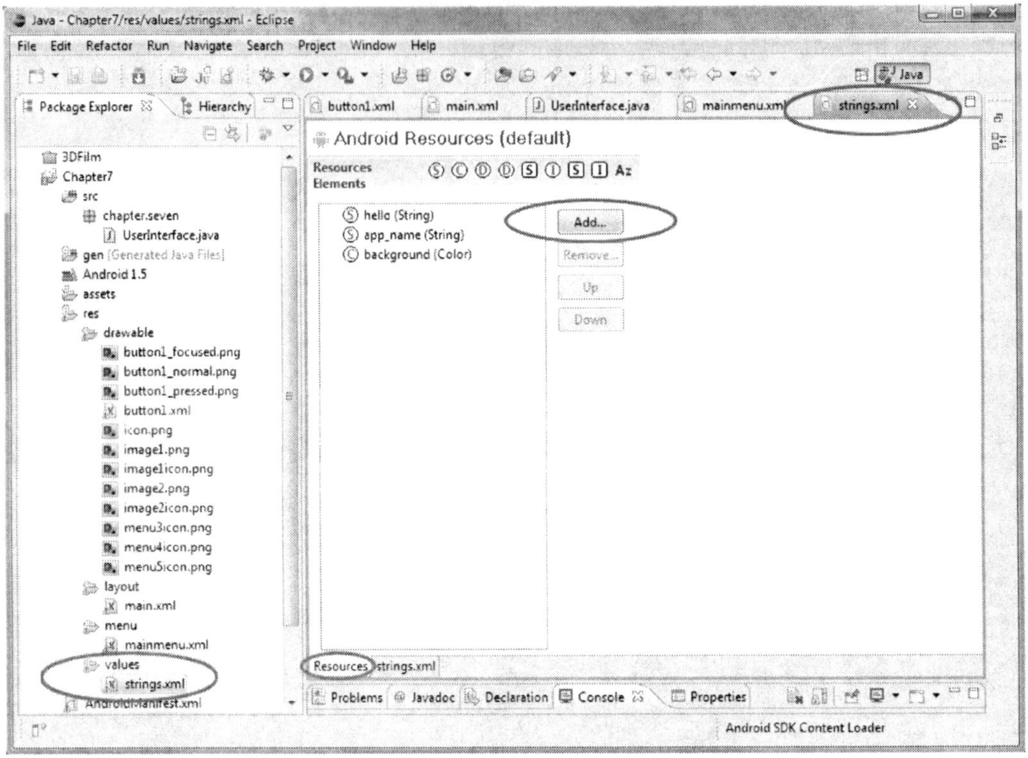

Figure 7–15. *Adding string values for our menu items in the visual editor in Eclipse IDE*

2. Click the Resources tab at the bottom of the pane to see a visual representation of the values in the *strings.xml* file.

TIP: Remember that if you want to see the XML, click the strings.xml tab next to it. You can switch back and forth between the code view and the helper view which is a great way to learn how to code XML UI elements!

3. Click the Add button to bring up the dialog shown in Figure 7–16. Select String and click OK to add a string to our *strings.xml* file.

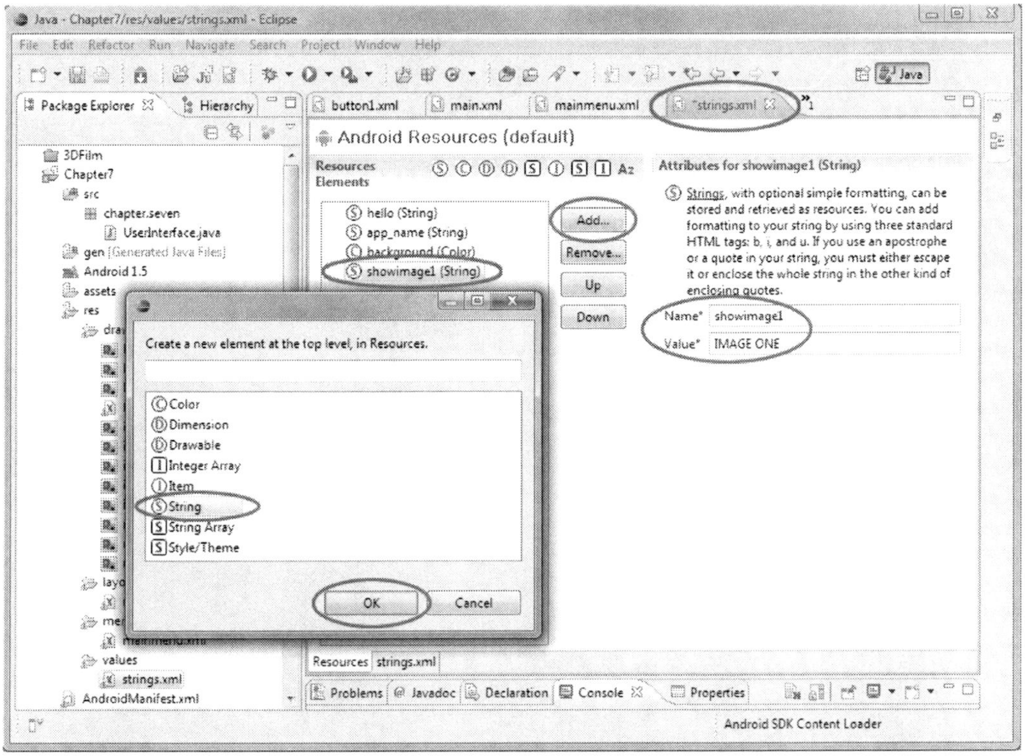

Figure 7–16. *Selecting a String element in the resource selection dialog in the add string resource work process*

4. In the area on the right, in the Name field, enter **showimage1**. In the Value field, enter **IMAGE ONE**. Click the Add button to add this string value to the *strings.xml* file.

5. Repeat steps 3 and 4 to add four more string values with the following names and values:

   ▓ showimage2, IMAGE TWO

   ▓ showwhite, USE WHITE

   ▓ showblack, USE BLACK

   ▓ showalert, SHOW ALERT

6. Set our default black background color of #000000 as a Color object, as shown in Figure 7–17.

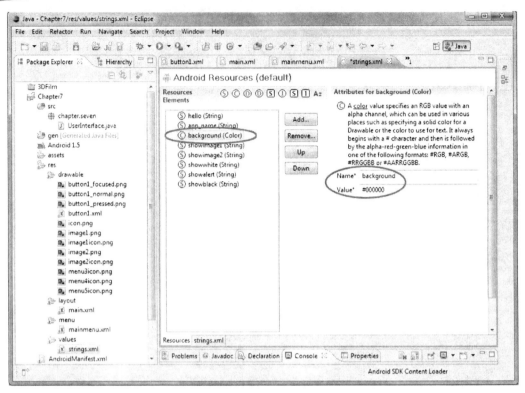

Figure 7–17. *Editing the background color resource in the strings.xml file via the Eclipse visual editor*

7.   Add a white background called background2, using a value of #FFFFFF.

Inflating the Menu Structure via Java

Now it is time to add in our Java code, which inflates our menu from the XML file into our application's memory. The term *inflating* a resource describes the process of the Android operating system taking the data described in an XML file and populating an object that can be accessed and used in Java. In this case, it is our mainmenu object, which contains five menu selection buttons, their icon resources, and the text captions.

Here is the Java code to add to our *UserInterface.java* file:

```
public boolean onCreateOptionsMenu(Menu menu) {
        MenuInflater inflater = getMenuInflater();
        inflater.inflate(R.menu.mainmenu, menu);
        return true;
 }
```

Android has a dedicated Java object for inflating XML code constructs into an object-based format for use with Java. This is precisely what you are seeing here inside the onCreateOptionsMenu() method, which uses the inflate() method and the *R.menu.mainmenu* path to our *mainmenu.xml* file. It creates the inflater MenuInflater object, which contains our inflated menu objects. The *R* equates to the *res* folder of our project, so *R.menu.mainmenu* is equivalent to *c:/Projects/Chapter7/res/menu/mainmenu.xml*.

We also added two `import` statements at the top of our code to tell Android which UI code we would be using. We specify `android.view.Menu` and `android.view.MenuInflater`, which form the foundation for our menu and its inflation from the XML format.

```
import android.view.Menu;
import android.view.MenuInflater;
```

Figure 7–18 shows the code added to *UserInterface.java*.

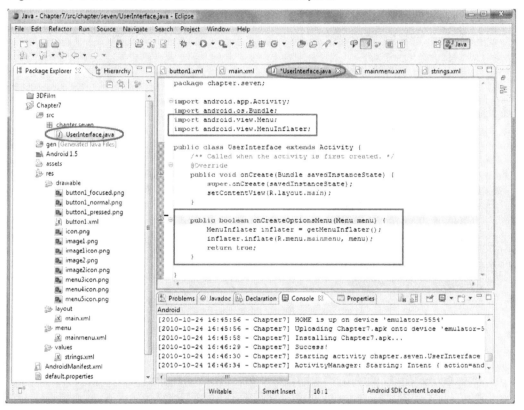

Figure 7–18. *Creating our menu using the MenuInflater in the Eclipse IDE Java editing pane*

Note that we have implemented our application's options menu in little more than a half-dozen lines of Java code. We have offloaded about 80% of the menu implementation coding to XML, and we can continue to add features and fine-tune menu options inside the XML markup as well.

Running the Application in the Android Emulator

Let's run our code and see our menu in action. Right-click the *Chapter7* folder in the Package Explorer pane and select **Run As…** ➤ **Android Application**. After the emulator loads and you start up your application, the emulator should look like Figure 7–19.

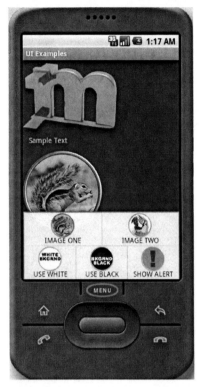

Figure 7–19. *Running our application in the Android 1.5 emulator*

As you can see, the Android phone has a prominent Menu button, which we can press to display our menu at the bottom of the screen. You can see the translucency of the menu. If you look closely at the first button, you will see the bottom of the ImageView behind the menu. If you click the various buttons, they will highlight in orange and close the menu, which you can reopen with the Menu button.

So, the default way an empty menu works is harmless to the application. It allows us to develop and test the way our menu looks via XML before we add in the Java logic to implement the actions that will be called when each button is pressed.

Making the Menu Work

Let's add our menu item implementations now. First, we need to give our LinearLayout an ID, so that we can find it in our code.

```
<LinearLayout xmlns:android="http://schemas.android.com/apk/res/android"
```

```
        android:id="@+id/uilayout"
    android:orientation="vertical"
    android:layout_width="fill_parent"
    android:layout_height="fill_parent"
    >
```

Now, we need to implement the onOptionsItemSelected() method, where we code the choices between our different menu item selections and what they do in our application if and when they are selected.

```java
public boolean onOptionsItemSelected(MenuItem item) {
    LinearLayout bkgr = (LinearLayout)findViewById(R.id.uilayout);
    ImageView image = (ImageView)findViewById(R.id.ImageView01);

    switch (item.getItemId()) {

    case R.id.buttonone:
                image.setImageResource(R.drawable.image1);
                return true;
    case R.id.buttontwo:
                image.setImageResource(R.drawable.image2);
                return true;
    case R.id.buttonthree:
                bkgr.setBackgroundResource(R.color.background2);
                return true;
    case R.id.buttonfour:
                bkgr.setBackgroundResource(R.color.background);
                return true;
    case R.id.buttonfive:
                // The Alert Code For Next Section Goes Here!
                return true;
    default:
            return super.onOptionsItemSelected(item);
    }

    }
```

This code is a bit more complex than our MenuInflater code. At its core, it implements a switch structure. The switch is a Java construct that says, "In the case of *this*, do *that*, and in the case of *this*, do *that*; otherwise, as a default, do *this*." This type of code construct is perfect for the main Android menu, as it usually has only five or six items.

Figure 7–20 shows the *UserInterface.java* code in the Eclipse editor in context with our previous two code blocks. In the figure, the new code is boxed. We will cover the top import statements, then the outer onOptionsItemSelected() method, and then its inner switch statement and programming logic for each button case statement and what it needs to do in the UI (switch images, background colors, and so on).

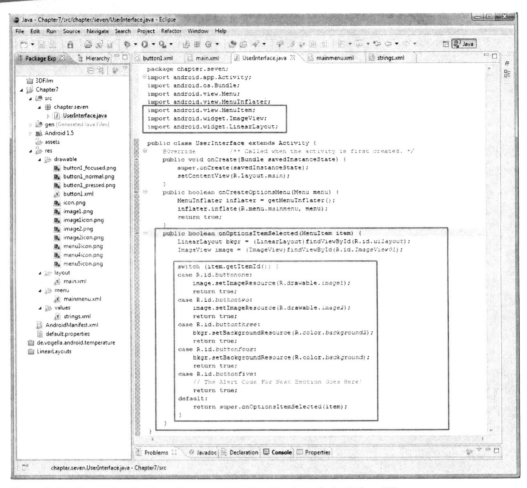

Figure 7–20. *Java code to implement our menu functionality shown in the Eclipse IDE*

First are the `import` statements for the Android classes that we are going to use in our `onOptionsItemSelected()` method (see the top box in Figure 7–20):

- Since we reference `MenuItem` in our `onOptionsItemSelected()` method, we need to import `android.view.MenuItem`.

- Since we are going to switch image resources in our `ImageView` UI object, we also need to import `android.widget.ImageView`.

- Since we are going to change our `LinearLayout` background color from black to white, we need to import `android.widget.LinearLayout` as well.

Remember that importing the class libraries that we are going to use in our Java code makes sure they are in memory when Eclipse needs to use them during the compilation of our Java code.

Next, let's examine our onOptionsItemSelected() code. First, we need to create references to our LinearLayout and ImageView objects, so that we can operate on these objects. This way, we can adjust their resource values to change our menu buttons' image and background color.

The first line creates a LinearLayout object called bkgr and sets it to the LinearLayout that is assigned the ID uilayout via the findViewById() method. The second line creates an ImageView object called image and sets it to the ImageView that is assigned the ID ImageView01 in the same way. These IDs can be seen in the *main.xml* file and tab, so you can check that everything matches up.

Finally, we have the Java switch statement. It starts with switch(item.getItemId()), which means "Decide between the following options (each case statement) based on the ID of the MenuObject that we named item. If nothing matches, just use the default action at the bottom of the statement decision tree list." The case statements work as follows:

- The first case statement says, "In the case of the item MenuItem with an ID of buttonone being passed, please set the image ImageView object's image resource to the 24-bit PNG image called *image1* in the */drawable* folder using the setImageResource() method."

- The second case statement says, "In the case of the item MenuItem with an ID of buttontwo being passed over, please set the image ImageView object's image resource to the 24-bit PNG image called *image2* in the */drawable* folder using the setImageResource() method."

- The third case statement says, "In the case of the item MenuItem with an ID of buttonthree being passed over, please set the bkgr LinearLayout object's background resource to the color resource called *background2* in the */values/strings.xml* resource using the setBackgroundResource() method."

- The fourth case statement says, "In the case of the item MenuItem with an ID of buttonfour being passed over, please set the bkgr LinearLayout object's background resource to the color resource called *background* in the */values/strings.xml* resource using the setBackgroundResource() method."

- The fifth case is left open for our next section, and thus the button does nothing at this point.

If none of the case statements match IDs passed over to operate on, then the default action is made, which is to pass over to the onOptionsItemSelected() method of the superclass.

Adding Dialogs

An Android dialog is always created as part of an activity, and is presented in the form of a small, gray pop-up window that appears on top of the current activity's UI. Android dims that UI so that it does not compete with the dialog box.

The Dialog class is used to create an interruption of your current activity in order to collect or relay information to your application's end user. Examples of uses for dialogs include alert notifications, end-user option selection, information data collection, date selection, time selection, task or processing progress bar monitoring, and so on.

Using Custom Dialog Subclasses

Four custom subclasses of the Dialog class are provided as part of the Android API:

- AlertDialog
- ProgressDialog
- DatePickerDialog
- TimePickerDialog

You can also subclass your own custom Dialog class (say, CustomDialog) so that it does exactly what you need it to do.

The general way to create a basic dialog within any given activity is via the onCreateDialog(int) method. Android uses this method to track the dialog created, which activity it belongs to, and its current state.

To display a dialog once it is created, you use the showDialog(int) method, specifying the number of the dialog you wish to display. To hide or dismiss a Dialog object, use the dismissDialog(int) method, and the Dialog object will be removed from memory and the application.

Here, we'll take a closer look at the most often used (and the recommended) Dialog class: AlertDialog. Android provides an easy and powerful way to construct alert dialogs with many features.

Displaying an Alert Dialog

The AlertDialog class provides a lot of built-in dialog features, such as a title, user message, up to three buttons, and a list of selectable items. You can even use check boxes and radio buttons in your list.

The AlertDialog works its magic via a dialog builder that provides a ready-made dialog code structure for you to create complicated dialogs via the AlertDialog.Builder class.

As shown in the boxed areas of Figure 7–21, there are four main parts to adding our AlertDialog to our existing Android application.

Figure 7–21. Java code for implementing our alert dialog builder in the Eclipse IDE

First, we add the import statements for the Android utilities we are going to leverage to provide our AlertDialog object:

```
import android.app.AlertDialog;
import android.content.DialogInterface;
```

Next, we create our AlertDialog.Builder object, which we name builder. This is a new (empty and initialized) AlertDialog.Builder object.

```
public boolean onOptionsItemSelected(MenuItem item) {
    LinearLayout bkgr = (LinearLayout)findViewById(R.id.uilayout);
    final ImageView image = (ImageView)findViewById(R.id.ImageView01);

    AlertDialog.Builder builder = new AlertDialog.Builder(this);
```

In order to work with the image object inside the builder dialog object that we are
constructing, we need to add the keyword final to our declaration of this object
variable (you'll see why in the next step). The final keyword is used for variables,
methods, and classes. A final variable cannot be given a new value after it has been
assigned one (although we can alter the variable object like any other object). A final
method cannot be overridden. Also, a final class cannot be extended, and is thus in a
sense protected from further programming modifications.

The preceding code basically says, "I want to declare an object named builder that is of
the type AlertDialog.Builder, and I wish to set it equal to this new AlertDialog.Builder
object that I am creating here. Therefore, please instantiate an empty
AlertDialog.Builder object for me to define and fill with my own custom parameters."

After this has been declared, builder exists as an empty AlertDialog ready to fill with
our own custom parameters. OK, on to the fun part and the third and major part of
AlertDialog definition.

Here is the code to customize our dialog:

```
builder.setTitle("Pick an Image!")
    .setMessage("Please Select Image One or Image Two:")
    .setCancelable(false)
    .setPositiveButton("IMAGE 1", new DialogInterface.OnClickListener()
    {
        public void onClick(DialogInterface dialog, int id) {
            image.setImageResource(R.drawable.image1);
        }
    })

    .setNegativeButton("IMAGE 2", new DialogInterface.OnClickListener() {
        public void onClick(DialogInterface dialog, int id) {
            image.setImageResource(R.drawable.image2);
        }
    });
```

We work with the image object, which we know can't be reassigned a value because it is
final. This is to deal with situations where the event listener is used after the
onOptionsItemSelected() method has terminated. In this case, a non-final image
variable would not be around to take a new assignment, whereas a final variable is
frozen in memory for access at all times (of course, this may never happen, but Java
was built this way just to be sure).

Notice in this block of code that sets our AlertDialog parameters (I am amazed that
they did not offload AlertDialog parameters to an *alert_dialog.xml* file) that a new
concept called *method chaining* is used. This allows a large number of parameters to be
set without the builder object being explicitly typed before each dot-notation construct.

In method chaining, the first method is attached to its object with dot notation. In our example, it looks like this:

```
builder.setTitle("Pick an Image!")
```

The follow-on methods that set the other parameters are simply .setMessage(), .setCancelable(false), and so on.

I've formatted the preceding code for ease of reading. But to give you a little more grip on method chaining, the first three method calls could be rewritten as follows, illustrating the chain:

```
builder.setTitle("Pick an Image!").setMessage("Please Select...").setCancelable(false)
```

Also note that between contiguous methods, there is no semicolon at the end of these parameter setting lines of code. Semicolons are required on only the last and final method call—in this case, after .setNegativeButton() to end the builder definition.

> **NOTE:** In this case, the order of the chained methods doesn't matter because each one returns an AlertDialog.Builder object with the new parameter set alongside all the other parameters that have been set so far. In other cases, the order of chaining matters. Android has been well designed to make chaining easy and convenient.

The code for setting the title, the message, and whether the Back button on the phone is able to cancel the dialog (in this case, it is not cancelable) is pretty straightforward here, so let's go over what is happening inside each button.

You can have up to three buttons in an AlertDialog object. These buttons are hard-coded into the Android operating system as follows:

- PositiveButton
- NeutralButton
- NegativeButton

This explains the setPositiveButton() and setNegativeButton() methods shown in the preceding code.

The convention here is to use PositiveButton for one-button dialogs, PositiveButton and NegativeButton for two-button dialogs, and all three for three-button dialogs. The code inside the two buttons in our dialog is nearly identical, so let's go over what is happening inside the first button, IMAGE 1.

```
.setPositiveButton("IMAGE 1", new DialogInterface.OnClickListener()
{
    public void onClick(DialogInterface dialog, int id) {
        image.setImageResource(R.drawable.image1);
    }
})
```

The setPositiveButton() method allows us to name the button IMAGE 1 and creates a new OnClickListener() implementation for the DialogInterface. Note that we declared android.content.DialogInterface in an import statement initially, and it is being used here to create a PositiveButton.

Inside the OnClickListener, we have a public method onClick(), which defines what will be done when the button is clicked. onClick() is passed a dialog object of type DialogInterface and an integer ID value that represents which of the buttons was clicked or the numerical order of the button that was clicked—both of which are what OnCLickListener wants to evaluate in the event the user clicks that button.

Inside this onClick container is where our code goes to change our ImageView object to the appropriate image resource. Since we have already done that in the menu code, we can simply copy the image.setImageResource(R.drawable.image1) code from down in our switch construct for ButtonOne.

Finally, down inside our switch statement, where before we had a placeholder comment, we can now display the dialog by calling the show() method of the builder object that we created earlier. This line of code could not be simpler:

```
builder.show();
```

Whenever the fifth menu button is clicked, our dialog will be shown. We can select between the two images, which will then be set on our screen appropriately.

Now, right-click your *Chapter7* folder and select **Run As…** ➤ **Android Application** to see your work. Figure 7–22 shows the dialog as it appears in the emulator after you click the ! button in the menu.

Figure 7–22. *Viewing our alert dialog in the emulator*

Summary

With the exception of dialogs, Android allows us to put together our designs using XML, and to implement them with just a half-dozen lines of code is some instances, such as when creating a system options menu. This allows designers to get one step closer to the coding process.

In this chapter, we created an application that has all of the primary UI objects that can be used to construct an application:

- ImageButtons allow us to create custom UI elements.

- TextView and ImageView objects allow us to put relevant information on the screen.

- Menu items allow us to use the Android Menu button to control our application.

- Alert dialogs interface with our users to gather information or inform about decisions.

In the next chapter, you will learn how to add graphics to provide even more new media user experiences in your Android applications.

Chapter 8

An Introduction to Graphics Resources in Android

This chapter will serve as an introduction to how to best integrate and optimize graphical elements in your Android apps. These include graphics such as bitmap images, tween animation (transform-based), bitmap animation (frame-based), image transitions (crossfades, or slow-blended image fades from one image into another) and digital video.

You will learn how to best use imaging techniques within your application's View objects that make up your UI, and how to support all three levels of Android screens (QVGA, HVGA, and WVGA) via custom resource assets.

> **NOTE:** Because VGA is 640 × 480 pixels, quarter VGA (QVGA) is 320 × 240 pixels, or one-quarter of a VGA screen; half VGA (HVGA) is 480 × 320, or one-half of a VGA screen; and wide VGA (WVGA) is 800 × 480, or a widescreen version of a VGA screen.

We'll cover the use of graphics objects in both the areas of UI design (custom buttons, for instance) and user experience design (the content itself, say music videos or an interactive children's storybook).

We'll look at two packages: the android.graphics.drawable package (I knew there was a reason that resource folder was called *drawable*) and the android.view.animation package. These are collections of useful classes for maximizing bitmap imagery and for working with images that support the fourth dimension (time) via animation. For fun, we'll play with a really cool 9-patch image auto-scaling feature that Android supports for the PNG format.

Finally, we'll take a look at digital video. Using the VideoView class makes playing digital video a snap. We'll also discuss which open source digital video formats are best to use, and how to optimize them for use on smartphones.

Introducing the Drawables

The central set of classes used to control the graphics-related content within your Android application is called the drawable package. This package handles classes and methods related to drawing the following onto the Android display screen:

- **Bitmaps**: In a bitmap, a collection of pixels make up an image—it's a map of image bits, if you will.

- **Shapes**: Shapes are line drawings. They also known as *vectors*, like the lines architects use in CAD drawings

- **Gradients**: Gradients are smooth transitions from one color to another color. They can be shaped in a straight line or circular.

- **Transitions**: Shape transitions are smooth vector changes between one shape to another shape. This process is sometimes referred to as *morphing*.

- **Animation**: Animation is an image that moves in some way.

- **Image transitions:** These are smooth fades between one image to another image. They are usually used to transition from one image to another image.

In Android development, graphics-related items like gradients, image transitions, animated transformations, and frame-based animation can all be termed *drawables*. With the exceptions of tweens and transformational animation, all center their resource assets in the */res/drawable* folder. (And you thought tweens were 12-year-olds, right?)

The */res/drawable* folder is also where you should put XML files that define things like frame-based image animations and crossfading image transitions (which we will look at later in this chapter). So get used to seeing *drawable* everywhere you look, because it will be one of the most used folders in your resources (*/res*) folder.

Implementing Images

The way that Android is set up to automatically implement your images via the project folder hierarchy is a bit hard to understand at first. But once you get used to it, you'll find that it is actually amazingly simple to use graphic resources, as major coding is all but eliminated. You will see that in this chapter when we implement features using as few as four lines of Java program logic.

I'm not sure what could be much simpler than this: put your imagery into the *project/res/drawable* folder, and then reference it by file name in your code. Yes, all you need to do is reference it in your XML and Java code, and you are finished, and with perfect results (assuming that your imagery is optimized correctly).

In this chapter, we will look at which image and video formats to use, which techniques to implement, and which work processes to follow as much as (or more than) we will be dealing with XML attributes and Java code snippets (although these are fun to play with as well).

Core Drawable Subclasses

Android offers more than a dozen types of customized drawable objects. In this chapter, we'll work with the following core subclasses of `android.graphics.drawable`:

- **`BitmapDrawable` object**: Used to create, tile, stretch, and align bitmaps.

- **`ColorDrawable` object**: Used to fill certain other objects with color.

- **`GradientDrawable` object**: Used to create and draw custom gradients.

- **`AnimationDrawable` object**: Used to create frame-based animations.

- **`TransitionDrawable` object**: Used to create crossfade transitions.

- **`NinePatchDrawable` object**: Used to create resizable bitmaps via custom stretchable areas.

> **NOTE:** If you want to review all of the drawable objects, look at the `android.graphics.drawable` package document on the Android Developers web site (`http://developer.android.com`). You'll find that there is a plethora of graphics power in Android's 2D engine.

The most pervasive and often used type of drawable is the bitmap. A *bitmap* is an image composed of a collection of dots called *pixels*, where "pix" stands for "pictures" and "els" stands for "elements". Yes, a bitmap is quite literally a map of bits. So, let's get started with adding bitmaps to your Android apps.

Using Bitmap Images in Android

How do we best optimize our static (motionless, or fixed-in-place) bitmap imagery for use within our Android applications? That's what this section is all about. We have already worked with bitmap images in the previous chapter, in the context of our `ImageButton` and `ImageView` objects, so you have a little experience with using truecolor 32-bit PNG (PNG32) files to obtain an excellent graphic result.

Android supports three bitmap image file formats: PNG, JPEG, and GIF. We'll talk about how Android truly feels about each one, so you can choose the right formats to meet your graphics-related design and user experience objectives.

PNG Images

The most powerful file format that Android supports, and the one it recommends using over all others, is Portable Network Graphics, or PNG (pronounced "ping"). There are two types of PNG:

- Indexed-color, which uses a limited 256-color image palette

- Truecolor, which uses a 32-bit color image that includes a full 8-bit alpha channel (used for image compositing)

PNG is a known as a *lossless* image file format, because it loses zero image data in the compression processing. This means that the image quality is always 100% maintained. If designers know what they are doing, they can get very high-quality graphics into a reasonably small data footprint using the indexed-color PNG8 and truecolor PNG32 image file formats.

Indexed-color PNG8 files use one-fourth of the amount of data (bits) that a truecolor 32-bit PNG32 image does. Remember the math we did in the previous chapter: 8 × 4 = 32. A smaller data footprint is achieved by using only 8 bits, or a 256-color palette of optimal colors best suited to represent the image, but with the same visual result. This is done primarily to save data file size, thereby decreasing the image's data footprint.

Truecolor PNG32 images use a full 32 bits of data for each of the image pixels to represent the four image data channels that are in most bitmap images: alpha, red, green, and blue (RGBA).

The alpha channel determines where the image is going to be transparent, and is used for image compositing. As you learned in Chapter 7, compositing is the process of using more than one image in layers to create a final image out of several component parts.

Another benefit of image compositing is that in your programming code, you can access different image elements independently of other image elements. For example, you might do this for game engine programming.

Note that at compile time, Android looks at your PNG32 graphics, and if they use less than 256 colors in the image, Android automatically remaps them to be indexed PNG8 images, just as you would want it to do. This means that you don't need to worry about analyzing your images to see if they should be in truecolor or indexed-color format. You can simply do everything in truecolor, and if it can be optimized into indexed-color with no loss of data, Android will do that for you—making your data footprint three to four times smaller.

If for some reason you don't want your images optimized at compile time, you can put them into the *project/res/raw* folder, which is for data that is accessed directly from your Java code. A good example of this is video files that have been well optimized for size and quality, and just need to be played. These come up in a video player example in Chapter 11, so stay tuned, as we will be using the */raw* folder soon enough.

JPEG and GIF Images

The next most desirable format to use is the JPEG image file type. This type does not have an alpha channel. It uses *lossy* compression, which means that it throws away data to get a better compression result.

If you look closely at JPEG images, you will see a lot of *artifacts*, such as areas of strange color variations or dirt on the image that was not on the camera lens. JPEG is useful for higher-resolution (print) images, where artifacts are too small to be seen. So, it is not really suitable for small smartphone screens. JPEG is supported but not recommended for Android apps.

Finally, we have GIF, an older 8-bit file format. The use of this file format is discouraged. Stay away from using GIFs for Android apps. Use PNG8 instead.

Creating Animation in Android

You've learned how to implement static bitmap images in previous chapters. So, let's get right into the fun stuff with animation.

Frame-based or Cel 2D Animation

Traditional 2D animation involves moving quickly among a number of what originally were called *cels*, or hand-drawn images, creating the illusion of motion. To steal a more modern term from the movie industry, each image, which is a little bit different from the next, is called a *frame*. This term refers back to the original days of film, where actual film stock would be run through a projector, showing 24 frames per second (fps).

In Android, frame-based animation is the easiest to implement and gives great results. You just need to define the XML animation attributes—what and where the frames are—in the correct place for Android to find them. Then you can control your animation via Java.

In our example, we are going to animate a 3D logo. It will come into existence via a fireworks-like particle animation.

Let's fire up a new project in Eclipse, and see how animation works in Android.

1. If you still have the *Chapter7* project folder open from the previous examples, right-click that folder and select **Close Project**. This closes the project folder in Eclipse (of course, it can be reopened later).

2. Select Eclipse **File ➤ New ➤ Project** and choose Android Project to open the New Android Project dialog. Fill it out as follows (and shown in Figure 8–1).

   ▪ **Project name**: Name this project Chapter8.

   ▪ **Build Target**: Choose Android 1.5.

- **Application name:** Let's call this application **Graphics Examples**.

- **Package name**: Name the package graphics.examples.

- **Create Activity**: Check this box and name the activity graphics.

- **Minimum SDK Version**: Enter **3**, which matches with our 1.5 compatibility Build Target setting.

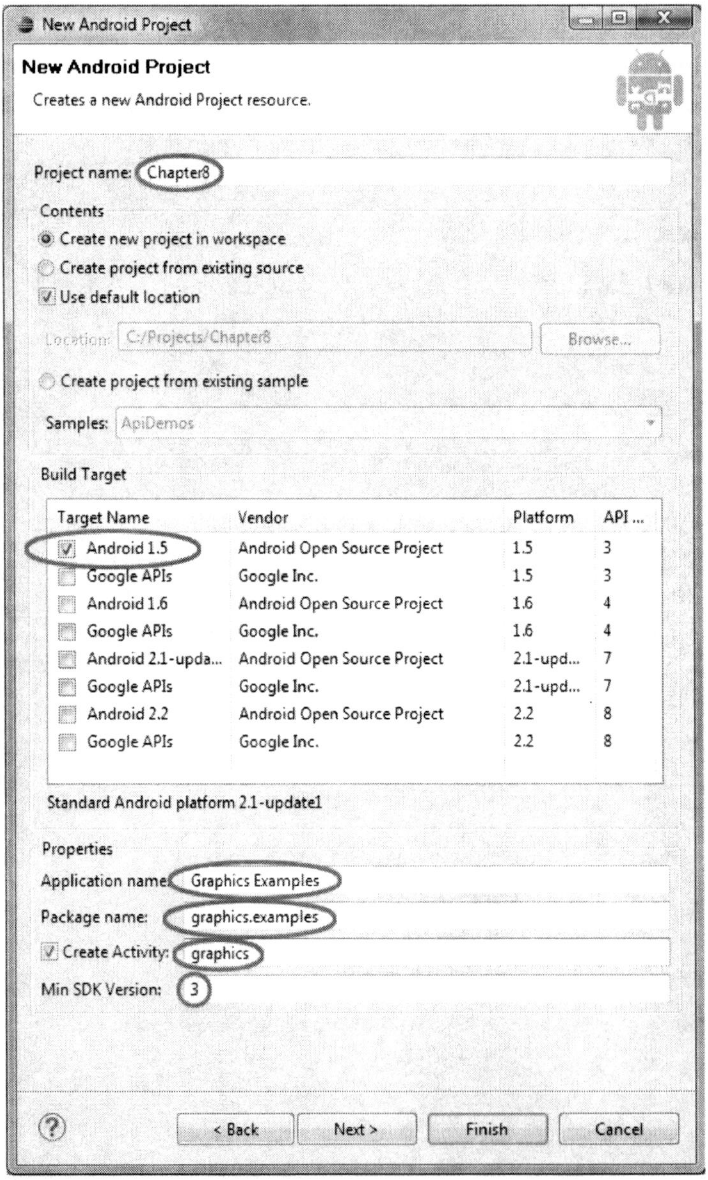

Figure 8–1. *Creating the Chapter8 Android project*

3. Now we need to define our animation's frames in an XML file, which we'll call *logo_animation*. Right-click your *Chapter8* folder and select **New ➤ File**. At the bottom of the dialog, enter *logo_animation.xml*. In the Chapter8 navigation pane in the middle of the dialog, expose your directory structure (via the arrows next to the folders), and select the *res/drawable* folder, so that the parent folder field above shows *Chapter8/res/drawable*. This places our *logo_animation* XML file in the correct folder. Figure 8–2 shows the completed New File dialog.

CAUTION: Since frame-based animation in Android uses bitmap images, you place the XML file that references these bitmap images into the same folder the images occupy: the */res/drawable* folder. Do *not* put frame animation images or XML specifications into the */res/anim* folder. That folder is for transform animation (covered in the next section of this chapter). This is an important difference in how frame-based animations and transform-based or tween animations are set up and created in Android.

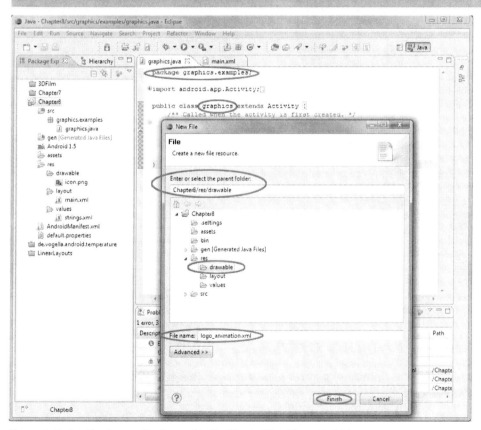

Figure 8–2. *Creating logo_animation.xml in the Chapter8/res/drawable folder*

4. Next, click the logo_animation.xml tab in Eclipse, and type in the following XML to define our frame-based animation for Android (Figure 8–3 shows the new file in Eclipse):

```xml
<?xml version="1.0" encoding="utf-8"?>

<animation-list xmlns:android="http://schemas.android.com/apk/res/android"
                android:oneshot="true">
    <item android:drawable="@drawable/mtlogo0" android:duration="200" />
    <item android:drawable="@drawable/mtlogo1" android:duration="200" />
    <item android:drawable="@drawable/mtlogo2" android:duration="200" />
    <item android:drawable="@drawable/mtlogo3" android:duration="200" />
    <item android:drawable="@drawable/mtlogo4" android:duration="200" />
    <item android:drawable="@drawable/mtlogo5" android:duration="200" />
    <item android:drawable="@drawable/mtlogo6" android:duration="200" />
    <item android:drawable="@drawable/mtlogo7" android:duration="200" />
    <item android:drawable="@drawable/mtlogo8" android:duration="200" />
    <item android:drawable="@drawable/mtlogo9" android:duration="200" />
</animation-list>
```

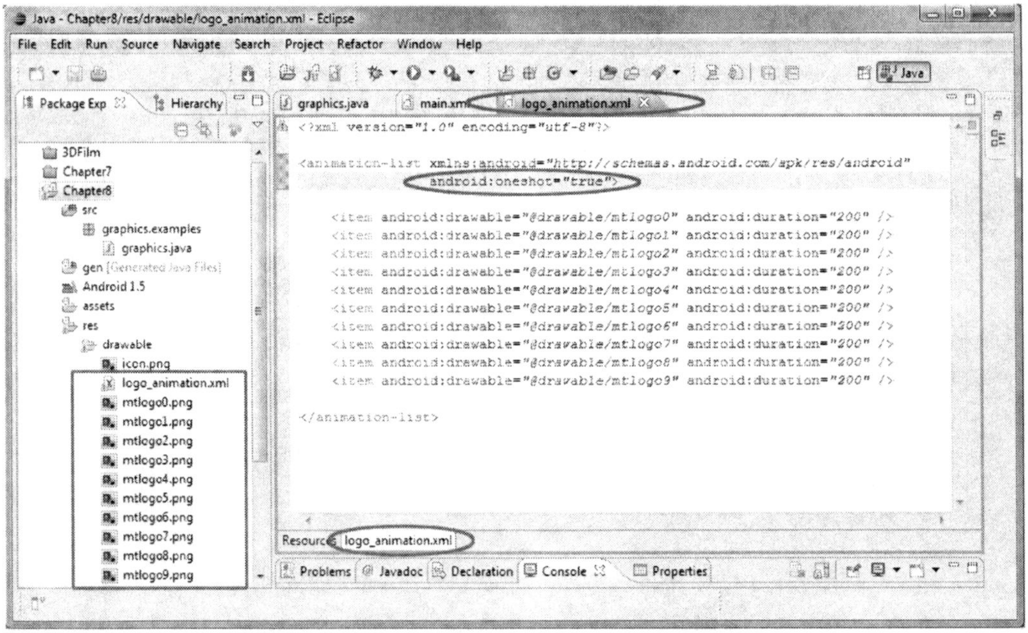

Figure 8–3. *Creating the XML mark-up for the logo_animation.xml file*

This is pretty straightforward XML tag mark-up logic here. We declare the XML version and add an animation-list tag for frame-based animation image (item) listings. This tag has its android:oneshot attribute set to true, which will prevent our animation from looping continuously. Setting oneshot equal to false will run the animation seamlessly as a loop.

Inside the animation-list tag, we have ten nested item tags (nested because the animation-list closing tag comes after these ten item tags). These specify the location of each image in our /res/drawable folder, where each image is a frame in the animation.

Using each item tag entry, we specify the name and location of each of our frames mtlogo0 through mtlogo9, as well as the duration of the frame display time in milliseconds (ms). In this case, we start off using 200 ms, or one-fifth second, for each frame, so that the entire animation plays over 2 seconds, and at 5 fps, just barely fast enough to fake movement. We can adjust frame times later, to fine-tune the visual result, as well as make the animation loop seamlessly to show this feature.

We need to put our animation frame images into the /res/drawable folder, so that the XML code can reference them successfully. As you know by now, in Android, everything needs to be in its correct place for things to work properly.

1. Copy the ten animation frames into the /res/drawable folder from the code download.

2. Right-click the Chapter8 folder in the Package Explorer and select **Refresh**, so that the IDE can see them.

3. If there are errors on your XML editing pane, right-click your Chapter8 folder and select **Validate** to clear these as well.

At this point, you should see a screen that looks similar to Figure 8–3.

Controlling Frame-based Animation via Java

Now we are going to write our Java code to access and control our 2D animation. If the graphics.java tab is not already open, right-click the graphics.java file and select **Open**.

> **NOTE:** In order to right-click the graphics.java file, the /src folder and subfolders need to be showing in the expanded Package Explorer project-tree view, so click those arrows to make your hierarchy visible.

Here is the code for our graphics.java file, which holds our graphics class from our graphics.examples package:

```
package graphics.examples;

import android.app.Activity;
import android.os.Bundle;
import android.view.MotionEvent;
import android.widget.ImageView;
import android.graphics.drawable.AnimationDrawable;

public class Graphics extends Activity {

        AnimationDrawable logoAnimation;
```

```
    @Override        /** Called when the activity is first created. */
    public void onCreate(Bundle savedInstanceState) {
        super.onCreate(savedInstanceState);
        setContentView(R.layout.main);

        ImageView logoImage = (ImageView) findViewById(R.id.iv1);
        logoImage.setBackgroundResource(R.drawable.logo_animation);
        logoAnimation = (AnimationDrawable) logoImage.getBackground();
    }
    public boolean onTouchEvent(MotionEvent event) {
        if (event.getAction() == MotionEvent.ACTION_DOWN) {
          logoAnimation.start();
          return true;
        }
        else return super.onTouchEvent(event);
    }
}
```

In Android Java code, AnimationDrawable is the class we need to use to implement our frame-based animation sequences. We import the android.graphics.drawable.AnimationDrawable class. Then we import the android.widget.ImageView class, which we will use as a view container to display the animation. Finally, we import the android.view.MotionEvent, which we will use to implement a touchscreen touch trigger to interactively start up the animation play cycle. We add the three new import statements to the ones that Android starts us out with (the first two).

Next, we add the object declaration for our AnimationDrawable object, which we are calling logoAnimation. This is as simple as writing the following:

```
AnimationDrawable logoAnimation;
```

Then we have our standard onCreate() method of our activity, using our *main.xml* UI layout specification. In this case, we're using a LinearLayout container with an ImageView called iv1 inside it to hold our frame animation.

Next, we create an ImageView object called logoImage, which we assign to ImageView iv1, which we will declare in the *main.xml* file.

After that, we set the background resource for this newly created ImageView to our *logo_animation* XML file, which specifies our animation sequence and timing. This is the bridge between display (ImageView) and animation data (*logo_animation.xml*) set up so that our animation will display through the background image setting for the ImageView. This leaves it open for us to have a source image in our ImageView that uses transparency (an alpha channel) to create cool effects. It essentially gives us two layers in the ImageObject, as we can set source and background images for any ImageView object.

Finally, we define the logoAnimation object that we declared in the first line of code in the graphics class. logoAnimation is an AnimationDrawable object that gets its data from the logoImage object via its getBackground() method, which grabs its background image. As you can see from the previous line, that image has been obtained from the *logo_animation.xml* file, where we define how everything should work.

To trigger our animation to play, we use a new method called onTouchEvent(). This method uses a MotionEvent event to detect if the touchscreen has been touched, which generates an ACTION_DOWN event. (Recall that an event is something that a Java class listens for and is programmed to react to, like a touchscreen touch event or a keyboard keystroke key event.)

In our code, if this ACTION_DOWN touch event is detected, then the logoAnimation object is sent a start() method trigger. It plays and returns true (I played it), or else it passes the event upward to the onTouchEvent method on the superclass from which it was subclassed.

It's pretty logical: a subclass is a specialization of a superclass. A superclass is a more general class than the subclass and serves as the foundation class. If a subclass is sent an event it is not specialized to deal with, it sends that event to its superclass for general handling.

Figure 8–4 shows the four logical sections of code that we need to add to the default graphics class and onCreate() code:

- Import the Android Java classes that we are leveraging in our code.

- Create and name an AnimationDrawable object that is accessible to every code construct in our graphics class.

- Create an ImageView object tied to our *main.xml* screen layout, set the background image resource of that ImageView to reflect our *logo_animation.xml* attributes, and then have our logoAnimation AnimationDrawable object take that frame data from the ImageView via getBackground().

- Trigger the animation with an ACTION_DOWN touchscreen event in our onTouchEvent() method.

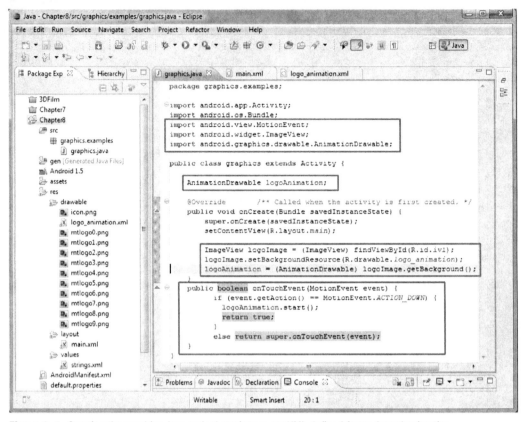

Figure 8–4. *Creating the graphics Java code that triggers our XML defined frame-based animation*

Finally, we need to put in place the ImageView named iv1, which ties the ImageView in our Java code to the ImageView defined in our XML document (*main.xml*) that defines our screen UI. Here is the code, which is also shown in Figure 8–5:

```xml
<?xml version="1.0" encoding="utf-8"?>
<LinearLayout xmlns:android="http://schemas.android.com/apk/res/android"
    android:orientation="vertical"
    android:layout_width="fill_parent"
    android:layout_height="fill_parent"
    >

    <ImageView
    android:layout_width="wrap_content"
    android:layout_height="wrap_content"
    android:id="@+id/iv1"/>

</LinearLayout>
```

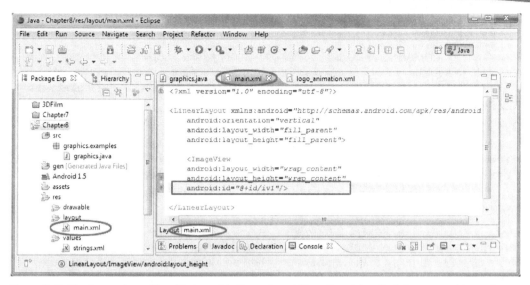

Figure 8–5. *Naming our ImageView UI element in the main.xml file so it matches the iv1 name used in our Java code*

In this case, we have a LinearLayout that contains an ImageView object named iv1. We set our ImageView to wrap_content (basically to conform the ImageView bounds to the 160 × 160 pixel dimension of our image, and thus our animation sequence).

Running the Frame-based Animation App in the Emulator

Now let's see our animation in action. Right-click your *Chapter8* folder and choose **Run As ▶ Android Application**. When the 1.5 emulator comes up with a black screen (the first frame of the animation is all black, so the effect loops seamlessly), tap the upper left of the screen, and the animation will play—amazing.

Since a screenshot cannot display an animation, we'll forego the screenshot of the 1.5 emulator. Now, here's a simple exercise to try after you run this version. Make the following changes, and then save the modified *logo_animation.xml* file:

1. Change the logo_animation values from 200 to 100 for all of the objects, except for the first frame and the last frame.

2. Set these to 1000 or 2000.

3. Change the animation-list tag's android:oneshot attribute to false.

To run our looping animation version, right-click the *Chapter8* folder and select **Run As ▶ Android Application**. Now when you touch the black screen in the upper-left portion, the animation will begin to play and will continue looping forever.

Next, let's add a transformational animation directly underneath our frame-based animation.

Tween Animation in Android

Tween animation is used for shape-based animation, where shapes are animated from one state to another without specifying the intermediate states. In other words, you define the start and end positions of the shape, and Android fills in the gaps to make the animation work.

This contrasts with frame-based animation, which uses a sequence of cels, or bitmap images, like the flipbook animations of days gone by. So frame animation does its work via pixels, while tween animation does its work via transforms that move, rotate, or scale a shape, image, or even text. Thus, tween animation is more powerful than frame-based animation. It can also be used in conjunction with frame-based animation to achieve even more spectacular results.

Tween animation in Android is completely different than frame animation. It is implemented with the set of classes found in the `android.view.animation` package. These classes represent the true power of tween animation in Android. They include things like advanced motion interpolators, which define how animation transformations accelerate over time; and animation utilities, which are needed to rotate, scale, translate (move), and fade `View` objects over time.

"Wait a minute," you must be musing, "does 'View objects' mean that I can apply all of this animation class power to, say, `TextViews`, for instance? Or even `VideoViews`?" Indeed it does. If you transform a `TextView` (rotate it, for instance), and it has a background image, that image is transformed correctly, right along with the text elements of the `TextView` and all of its settings.

> **NOTE:** Here, the word *transformation* refers to the process of rotation (spinning something around a pivot point), scaling (resizing in x and y dimensions relative to a pivot point or reference point), and x or y movement, which is called *translation* in animation.

As you might imagine, tween animation definitions can get very complex. This is where the power of using XML to define complicated things, like transformational animation constructs, becomes very apparent. Again, we thank Android for off-loading work like this from Java coding to XML constructs. In XML, the animation transforms are simple lists of nested tags; they are not called classes and methods. It is certainly easier to fine-tune and refine these types of detailed animations via XML line-entry tweaks rather than in Java code.

The XML for tween animations goes in an entirely different directory (folder) than frame animation (which goes in */res/drawable*). Transform animation goes in the */res/anim* folder.

Creating the text_animation.xml File

We will use a different XML file-creation method to create our transform animation XML file and its folder, so let's get into that right now.

1. Right-click your *Chapter8* folder in the Eclipse Package Explorer pane at the left and select **New ➤ Other… ➤ Android ➤ Android XML File**, as shown in Figure 8–6. Then click Next.

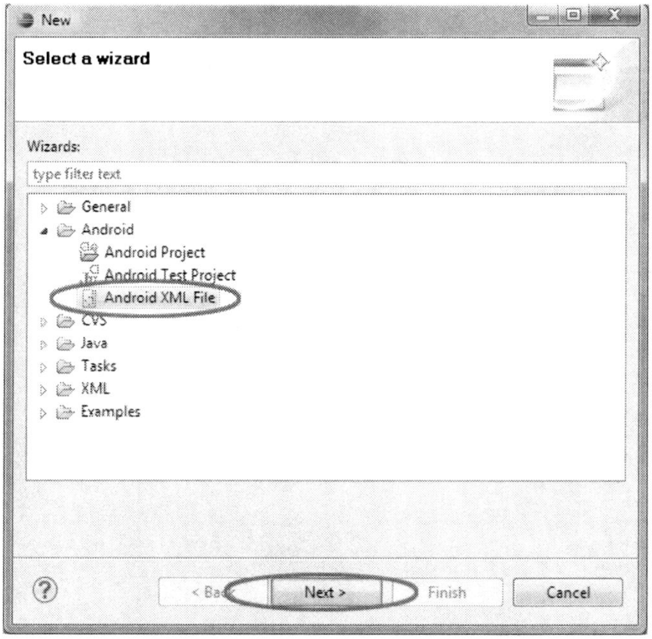

Figure 8–6. *Selecting to create a new XML file via the Eclipse New ➤ Other right-click menu selection route*

2. As you can see by the options in the New Android XML dialog, Android in Eclipse has a powerful XML file-creator utility that supports seven different genres of XML files, including animation. Fill out the dialog as follows (and shown in Figure 8–7):

   - **File:** The first field we want to fill out is the name of the animation XML file, which is *text_animation.xml*.

   - **What type of resource would you like to create?:** Select Animation as the XML file type, which automatically puts */res/anim* as the Folder field at the bottom of the dialog.

- **Select the root element for the XML file**: Make sure that set is selected as the root element in the file. (The root element is the outermost tag in an XML file and contains all the other tags.) <set> is used to group and nest transforms to achieve more powerful and flexible results, as you will see in our transform XML markup.

3. Now click Finish. You will see the */res/anim* folder appear in your project hierarchy tree in the Package Explorer pane, with the *text_animation.xml* file under that.

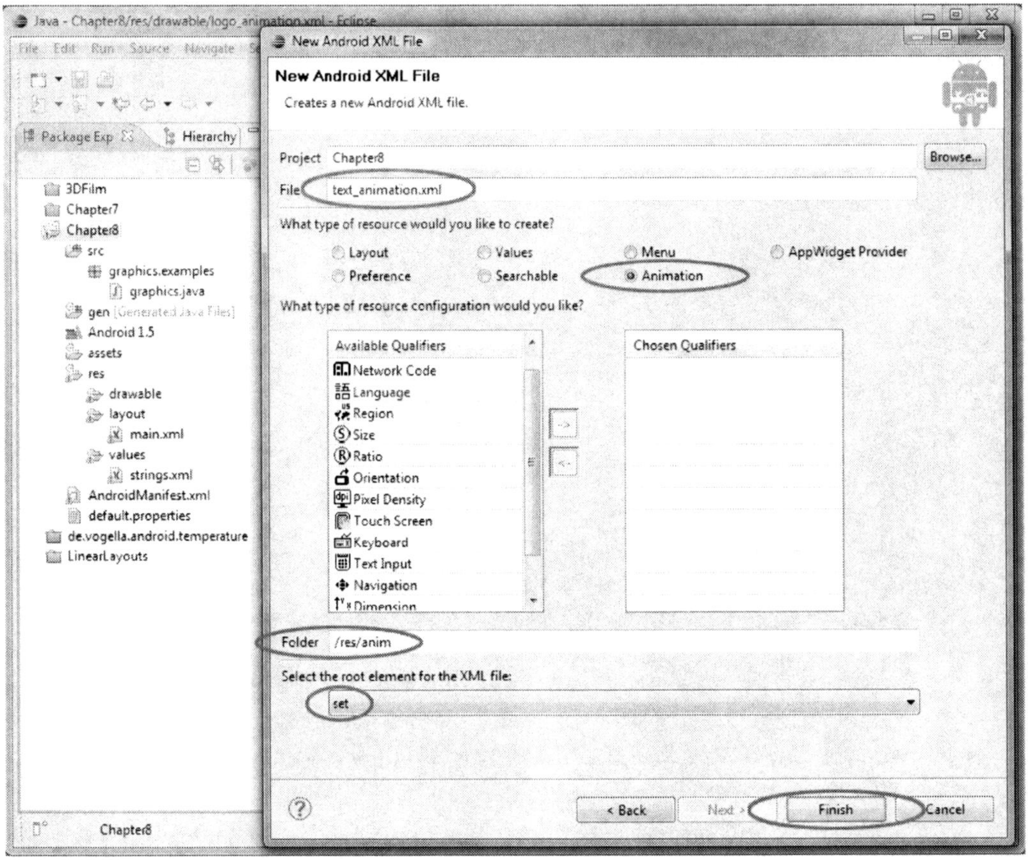

Figure 8–7. *Filling out the New Android XML File dialog*

4. Now let's add in our XML tags to define our scale and rotation transforms, as shown in Figure 8–8. (Click the Source tab at the bottom of the main window to open the XML code editing window if it does not appear automatically.)

```
<?xml version="1.0" encoding="utf-8"?>

<set xmlns:android="http://schemas.android.com/apk/res/android"
```

```
        android:shareInterpolator="false">

    <scale android:interpolator="@android:anim/accelerate_decelerate_interpolator"
          android:fromXScale="1.0"
          android:toXScale="1.4"
          android:fromYScale="1.0"
          android:toYScale="0.6"
          android:pivotX="50%"
          android:pivotY="50%"
          android:fillAfter="false"
          android:duration="700" />

    <set android:interpolator="@android:anim/decelerate_interpolator">
        <scale android:fromXScale="1.4"
               android:toXScale="0.0"
               android:fromYScale="0.6"
               android:toYScale="0.0"
               android:pivotX="50%"
               android:pivotY="50%"
               android:startOffset="700"
               android:duration="400"
               android:fillBefore="false" />

        <rotate android:fromDegrees="0"
                android:toDegrees="-45"
                android:toYScale="0.0"
                android:pivotX="50%"
                android:pivotY="50%"
                android:startOffset="700"
                android:duration="400" />
    </set>
</set>
```

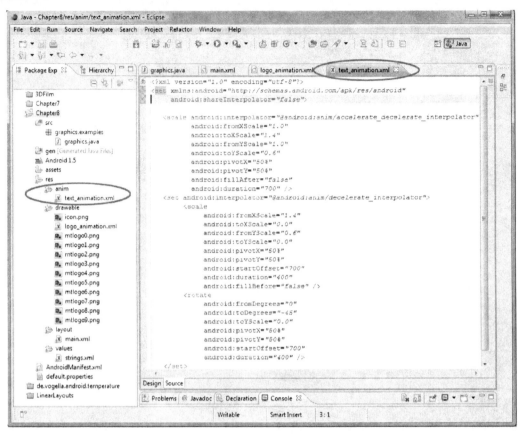

Figure 8–8. *Coding our tween animation tags and their parameters in the text_animation.xml file*

Notice that there are quite a few attributes for the tags that allow transformational animation over time. For instance, our scale tags allow us to specify to and from values for both x and y dimensions, pivot points (where the scale emanates from, or from which location on the object the scale is performed), scale offsets for nonuniform scaling, time duration, and whether to fill before or after the transformation.

For rotation tags, we have rotation to and from degree specifications, as well as x and y pivot point settings. We also have both an offset for skewed rotations and a duration attribute that controls the speed of the rotational transformation. The pivot point defines the center point of the rotation, and an offset defines how to skew the rotation from that point, much like the old Spirograph set that created cool flower-like graphics.

Controlling Tween Animation via Java

Now that our TextView transform animation XML data is in place inside our newly created */res/anim/text_animation.xml* file, we can insert a half dozen lines of Java code into our *graphics.java* file, to implement the transform animation within our application, directly underneath our frame-based animation.

1. As shown in Figure 8–9, the first thing we must do is to import the
   Android classes that are going to be used in the text animation
   transformation: android.widget.TextView and the
   android.view.animation classes called Animation and AnimationUtils.

```
import android.widget.TextView;
import android.view.animation.Animation;
import android.view.animation.AnimationUtils;
```

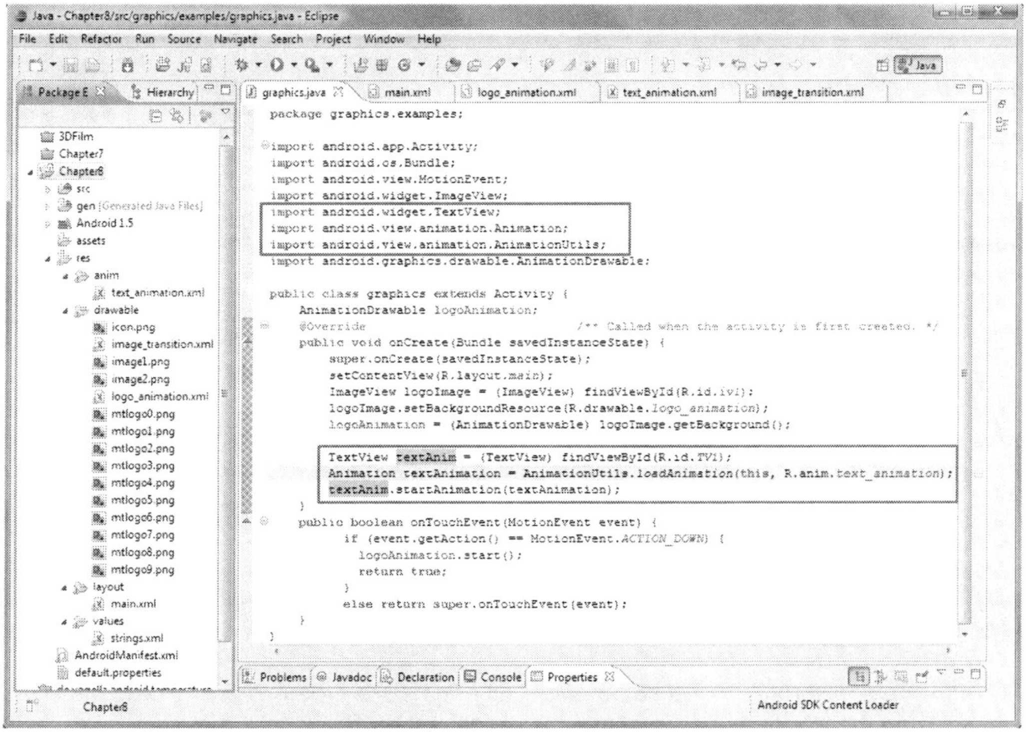

Figure 8–9. *Triggering our tween animation in our graphics.java code*

2. Then down in our onCreate() method, we specify the TextView object
   textAnim and the Animation object textAnimation.

```
TextView textAnim = (TextView) findViewById(R.id.TV1);
Animation textAnimation = AnimationUtils.loadAnimation(this, R.anim.text_animation);
```

3. We then call the startAnimation() method on the TextView object,
   specifying that we want to use the textAnimation Animation object.

```
textAnim.startAnimation(textAnimation);
```

4. Finally, we need to add a TextView object named TV1 to our
   LinearLayout tag and UI container in our *main.xml* file, as shown in
   Figure 8–10.

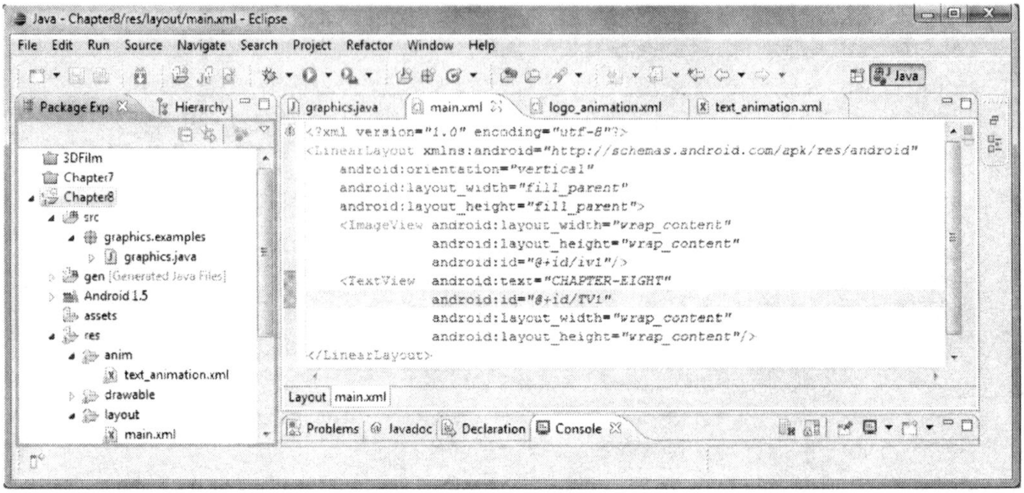

Figure 8–10. *Adding a TextView UI object to our main.xml file*

5. Now we can try out the tween animation. Right-click the *Chapter8* folder in the Package Explorer pane and select **Run As…** ➤ **Android Application**.

6. It runs pretty fast. Let's add a zero on the time values in our *text_animation.xml* file, changing 400 to 4000 and 700 to 7000.

7. Compile and run the app again. You'll see that the animation runs ten times slower.

Using Transitions

Transitions are preprogrammed custom special effects like crossfades and directional wipes. Using these effects can increase the perceived professionalism of your application.

You can use XML to set up such graphics transformations.

Android provides the `TransitionDrawable` class. Here, we will use it in conjunction with an XML file in the */res/drawables* directory, just as we did in the frame-based animation example, since we are working solely with bitmap images.

So let's get started.

1. Right-click the *Chapter8* folder and select **New** ➤ **File** to create a standard text file for our XML in the */res/drawable* folder (since we are working with bitmap images).

2. Name the file *image_transition.xml*, as shown at the bottom of the New File dialog in Figure 8–11.

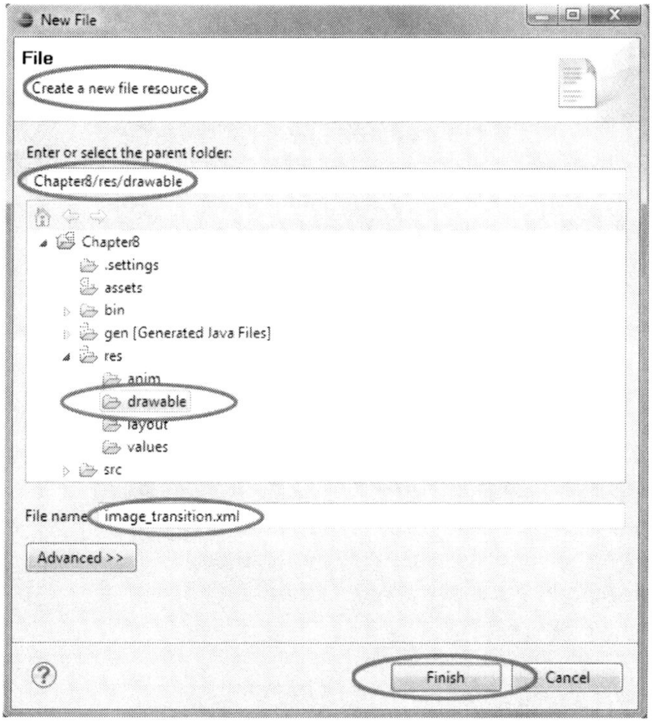

Figure 8–11. *Creating the image_transition.xml file in the drawable folder via the New File dialog*

3. Next, add the `<transition>` tag as follows. The `<transition>` tag has the usual `xmlns` reference (to make our file valid Android XML). Inside the tag, we specify two `<item>` tags referencing the images that we need to transition from and transition to. We are using the two images from Chapter 7 here to show that the transitions will accommodate the alpha channel and more complicated masking of images, which is important for advanced designs:

```
<?xml version="1.0" encoding="utf-8"?>

<transition xmlns:android="http://schemas.android.com/apk/res/android">

        <item android:drawable="@drawable/image1"/>
        <item android:drawable="@drawable/image2"/>

</transition>
```

4. Add the two images to the *drawable* folder. Figure 8–12 shows what your screen should look like once you have added the two images, refreshed the IDE, and typed in your tags.

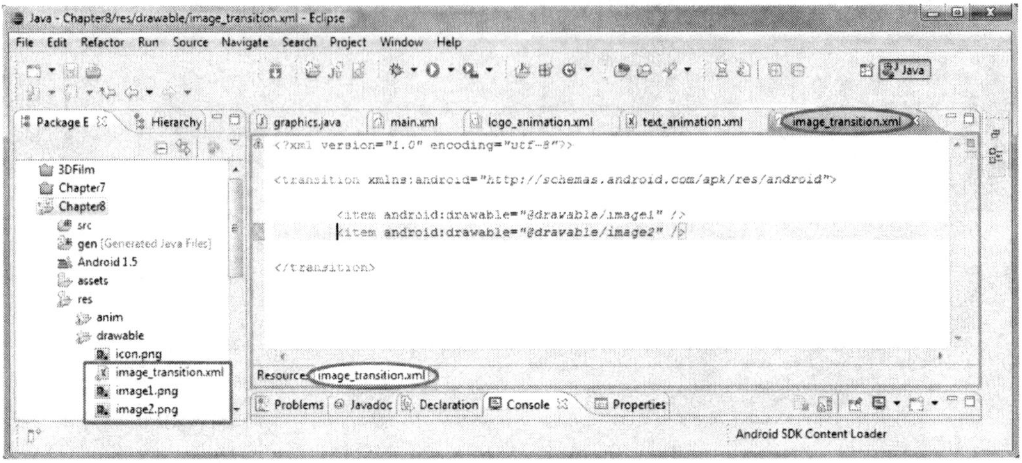

Figure 8–12. *Writing our XML mark-up to transition between two images in our image_transition.xml file*

5. Now we need to add an ImageView in our LinearLayout to hold our image transition. Put the following in the *main.xml* file underneath our animated TextView, as shown in Figure 8–13.

```
<ImageView android:layout_width="wrap_content"
        android:layout_height="wrap_content"
        android:src="@drawable/image1"
        android:id="@+id/imgTrans"/>
```

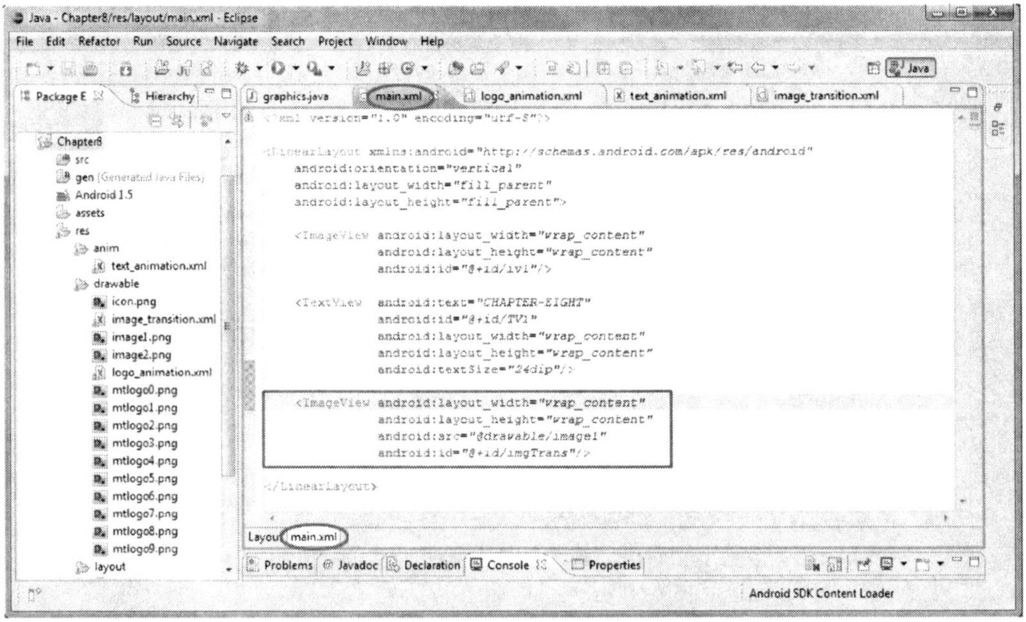

Figure 8–13. *Adding an ImageView UI object to our main.xml file to hold our image transition*

We are specifying the first image (the "from" image) of our transition as the source image to use in the ImageView object, and we are naming it imgTrans via the now familiar @+id/imgTrans notation.

Now we are ready to drop a few lines of Java code (a whopping four this time) into *graphics.java* to add the ability to do a fade transition from one image slowly into another.

Here is the code to set up the ImageView we just added to access the transition:

```
TransitionDrawable trans = (TransitionDrawable)
    getResources().getDrawable(R.drawable.image_transition);
```

This is all on one line, as shown in Figure 8–14.

> **TIP:** We have no new import statements to add, so the import statements block of code is closed in Figure 8–14. This is indicated by a plus sign (+) next to the block, which signifies that this code block can be expanded (just click the +). You can click any of the minus signs (–) in your Java code window to close classes you are finished editing, if you want to see a higher-level view of your code. Once your code becomes long and involved, you will find that you use this simple feature regularly. Try it, and get used to making it a part of your work process inside the Eclipse IDE.

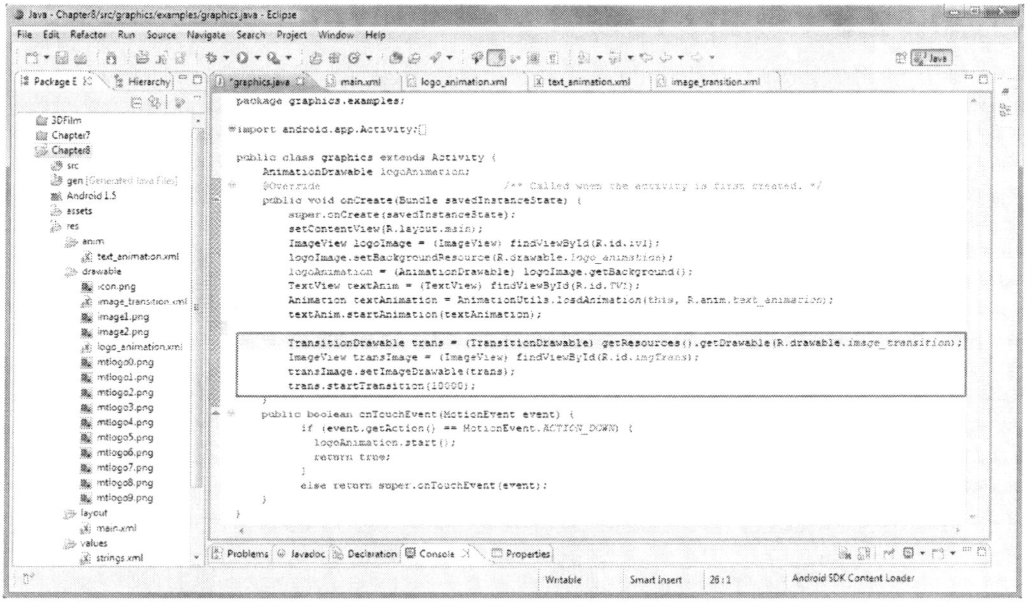

Figure 8–14. *Adding our Java code to graphics.java to define and trigger our image transition*

This code declares our TransitionDrawable object, which we name trans. It sets trans to the results of the call to the getDrawable() method of the object returned by the getResources() method. This obtains the *image_transition.xml* transition drawable specification, which points to our two circular images.

Setting up that TransitionDrawable object and loading it with our XML file is the hardest line of code in this quartet. The next three are more familiar and straightforward:

```
ImageView transImage = (ImageView) findViewById(R.id.imgTrans);
transImage.setImageDrawable(trans);
trans.startTransition(10000);
```

We create an ImageView object called transImage and, via the findViewById() method, we link it to the imgTrans ID, from the second ImageView XML tag we added to *main.xml* earlier. We then use the setImageDrawable() method to set the transImage ImageView object to the trans TransitionDrawable object that we just created above it.

This second and third lines of Java code bridge our ImageView object with our TransitionDrawable object, and thus complete our wiring together of the various UI view and animation effect objects.

Finally, we can now talk to the trans TransitionDrawable object via its startTransition(milliseconds) method. We will use that method to tell the transition to begin and to take place over 10,000 ms, or 10 seconds, (slow fade) to complete.

Select **Run As...** ➤ **Android Application** and watch the fun.

Creating 9-Patch Custom Scalable Images

Another type of drawable utility subclass in android.graphics.drawable package is NinePatchDrawable. A NinePatch is a resizable bitmap whose scaling during resize operations can be controlled via nine areas that you can define in the bitmap image (think tic-tac-toe). This type of image could be used for anything from a scalable button background to a UI background that scales to fit different screen resolutions.

The advantage to the NinePatch drawable object is that you can define a single graphic element (in our example, that will be a 2.7KB PNG file) that can be used across many different UI elements, including buttons, sliders, backgrounds, and similar items. Screen or button backgrounds can use this technology.

Android comes with a tool for editing NinePatch objects. In the *Android SDK tools* folder (as shown in Figure 8–15, this is under *android-sdk-windows* on Windows), you will find a *draw9patch.bat* batch file. Running this file (from the command line or by using a right-click context-sensitive menu) starts the Draw 9-patch utility.

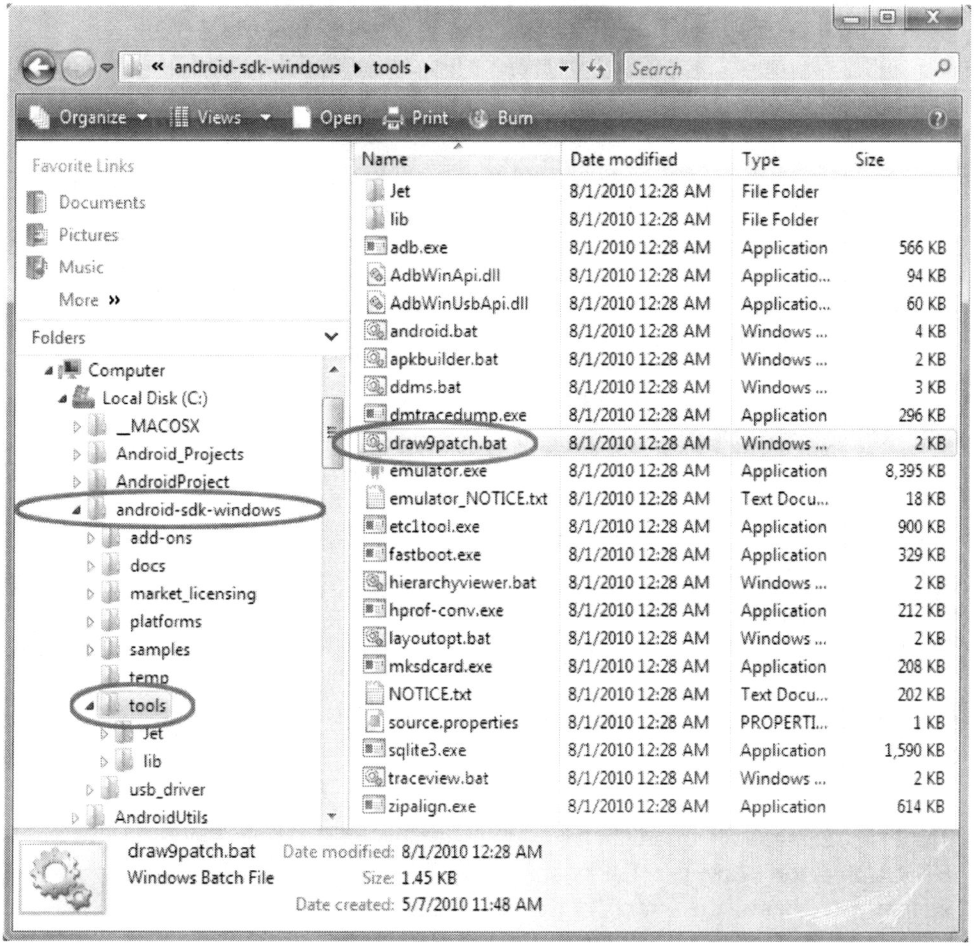

Figure 8-15. *Locating the Android 9-patch editing tool in your operating system directory structure for the Android SDK*

> **TIP:** This chapter uses screen images from Adobe Photoshop. If you don't have PhotoShop, there a free open source software called GIMP (for the GNU Image Manipulation Program), which is similar to Photoshop and available for Mac, Linux, and Windows systems. For more information and to download GIMP, go to `http://gimp.org`.

Let's try creating some 9-patch buttons.

1. To launch the 9-patch editor from Windows, right-click the *draw9patch.bat* file (in Linux and Mac systems, the file name extension may be different) and select **Run as Administrator**. You will see the Draw 9-patch startup screen.

2. Select File ➤ Open 9-patch from the menu bar, as shown in Figure 8–16. In the dialog that appears, go to your *project/res/drawable* folder and open the *chromebutton.png* file.

Figure 8–16. *Draw 9-patch startup screen*

3. The PNG32 image file opens in the 9-patch editor, as shown in Figure 8–17. Select the Show patches check box at the bottom of the window, so that you can see the effects of the patch areas as colored, translucent surfaces over the top of the image.

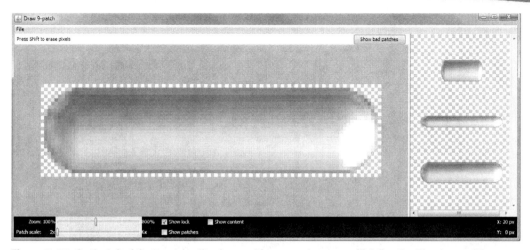

Figure 8–17. *On the left of the 9-patch editor is a working area where you will define the tiling areas of the 9-patch. On the right is a real-time preview area, showing how the image will tile when stretched in different dimensions.*

4. Draw boundaries with your mouse by dragging the mouse within the 1-pixel wide transparent border area above and to the left of our graphic, as shown in Figure 8–18. The Draw 9-patch utility adds this 1-pixel border area inside the image.

NOTE: As you add points to this line with a left-click (or subtract with a right-click or Shift-click for Mac), be sure to look at the images on the right. You'll see how they change the way that Android scales your background in real time as you work on the image.

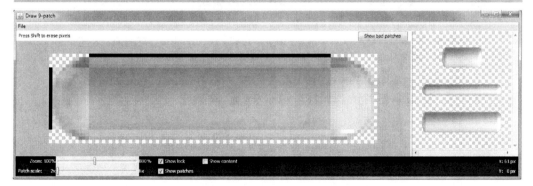

Figure 8–18. Tileable areas in the 9-patch editor are defined by different colors.

5. Bring the original and the newly created 9-patch image into Photoshop, as shown in Figure 8–19. Now, you can see what the 9-patch editor is doing to tell Android which parts of the image to tile or scale and which parts of the image to preserve (usually edges).

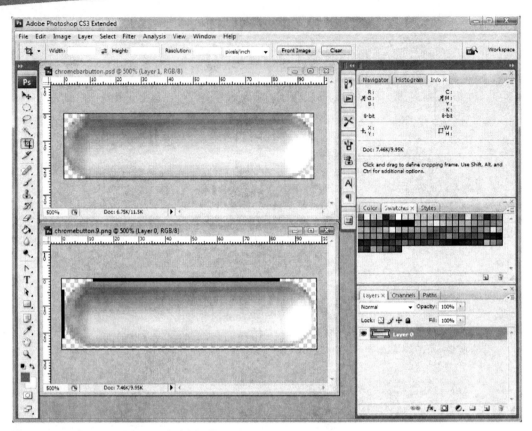

Figure 8–19. *The 9-patch images in Adobe Photoshop*

6.   Select File ➤ Save and save the 9-patch image in your
     /project/res/drawable folder as *chromebutton.9.png*. It is now ready to
     implement as a background image in the test buttons that we are going
     to add to our *main.xml* file.

7.   Add the following code to the bottom of our LinearLayout container (it
     can also be seen in Figure 8–21 later in the exercise):

```
<Button android:id="@+id/Button1"
               android:layout_width="wrap_content"
               android:layout_height="wrap_content"
               android:background="@drawable/chromebutton"
               android:textColor="#770000"
               android:padding="3dip"
               android:text="CLICK HERE!"
               android:layout_gravity="center"/>
<Button android:id="@+id/Button2"
               android:layout_width="wrap_content"
               android:layout_height="wrap_content"
               android:background="@drawable/chromebutton"
               android:textColor="#007700"
               android:padding="30dip"
```

```
android:text="NOW LETS REALLY SCALE THIS UP!"
android:layout_gravity="center"
android:textSize="17dip"/>
```

8. Click the Graphical Layout tab at the bottom of the *main.xml* editing window, and switch Eclipse into preview mode (as you've done in earlier examples). As shown in Figure 8–20, you can readily see the different effects of scaling the 9-patch image that were previewed in the Draw 9-patch tool.

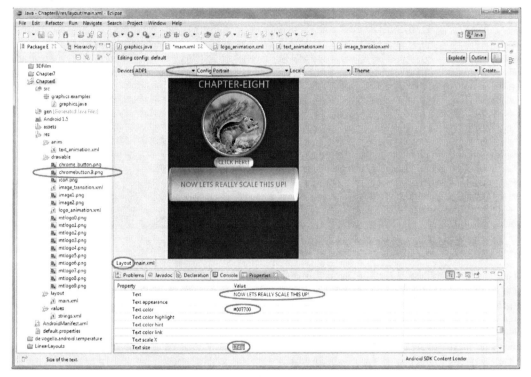

Figure 8–20. *Setting UI parameters and portrait mode in the Eclipse layout editor*

In this case, small padding values preserve the round ends of the button, and ten times larger padding values scale the image to look more like a piece of chalk. Both different button treatments are culled from the same 2.7KB PNG image using the NinePatchDrawable object.

Note how easy it was for us to define and use the NinePatchDrawable class, without any Java code at all. We simply need to put the *chromebutton.9.png* 9-patch-compatible image into the */res/drawable* folder, so it can be found and accessed by our XML.

Figure 8–21 shows the additions to *main.xml*. Notice that we added an attribute in each of our UI tags (ImageView and TextView):

```
android:layout_gravity="center"
```

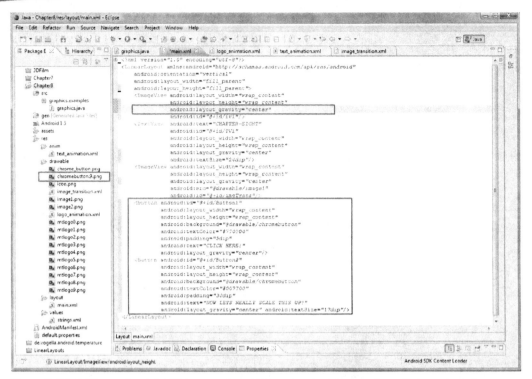

Figure 8–21. *Adding our 9-patch PNG in our main.xml UI layout and setting layout_gravity to center buttons*

Layout gravity is like the alignment feature in word processors and browsers. It allows you to snap a layout container or a UI element to the left, right, top, bottom, or center. It's handy for designing the visual screen layout.

Now choose **Run As ➤ Android Application** and check out our 9-patch buttons at the bottom of the emulator screen. Take a good look at them, because we are going to replace them with a VideoView in the next section.

Playing Video in Your Android Apps

As our final topic, we'll look at how to simply and effectively play video files in your Android applications. You do this through a very handy class called VideoView. We are going to add the ability to play video in our application using only three lines of XML code and eight lines of Java code, or less than a dozen lines of code in total.

Adding a VideoView Object

For video playback, we will use the VideoView class. Like TextView and ImageView objects, VideoView objects make it easy to access MPEG-4 H.264 video in your Android applications. Your video can be easily streamed from a remote server, keeping your application download size to a minimum.

To add a VideoView to our LinearLayout, *in main.xml,* place the following new tag underneath the last ImageView tag (and in place of our two Button tags, which should be deleted and replaced with the following):

```
<VideoView android:layout_height="fill_parent"
           android:layout_width="fill_parent"
           android:id="@+id/VideoView"/>
```

This names our VideoView and tells it to fill its parent container using fill_parent. The fill_parent value does the opposite of wrap_content. It blows the content up to fit the layout container, rather than scaling the layout container down around the content.

With this in our LinearLayout for our *Chapter8* project, replacing the two Button tags, we will now have video at the bottom of our app screen, under our transition object. Since in our vertical layout our VideoView object is getting pushed off the bottom of the screen, let's temporarily disable our frame-based animation while we develop our VideoView code. We do this by commenting out a block of code, as follows:

```
<!--
    <ImageView android:layout_width="wrap_content"
               android:layout_height="wrap_content"
               android:layout_gravity="center"
               android:id="@+id/iv1"/>
-->
```

So, to comment out a block of code in XML, simply add the <!-- opening tag and the --> closing tag, as shown here.

Your new *main.xml* code should look like Figure 8–22. You can see that once this block of code is commented out, Eclipse changes the color of the code, and the Android compiler no longer sees that code. As far as it's concerned, the code is not there anymore. We'll do the same thing in our Java code as well, except using a different comment method.

> **TIP:** Commenting is a useful technique when you want to temporarily change a file without deleting some content, or as a way of leaving notes to yourself. You will see this latter approach used extensively in Java code. Commenting is a good habit for developers.

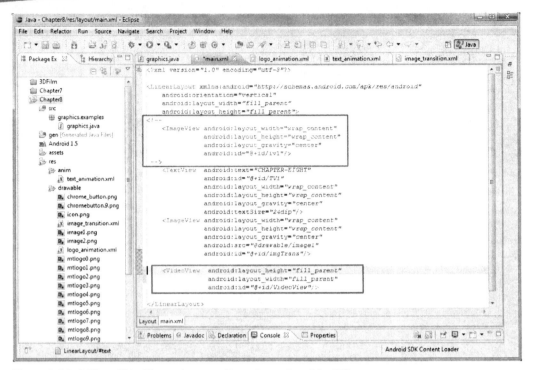

Figure 8–22. *Adding a VideoView and commenting out a section of the XML*

Adding the Java for Video

In Java, a line of code is commented out by adding two forward slashes (//). In *graphics.java*, we begin by commenting out our import android.view.MotionEvent statement, as shown in Figure 8–23. Eclipse turns the commented code green to show it is no longer recognized by the compiler.

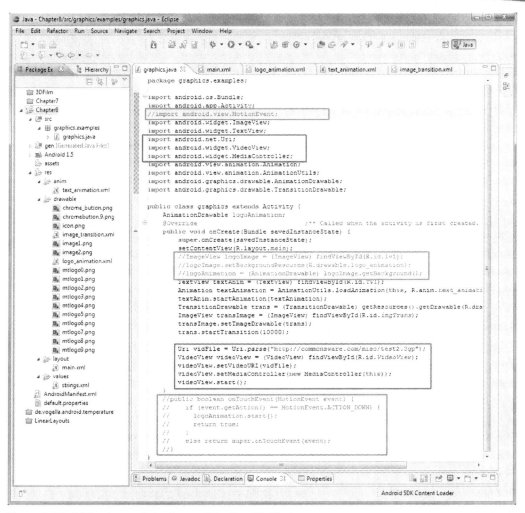

Figure 8–23. *Adding Java code to play our VideoView UI object*

Remember that we commented out the code for our frame-based animation in our XML file. Let's now comment out the code that implements that frame-based animation in our Java file. We also comment out the touchscreen code, as follows (and shown in Figure 8–23):

```
//ImageView logoImage = (ImageView) findViewById(R.id.iv1);
//logoImage.setBackgroundResource(R.drawable.logo_animation);
//logoAnimation = (AnimationDrawable) logoImage.getBackground();
```

Now, add three new import statements for the classes we need:

```
import android.net.Uri;
import android.widget.VideoView;
import android.widget.MediaController;
```

To get the video from our server, we also need to define its path using a Uri object, so we must import the android.net.Uri class. We next import the VideoView widget (android.widget.VideoView). Finally, to play the video in the VideoView, we will use a MediaController object, so we import the android.widget.MediaController class as well.

Next, add the following to create our VideoView object (see Figure 8–24):

```
Uri vidFile = Uri.parse("http://commonsware.com/misc/test2.3gp");
VideoView videoView = (VideoView) findViewById(R.id.VideoView);
videoView.setVideoURI(vidFile);
videoView.setMediaController(new MediaController(this));
videoView.start();
```

First, we create the Uri reference object, which holds the path, or address, to the video file on the server. The Uniform Resource Identifier (URI) can use the familiar HTTP server paradigm or a more advanced real-time streaming protocol. As you can see, here we are using the HTTP protocol, which works fine and is the industry standard, thanks to the Internet. We create a Uri object called vidFile using the parse() method with the HTTP URL to any valid path and file name in quotes. Here, the Uri object points to the content at http://commonsware.com/misc/test2.3gp, so that we have some video to play.

Now we have an object called vidFile that contains a reference to our video file.

Next, we set up our VideoView object, calling it videoView and using findViewById() to locate the VideoView we created in our XML layout file. This is the same thing we have been doing with the other View types, and should be pretty familiar to you at this point.

Now that we have a videoView object, we use the setVideoURI() method to pass the vidFile Uri object to the videoView VideoView object, so that the VideoView is loaded with the file path to use to retrieve the video. Now our Uri is wired into our VideoView, and we need only to wire the MediaController into the VideoView so that the video can be played.

The next line of code connects the videoView object to the MediaController object using the videoView object's setMediaController() method, and invokes a cool code-optimization trick of declaring a new MediaController object inside the setMediaController() method. The long form of this would require two lines of code and an additional object variable, like so:

```
MediaController mediaControl = new MediaController(this);
videoView.setMediaController(mediaControl);
```

Finally, to start our videoView object playing, we send it a start() method call via the last line of code:

```
videoView.start()
```

We are finished setting up our VideoView object. Now select **Run As ➤ Android Application** and watch our video stream over the Internet into your 1.5 emulator.

Summary

In this chapter, we took a look at the more advanced graphics capabilities that Android offers, including two different types of animation, image transitions, and digital video. You also learned a little more about the Eclipse IDE, code commenting, and image file formats that are optimal for Android apps.

Here are some important points to remember:

- Always use PNG24 (which is really PNG32) format.

- Bitmap animation and tween animation are two completely different things as far as Android is concerned. Bitmap-related animation and transitions are handled through the */res/drawable* folder. Tween animation is handled via XML files defined in the */res/anim* folder.

- Don't limit yourself when using tween animation. Use it on any type of View container you like—text, image, video, or whatever; wax creative.

In the next chapter, we'll start looking at how to make things interactive by setting up our applications to handle events and to listen for those events via event listeners.

Adding Interactivity: Handling UI Events

In this chapter, we will explore how to wire up those super-cool UI designs that you have seen in the previous chapters, so that your UI design becomes highly functional within your Android application. With Android's convenient event listeners, you can easily add in your own custom programming logic. Using the event handling described in this chapter, you'll be able to have your UI and graphical elements actually do something productive or impressive after they are tapped on (touchscreen), navigated to (navigation keypad), or typed into (keyboard).

We'll begin with an overview of how Android listens to its touchscreen and keyboard, and how to harness the power of input devices.

An Overview of UI Events in Android

The way that we talk to all of the input devices in Java, and thus in Android, is via events for each type of input device (touchscreen, keyboard, and navigation keys). Events are actually system-generated messages that are sent to the View object whenever a UI element is accessed in some fashion by a user. *Event* refers to something that you attend or otherwise recognize as being significant, and thus is the perfect term for these UI occurrences via Android input devices.

Listening for and Handling Events

Handling and *handlers* are two other terms used in conjunction with events in Java and Android. Once these events are triggered by a user's touch, keystroke, or navigation key, they must be handled within your application. This is accomplished inside a method (such as onClick() or onKeyDown()) that specifies exactly what you want to happen when one of these input events is detected by Android and is sent over to your appropriate event handler for processing.

This concept of handling events is termed *listening* in Android. You will see the terms *event listeners* and *event handlers* throughout this chapter. That's because they are what the chapter is all about: how to put into place the proper event listeners and event handlers to cover your app users' interaction via touchscreen, navigation keys, and keyboard input devices that are part of a smartphone's hardware.

Handling UI Events via the View Class

Each of the UI elements in your application is a View object of one incarnation or another, and each has events that are unique to that element. This is how user interaction with specific UI elements is kept separate and organized. Each of these View objects keeps track of its own user-input events.

The way that a View object within your layout talks with the rest of your application program logic is via a public callback method that is invoked by Android when a given action occurs in that UI View object. For instance, if a Button is touched, an onTouchEvent() method is *called* on that object, because Android knows to call a method of that name when that event occurs. In other words, Android calls back to the object that received an event so that the object can handle it.

For this callback message to be intercepted by your Java code and program logic, you need to extend your View class and override the method from the View class that your UI widget was spawned (subclassed) from. To *override* a method means to declare and define that method specifically within your class, and have it do something via your own custom program logic.

Since your UI design is made up of a collection of View objects in one or more ViewGroup layout containers, you can see how this might represent a gaggle of coding just to make sure all of your UI elements are properly listening to the keyboard, touchscreen, and navigation keys. Has Android done anything here to make things easier on us, as it has in other areas of app development?

Yes, Android has provided a way to facilitate event handling. The View class from which all of our UI widgets are subclassed contains a collection of nested interfaces featuring callbacks that are far easier to define, as they are part of the system that makes up the View class and all of its methods.

These nested interfaces that are already a part of all of your View class-based widgets are called *event listeners*. They provide the easiest way to quickly set in place code that will capture user-input events and allow them to be processed right there in your application program logic.

Event Callback Methods

In the most simple of terms, an *event listener* is a Java interface in the View class that contains a single callback method to handle that type of user-input event. When you implement a specific event listener interface, you are telling Android that your View class will handle that specific event on that specific View.

These callback methods are called by Android when the View object that the callback method is *registered* to is triggered by the user-input device used to access that UI interface element. (I like to say the method is *wired up* to the View object, but then again, I am a programmer and drink far too much coffee.)

The callback methods that we are going to cover in this chapter are the most common ones used in Android application development. They are listed in Table 9–1.

Table 9–1. *Common Android Callback Methods*

Method	From	Triggered By
onClick()	View.OnCLickListener	Touch of screen or click of navigation keys
onLongClick()	View.OnLongClickListener	Touch or Enter held for 1 second
onKey()	View.OnKeyListener	Press or release of key on phone
onTouch()	View.OnTouchListener	Touch, release, or gesture events
onFocusChange()	View.OnFocusChange	Focus change
onCreateContextMenu()	View.OnTouchListener	Context menu

In the table, two of the methods are not directly triggered by user input, but they are related to input events. These are onFocusChange() and onCreateContextMenu(). onFocusChange() tracks how the user moves from one UI element to the next. The term *focus* refers to which UI element the user is using or accessing currently. When a user goes from one UI element to another one, the first UI element is said to have "lost focus," and the next element is said to now "have the focus." The onCreateContextMenu() method is related to the onLongClick() callback method, in the sense that context menus in Android are generated via a long-click user action. This is the touchscreen equivalent of a right-click on most computers.

To define one of these callback methods to handle certain types of events for one of your View objects, simply implement the nested interface in your activity or define it as an anonymous class within your application. If you define it as an anonymous class, you pass an instance of your implementation of the listener to the respective set…Listener() method, as you'll see in the next section.

In the rest of this chapter, you'll learn how to leverage the main event listeners in Android so you can make your applications interactive and useful.

Handling onClick Events

The onClick() method is triggered when the user touches a UI element. As you might guess, it's the most commonly used event handler out there. So, it only makes sense to start with handling onClick events.

Implementing an onClick Listener for a UI Element

First, let's create an anonymous OnClickListener:

```
final OnClickListener exampleListener = new OnClickListener()
{
    public void onClick(View v) {
        //Code here that does something upon click event.
    }
};
```

This is an example of an anonymous class. This line of code sets up a variable called exampleListener as a new OnClickListener object, which listens for onClick events.

> **NOTE:** Recall from Chapter 7 that a final variable cannot be reassigned a value once it has been set. This ensures that another listener does not get assigned.

It is logical, then that inside this class definition there would be a public onClick(View v) handler to handle the onClick event. The public onClick handler is passed an ID reference to the View object that was clicked on, so that it knows which View object to handle. Note that the View that has been clicked is named v, so if you want to reference the View object in the code inside this method, it is ready to go and must be referenced via a variable "v".

How any given onClick handler handles a click event is up to the code inside the onClick handler. That code basically explains what to do if that UI element was clicked on or touched, or typed with a keystroke.

If you want to come off as really cool right now, simply look up casually from the book and exclaim to your family, "I'm coding an onClick handler in Java right now," and then look back down and continue reading.

We have defined an OnClickListener, but we need to wire it to a UI element (attach it to a UI View object) before that code can be triggered. Usually, this will go inside the onCreate() method (which you have become familiar with in the first two-thirds of this book).

It takes only two lines of code to connect a button to the exampleListener object. The first is simply our Java declaration of the Button UI object in our *main.xml* UI layout definition:

```
<Button android:text="First Button"
        android:id="@+id/firstButton"
        android:layout_gravity="center"
        android:layout_width="wrap_content"
        android:layout_height="wrap_content"/>
```

The second line is where we connect the button construct with the event listener construct, by using the Button widget's setOnClickListener() method, like so:

```
Button exampleButton = (Button)this.findViewById(R.id.firstButton);
exampleButton.setOnClickListener(exampleListener);
```

Adding an onClick Listener to an Activity in Android

You will probably not be surprised when I tell you that there is an even sleeker way to define your event listeners for your activities, using even fewer object references and lines of code. This is normally how you will want to do things in your Android applications programming activities.

You can implement an event listener directly inside the declaration of your activity within the actual class declaration. Wow. Event listeners must be *muy importante*.

Here is a class declaration that uses the `implements` keyword to embed an `OnClickListener` directly into the class via its declaration:

```
public class ActivityExample extends Activity implements OnClickListener() {…}
```

The previous two lines of code declaring the `Button` and wiring via `setOnCLickListener()` would still exist inside the `onCreate()` code block, but the declaration of the `exampleListener` object and class would not be necessary.

Now it's time to create our *Chapter9* project folder and implement a button and `onClick` listener so that you can see event handling in action.

Creating the Event Handling Examples Project in Eclipse

For our first example, we'll set up the button so that when it is clicked, the text on a `TextView` changes.

In Eclipse, close the *Chapter8* project folder (right-click it in Package Explorer and select **Close Project**), if it's still open. Also close all the empty tabs at the top of the Eclipse IDE, using the x icons in the top-right side of each tab.

Select **File ➤ New ➤ Project** and choose Android Project to open the New Android Project dialog. Fill it out as follows (and shown in Figure 9–1):

- **Project name**: Name the project *Chapter9*.

- **Build Target:** Choose Android 1.5.

- **Application name:** Name the application **Event Handling Examples**.

- **Package name:** The package name should be event.handling.

- **Create Activity**: Check the box and name the activity `HandlerExamples`.

- **Minimum SDK Version**: Set this to 3, which matches our Android 1.5 build target and emulator.

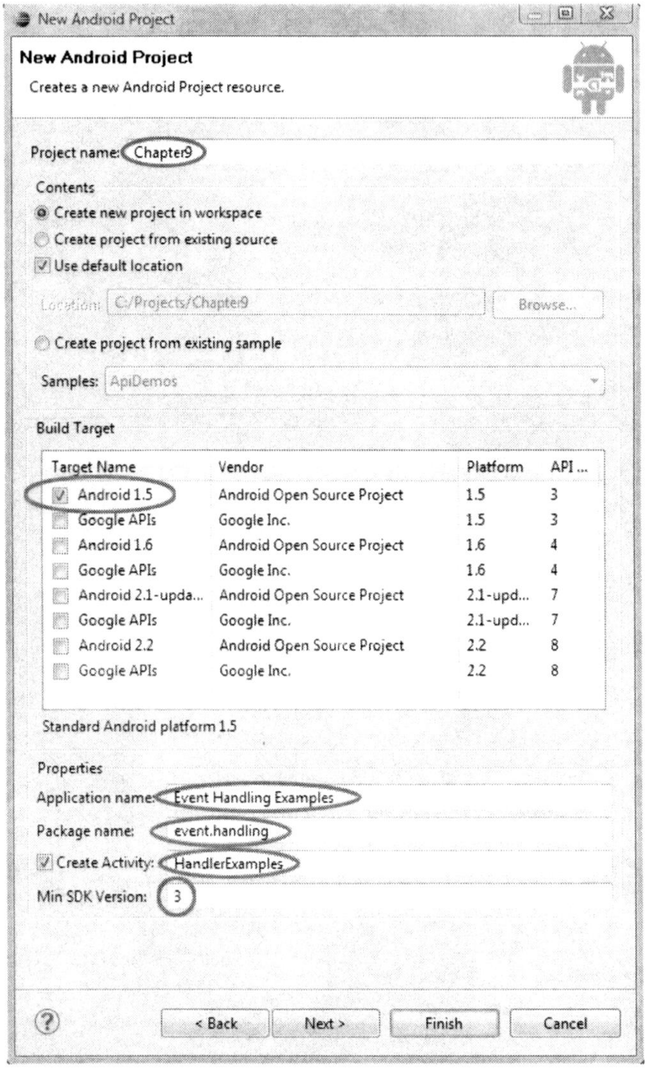

Figure 9–1. *Creating the Chapter9 Android project*

Editing the HandlerExamples.java File

Now let's edit the java code:

1. In the Package Explorer, open your project tree hierarchy by clicking the arrows next to the */src* and */res* folders, so that you can see their contents. Select the *HandlerExamples.java* file under the */src/event.handling* folder by clicking once on it (it will turn blue), and then hit the F3 key on your keyboard. This is the keyboard shortcut for the Open option.

2. Notice that some code has been written for us. The first thing we need to do is to implement `OnClickListener`. Add `implements OnClickListener` to the end of the class declaration, as shown in Figure 9–2. (Note there is a deliberate typo here, so I can show off some features of Eclipse. See if you can spot it.)

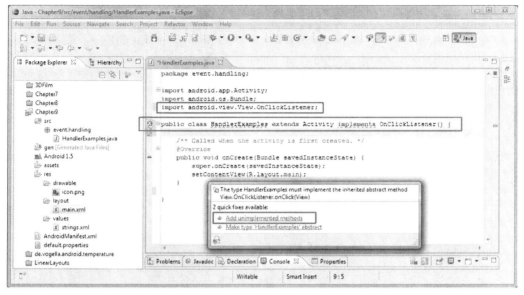

Figure 9–2. *Editing HandlerExamples.java*

3. As you can see in Figure 9–2, Android and Eclipse have alerted us that something is amiss. If you hold the mouse over the red-underlined keywords, Eclipse will tell you what it thinks is wrong. When you mouse-over the `HandlerExamples` keyword in the class definition, up pops a box (shown in Figure 9–2) saying that Eclipse wants to see an `onClick()` method. To fix this, click the Add unimplemented methods link (the first one), and Eclipse will add the method for you (see Figure 9–3), as follows:

```
@Override
public void onClick(View v) {
        // TODO Auto-generated method stub

}
```

NOTE: Since the `onClick` code uses a `View` object, Eclipse imports `android.view.View`, which is shown at the top of the file.

4. There is nothing better than having our IDE write some code for us. Let's try it again. Mouse-over the `OnClickListener` keyword, and Eclipse will tell you that you need an `import` statement. Click the Add import link, and Eclipse will add the `import` statement (highlighted at the top of Figure 9–3).

Figure 9–3. *Implementing a listener in our class definition via the implements keyword*

> **NOTE:** You need to get used to looking at what Eclipse is telling you as you code. This awareness is especially useful while you are learning the programming language and the development environment. That is why I am showing you some mistakes here, rather than writing perfect lines of code every time. One of the things you need to master is your process of working with the Eclipse IDE.

5. But there is still an error in the class declaration. This is because when you implement an `OnClickListener`, you do *not* need to add the `()` at the end. I removed the typo, and then I got a clean bill of health from Eclipse, as shown in Figure 9–4.

```
public class HandlerExamples extends Activity implements OnClickListener {
```

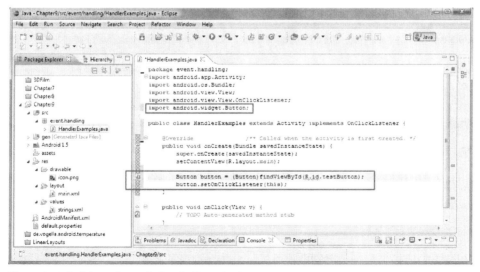

Figure 9–4. *A listener implemented correctly in Eclipse*

6. Now let's define our `Button` and attach our `setOnClickListener()` to it. We talked about this earlier in the chapter, but this time, the containing activity is the event listener, so we use this to refer to the containing object.

```
Button button = (Button)findViewById(R.id.testButton);
button.setOnClickListener(this);
```

This is shown in Figure 9–5, along with the `import android.widget.Button;` statement that we need in order to use the `Button` in our code.

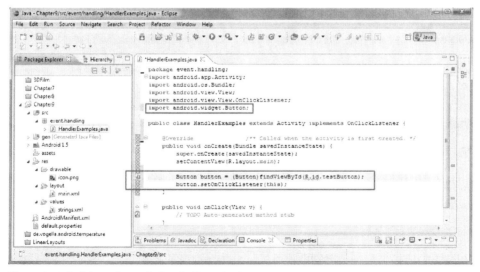

Figure 9–5. *Defining a Button in HandlerExamples.java*

Editing the main.xml File

Now it's time to set up the XML mark-up in our *main.xml* file.

1. Select the *main.xml* file under the */res/layout* folder and hit F3 to open it in the IDE in its own tab.

2. Click the Layout tab at the bottom of the IDE to show the layout visually (see Figure 9–6), Then drag the `Button` widget (shown circled and selected in Figure 9–6) onto the screen to the right, and drop it into place under the `TextView` widget.

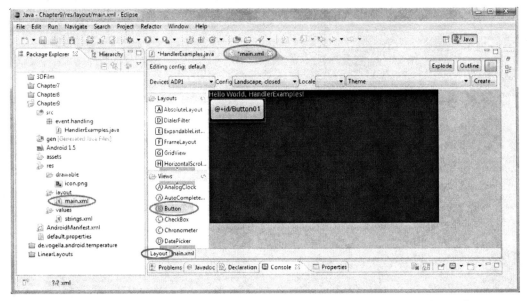

Figure 9–6. *Adding a Button via a drag-and-drop operation the Eclipse layout editor in our main.xml file*

3. Now click the main.xml tab at the bottom of the IDE to switch the view from visual layout to coding view. Cut and paste the `Button` code so that it comes before the `TextView` code (but after the `LinearLayout` tag). The `Button` should be the first thing at the top of the screen.

4. Add the `"CLICK TO GENERATE EVENT"` text, `testButton` ID, and centering attribute you learned about in the previous chapter. Let's also add a few `TextView` attributes to improve visibility (see Figure 9–7).

```
<?xml version="1.0" encoding="utf-8"?>
<LinearLayout xmlns:android="http://schemas.android.com/apk/res/android"
    android:orientation="vertical"
    android:layout_width="fill_parent"
    android:layout_height="fill_parent"
    >

<Button android:text="CLICK TO GENERATE EVENT"
```

```
        android:id="@+id/testButton"
        android:layout_gravity="center"
        android:layout_width="wrap_content"
        android:layout_height="wrap_content"/>

<TextView android:layout_width="wrap_content"
        android:layout_height="wrap_content"
        android:id="@+id/testText"
        android:text="BEFORE CLICK TEXT!"
        android:textColor="#FFCC99"
        android:textSize="24px"/>
</LinearLayout>
```

Figure 9–7. *Adding Button and TextView attributes in our main.xml file*

Updating HandlerExamples.java

Now let's go back into our Java code.

1. Click the HandlerExamples.java tab at the top of the code editor pane.

2. Add the code that responds to a click on the button, as follows (see Figure 9–8):

```
public void onClick(View v) {
        TextView text = (TextView)findViewById(R.id.testText);
        text.setText("BUTTON HAS BEEN CLICKED. EVENT PROCESSED.");
}
```

We add our TextView object declaration into onClick(). We also add a setText("BUTTON HAS BEEN CLICKED. EVENT PROCESSED.") call to the TextView object we named text, created in the previous line.

Figure 9–8. *Defining the onClick() event Handler Code for a TextView in HandlerExamples.java*

Running the Event Handling Examples App in the Emulator

To run this example, right-click your *Chapter9* folder in the Package Explorer pane and select **Run As ➤ Android Application**. We have our first UI that responds to the most common event handler out there: the onClick handler. Figure 9–9 shows the results.

Figure 9–9. *Running the onClick event example in the Android 1.5 emulator*

Android Touchscreen Events: onTouch

Android handsets that feature touchscreens—the vast majority of them today—can take advantage of advanced touchscreen features, such as gestures.

> **NOTE:** *Gestures* are movements with the user's finger across the touchscreen that invoke certain program functions. They are popular for interaction on large screen smartphones and tablets. You will want to learn about implementing gestures when you become a more experienced Android developer. You have already been introduced to the onTouch event handler in the previous chapter, where we used it to trigger the start() method of a frame animation sequence of bitmap images. Gestures became available in Android 1.6 and thus do not work in Android 1.5 which is the version we are developing for in this book to provide the widest audience of user compatible devices.

It is important to note that an onClick event handler also works on a touchscreen, but an onTouch handler does not work with the navigation keys or selector key (the center selector Enter key). Therefore, it may be wise to use the onClick() method for most UI operations, and use onTouch() specifically when working with more advanced touch events such as gestures that involve only the touchscreen.

Since we have already covered implementing onTouch() (you can revisit it in Chapter 8 if you like), we'll continue here with the other important event handlers. These are the ones you will use more frequently in your application's design and coding.

Touchscreen's Right-Click Equivalent: onLongClick

After OnClick, OnLongClick is the next most used interface event. It is generated by the most input hardware and also the basis for the context menu in Android.

The onLongClick() method works with the following:

- When the user touches and holds on the touchscreen for 1 second
- When the user holds down the Enter button on the phone
- When the user holds down the center navigation key for 1 second

Any of these will generate an OnLongClick event for whatever UI widget has the focus.

Since any View object can trap an onLongClick() callback, the most elegant way to show this event handling is to add it to our Button UI object in our current *Chapter9* example code. This will also allow you to see the common scenario of more than one type of handler being used right alongside other types of event handlers in the same View and class.

1. In *HandlerExamples.java*, add a comma after `OnCLickListener` in the public class `HandlerExamples` definition and add `OnLongClickListener`, as shown in Figure 9–10. Then mouse-over the red-underlined `OnLongClickListener` and select to add the `import` statement (boom bam—there is our `import` code for this listener). Then mouse-over the red-underlined `HandlerExamples` class name and select to implement handler code. Voila, we now have the following:

```
public boolean onLongClick(View arg0) {
    // TODO Auto-generated method stub
    return false;
}
```

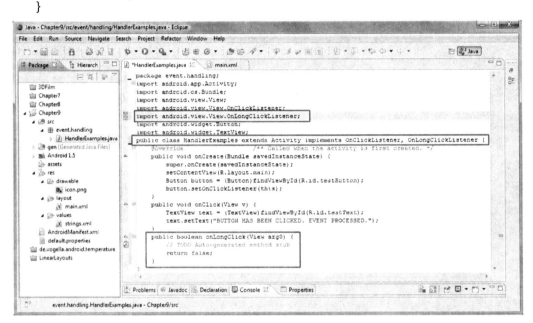

Figure 9–10. *Implementing an OnLongClick listener in HandlerExamples.java*

2. Now copy the `text` object and `text.setText()` code from the `onClick` handler and paste it into the `onLongClick` handler, where the placeholder comment code is. Change the text message to reflect the hold and long-click, as shown in Figure 9–11. Note that we can use the same object name `text` in both handlers. Since it is a local variable to each handler, neither `text` object sees the other reference.

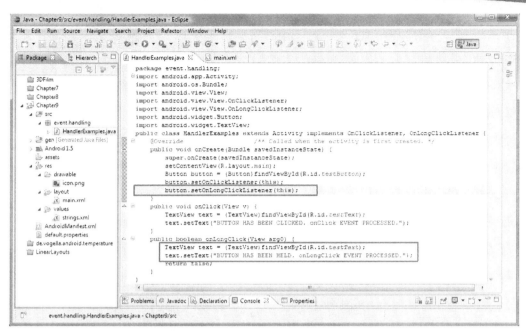

Figure 9–11. *Attaching an OnLongClick listener to our Button object in HandlerExample.java*

3. Now try the new functionality. Right-click the *Chapter9* folder and choose **Run As ➤ Android Project**. This time, you get an app that displays one message when you click and another when you hold the click. But when you release the long-click, the onClick message appears. The onLongClick message does not stay on the screen. Why is this?

4. Well, we forgot to change the default onLongClick() code, which returns false. This tells Android that nothing has been handled in that code block, so we are happy for Android to pass the event on to any other handlers that might be interested. But we don't want this to happen in our example. Instead, we need to return true when we handle the event, as follows (see Figure 9–12):

```java
public boolean onLongClick(View arg0) {
    TextView text = (TextView)findViewById(R.id.testText);
    text.setText("BUTTON HAS BEEN HELD. onLongClick EVENT PROCESSED.");
    return true;
}
```

This tells Android that we handled the event successfully, and sets the text that we wanted.

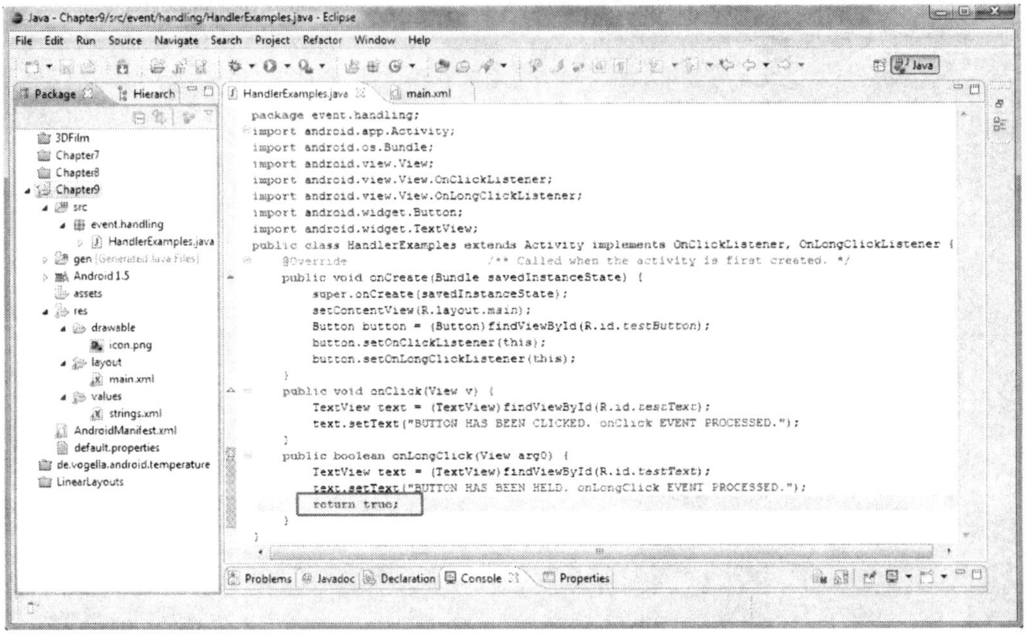

Figure 9–12. *Returning a true flag from our handled onLongClick() method*

Some of the event handlers return a Boolean (true or false value) to tell the calling code whether or not your listener has handled the code (or *consumed* the event as the programming terminology goes). So return true if you have handled the event (in our case, setText() has been done) and processing should stop here. Return false if you have not handled it or if you want the event to bubble up—that is, to be passed to other event handlers.

Now compile and run our OnLongClick app version. It works perfectly. A click displays the proper message and stays on the screen, and a long-click displays the proper message that stays on the screen until a short-click changes it.

Now let's add an onKeyListener and trap some keystroke events.

Keyboard Event Listeners: onKeyUp and onKeyDown

Events that will become familiar to you in Android app programming are onKey or onKeyUp (key released) and onKeyDown (key pressed down).

These events are commonly used for games and to implement shortcuts in your application, much like the F5 shortcut we use for **Refresh** or the F3 shortcut we use for **Open**.

To show how easy the keyboard event listeners are to implement, we are going to go back to our bootstrap code (the code that Android wrote for us in the beginning of this chapter) and add a couple lines to our *main.xml* file and our Java code to listen for a key event (the Enter key, of course). In other words, we are starting from scratch with a blank activity.

Adding the XML for Keyboard Events

First, let's go into our TextView object and add in a pre-Enter key "BEFORE KEYSTROKE DETECTED TEXT!" string, as well as a brighter color and larger text size. Here is the XML markup for our *main.xml* file (see Figure 9–13):

```xml
<?xml version="1.0" encoding="utf-8"?>

<LinearLayout
xmlns:android="http://schemas.android.com/apk/res/android"
        android:orientation="vertical"
        android:layout_width="fill_parent"
        android:layout_height="fill_parent">

    <TextView android:layout_width="fill_parent"
                android:layout_height="wrap_content"
                android:id="@+id/testText"
                android:text="BEFORE KEYSTROKE DETECTED TEXT!"
                android:textColor="#FFDDAA"
                android:textSize="19px"/>

</LinearLayout>
```

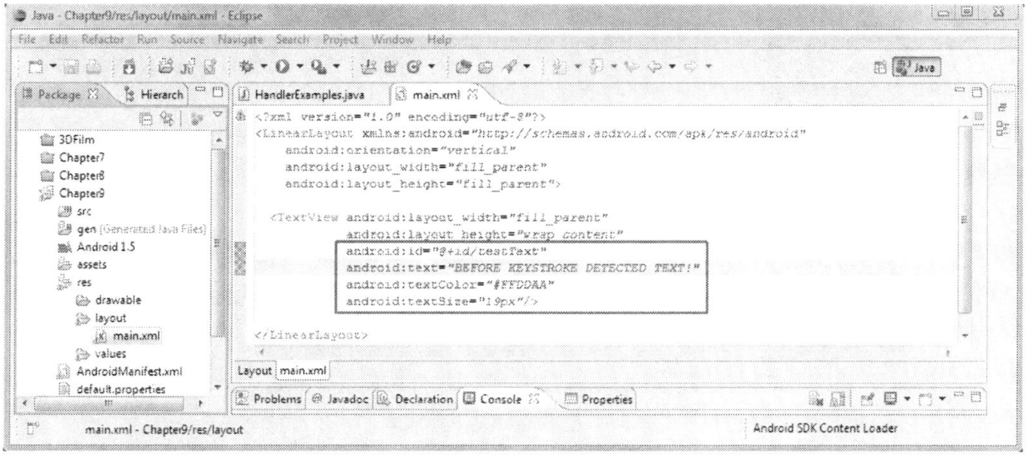

Figure 9–13. *Adding our TextView attributes in the main.xml file*

Adding the Java for Keyboard Events

In our *HandlerExample.java* file, we want to add two simple import statements and two basic blocks of code to allow us to handle keyboard events via the OnKeyDown handler. We will add about a dozen lines of code to be able to handle key events.

Here is the code, including the import statements and onCreate() method that was written for us by Eclipse (see Figure 9–14):

```java
package event.handling;

import android.app.Activity;
```

```java
import android.os.Bundle;
import android.view.KeyEvent;
import android.widget.TextView;

public class HandlerExamples extends Activity {
    @Override    /** Called when the activity is first created. */
    public void onCreate(Bundle savedInstanceState) {
        super.onCreate(savedInstanceState);
        setContentView(R.layout.main);
    }

        public boolean onKeyDown(int keyCode, KeyEvent event) {
                if (keyCode == KeyEvent.KEYCODE_ENTER) {
                        textUpdate();
                        return true;
                }
                    return false;
        }

        public void textUpdate() {
                TextView text = (TextView)findViewById(R.id.testText);
                text.setText("ENTER KEY PRESSED!");
        }
}
```

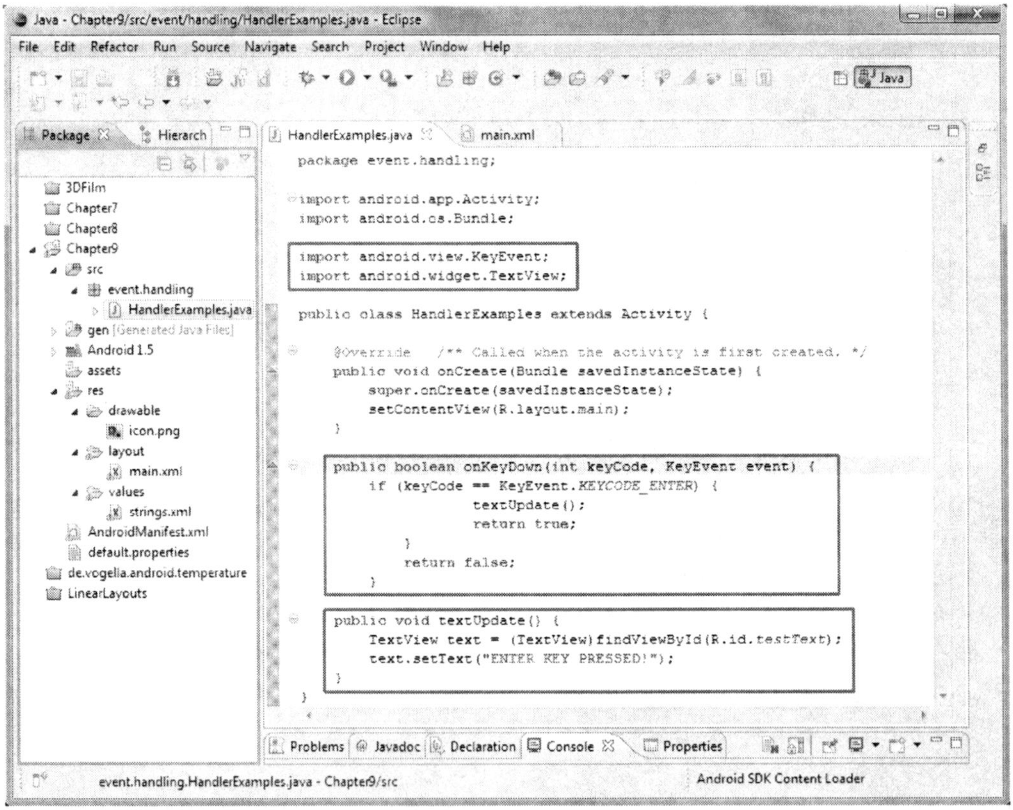

Figure 9–14. *Adding an onKeyDown listener to our Java code*

We need to import android.view.KeyEvent for the onKeyDown handler (first code block) and import android.widget.TextView for the textUpdate() method that we write in our second code block.

We leave the class declaration and onCreate() block of code (after the import statements) exactly as is.

The first block of code we write is the onKeyDown handler, which is a public method that returns a Boolean value that tells us if the event was handled (true) or not handled and needs to be passed along (false). The onKeyDown() method takes two parameters: the keyCode (the key that was pressed) and details of the event (event).

Our program logic inside the onKeyDown handler looks at the keyCode passed into the handler. If it is equal to the Enter key, signified by the KEYCODE_ENTER constant, it runs the textUpdate() method, and then returns true to signify we handled the event. Otherwise, onKeyDown() returns false to signify that an event was not handled.

This is the first time we have written our own method: the textUpdate() method that is called from inside onKeyDown(). This demonstrates some standard Java programming. The two lines of code that are in the textUpdate() routine could have been written where the textUpdate(); line of code is inside the onKeyDown() handler:

```
public boolean onKeyDown(int keyCode, KeyEvent event) {
        if (keyCode == KeyEvent.KEYCODE_ENTER) {
                TextView text = (TextView)findViewById(R.id.testText);
                text.setText("ENTER KEY PRESSED!");
                return true;
        }
                return false;
        }
```

This means that the textUpdate() method can contain all the things you want to do when someone clicks the Enter key. You can use this method, rather than putting them all inside the onKeyDown handler, where they could be in among actions for other keys. This makes things more organized and modular, and really comes in handy when you get into more complex code constructs.

Now compile and run the application.

You'll see a text field that says "BEFORE KEYSTROKE DETECTED TEXT!" that changes after you click the Enter key in the emulator.

TIP: If you want to detect a range of keystrokes and send them to different custom methods, a good programming construct to use is the switch construct, which allows you to outline different cases from which to select. We used switch in Chapter 7's examples.

Context Menus in Android: onCreateContextMenu

The concept of the context menu is a very clever one. Unfortunately, it is often underutilized both in PC and smartphone applications.

A context menu provides quick and easy access to all methods related to a UI object.

For instance, when I right-click here in my word processor, I get a context-sensitive menu with options for cut, copy, paste, font, paragraph, bullets, hyperlink, lookup, synonyms, and translate.

The context menu in Android is always accessed by a LongClick event (covered earlier in the chapter), just as on a PC it is accessed via a right-click.

To demonstrate, we will add context menus to this chapter's example project. We'll add two classes, along with two custom methods, to implement our context menus. We'll are take a look at the Android Toast widget, which is handy to use to blast quick little messages to the user. This way, you don't need to use a full-blown dialog implementation, as we did in Chapter 7.

Adding the XML for Context Menus

First, let's add a Button tag to our *main.xml* LinearLayout so that we have a UI element (button) to long-click on.

1. Click the main.xml tab, and then click the Layout tab at the bottom of that pane. Now add a Button view to the pane under the TextView.

2. Once the button appears under your text, switch back into XML editing mode via the main.xml tab at the bottom of the pane. Now we'll edit our Button tag attributes. The first one is android:text. Let's change that to "Long-Click Here to Access Context Menu" and change our ID from Button01 to contextButton.

3. Let's also center our button using the android:layout_gravity = "center" attribute, as we have done previously. But let's do it a different way this time. Put your cursor at the end of the android:id tag after the end quote and hit Return to put the attribute on its own line. Type in **android:**, and then wait.

4. Up will pop a little dialog listing *every* attribute that can be used in the Button tag. This represents more work being done for us. Double-click android:layout_gravity to select it. Then type = and wait again.

5. Again, a little dialog pops up, showing *every* value that can be used with android:layout_gravity. Double-click center, and you have the tag attribute written for you. (Make sure to use android:layout_gravity and not android:gravity, or it will not work.)

Here is what your XML tags should look like (see Figure 9–15):

```xml
<?xml version="1.0" encoding="utf-8"?>
<LinearLayout
xmlns:android="http://schemas.android.com/apk/res/android"
android:orientation="vertical"
android:layout_width="fill_parent"
android:layout_height="fill_parent">

<TextView android:layout_width="fill_parent"
        android:layout_height="wrap_content"
        android:id="@+id/testText"
        android:text="BEFORE KEYSTROKE DETECTED TEXT!"
        android:textColor="#FFDDAA"
        android:textSize="19px"/>

    <Button android:text="Long-Click Here to Access ContextMenu"
            android:id="@+id/contextButton"
            android:layout_gravity="center"
            android:layout_width="wrap_content"
            android:layout_height="wrap_content"/>
</LinearLayout>
```

We will reference the testText and contextButton inside our Java code.

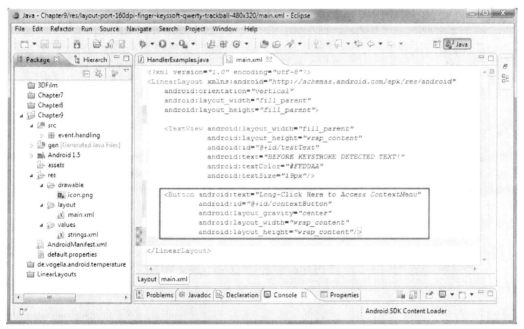

Figure 9–15. *Adding a Button object in our main.xml file to receive the long-click event*

Adding the Java for Context Menus

The main two Java methods that we override are onCreateContextMenu() and onContextItemSelected(), which replace Android's default methods of this same name. The use of the super object in the first one allows us to reference a method in the parent class that we are overriding. Note that overriding does not replace a class; it just allows us to customize it, leaving the original class that was extended intact and usable.

Now let's add the code for our onContextMenu event handling in *HandlerExamples.java*. We'll add the new code in with the previous code that we wrote in the onKey() section in order to handle onKeyDown events.

First, we need to use an import statement to import the Java classes that we are going to reference in the code we are about to write. Three of the six are related to our UI elements (android.view.View, android.widget.Button, and android.widget.Toast), and the other three are related to our implementation of our LongClick context menu.

```
import android.view.ContextMenu;
import android.view.MenuItem;
import android.view.View;
import android.view.ContextMenu.ContextMenuInfo;
import android.widget.Button;
import android.widget.Toast;
```

ContextMenu contains the methods that are related to the top level of the menu, such as what it is called, how it looks, and so forth. ContextMenuInfo relates to the information about any one given ContextMenu, which is really a collection of options. Within that container or level, we have the MenuItems, which are their own level of objects. Each MenuItem can have a name and styling, and can call methods once it is selected.

Now, let's see how Android attaches to a ContextMenu.

First, we need to add two key lines of code to our onCreate() method for our activity. The first declares and establishes a Button object, which we call contextButton and which we find by its contextButton ID from the *main.xml* file. The next line of code wires our newly created contextButton Button object to the ContextMenu system in Android.

```
public void onCreate(Bundle savedInstanceState) {
    super.onCreate(savedInstanceState);
    setContentView(R.layout.main);
    Button contextButton = (Button) findViewById(R.id.contextButton);
    registerForContextMenu(contextButton);
}
```

> **TIP:** When I first started working with Android, I wondered which class contained the registerForContextMenu() method. To again demonstrate how to use Eclipse as a learning tool, I'll tell you how to answer a question like that. Place your cursor over the method you are interested in, and Eclipse will pop up a box full of information about the method in question, which includes the class that contains the method.

Now let's get into our custom logic for creating our ContextMenu and its content. The first of the two menu methods is onCreateContextMenu(), which takes three objects as parameters:

- The ContextMenu object named menu

- The View object that called it

- The ContextMenuInfo object named menuInfo, which contains information about the menu configuration

The first line of code inside this code block simply passes our three parameters up to the parent class, which is referenced via the super keyword.

```
public void onCreateContextMenu(ContextMenu menu, View view,
                                ContextMenuInfo menuInfo) {
    super.onCreateContextMenu(menu, view, menuInfo);
```

The next three lines of code call methods against or on the menu object, which is of type ContextMenu. This code is configuring our top-level ContextMenu object by giving it a title using menu.setHeaderTitle() and adding two menu items via the two menu.add() methods.

```
public void onCreateContextMenu(ContextMenu menu, View view,
                                ContextMenuInfo menuInfo) {
    super.onCreateContextMenu(menu, view, menuInfo);
    menu.setHeaderTitle("Android Context Menu");
    menu.add(0, view.getId(), 0, "Invoke Context Function 1");
    menu.add(0, view.getId(), 0, "Invoke Context Function 2");
}
```

The second context menu method is onContextItemSelected(), which is passed a single parameter of type MenuItem named item. Note that this method has a Boolean return type, which means we need to return a true (handled) or false (not done yet) reply.

To start with, we have an if-then-else loop that compares the title of each MenuItem to a string. If the title matches, it runs the appropriate contextFunction1 or contextFunction2 (which we will code next).

```
public boolean onContextItemSelected(MenuItem item) {
    if(item.getTitle()=="Invoke Context Function 1") {
        contextFunction1(item.getItemId());
    }
    else if(item.getTitle()=="Invoke Context Function 2"){
        contextFunction2(item.getItemId());
    }
    else {
        return false;
    }
    return true;
}
```

Recall that the first code after the if in parentheses is the condition. It reads, "If the title that we are getting from the item object is equal to the text string "Invoke Context Function 1", then perform the statements in the curly braces that follow this conditional statement."

> **NOTE:** Remember that == means is equal to, and = means set the value of a variable or constant.

If this does not equate to true for the first if condition, then the next else block is encountered, along with a second (nested) if statement that is almost completely identical to the first, except that it is looking for the 2 option rather than 1. If this is also not satisfied or matching, the second else returns a false from the method to the calling code, telling it, "Sorry, no menu options here that match that!" If one of the if conditions is met, the true that is under the conditional code block is returned, because we have not jumped out of the method by returning a value yet.

Now we need to write our own methods for the two options, which we'll call contextFunction1() and contextFunction2(). We declare the first method as public and as void, as it does not return any values. It simply carries out a task with no result to report back. We name the method contextFunction1() and define one integer data parameter to pass, in this case an ID.

```
public void contextFunction1(int id){
```

Inside this method, we make a call to the Toast widget, which allows us to send brief messages to our end users during their use of the application. To do this, we use the makeText() method and access it directly from the Toast class via the following one (admittedly dense) line of code:

```
Toast.makeText(this, "function 1 invoked!", Toast.LENGTH_SHORT).show();
```

This is another one of those lines of code that does several things with a single construct. Once you get really good at programming, this type of coding becomes a really nice thing.

So we call the makeText() method and pass it three parameters:

- The activity that is running this Toast alert
- What the message should be
- How long to show the Toast pop-up

After the Toast.makeText(), another show() is appended. This displays the message we just specified with makeText(). One line of code does everything. And the best part is you can now use this code to pop up little messages to your users whenever you want to do that.

No, the context menu stuff that we did earlier has *nothing* to do with this one-line Toast construct, which will send a message to your screen anyplace in your code. Some people use this for debugging, with messages like, "Setting X variable to 7" or similar, so that you can see on the screen a visual progress through the code logic.

After our contextFunction2 code construct, which is similar to contextFunction1, we have our key event handlers from the previous section working at the same time as our ContextMenu.

The entire body of code in *HandlerExamples.java* should now look like the following (see Figure 9–16).

```java
package event.handling;

import android.app.Activity;
import android.os.Bundle;
import android.view.KeyEvent;
import android.widget.TextView;
import android.view.ContextMenu;
import android.view.MenuItem;
import android.view.View;
import android.view.ContextMenu.ContextMenuInfo;
import android.widget.Button;
import android.widget.Toast;

public class HandlerExamples extends Activity {

    @Override                          /** Called when the activity is first created. */
    public void onCreate(Bundle savedInstanceState) {
        super.onCreate(savedInstanceState);
        setContentView(R.layout.main);
        Button contextButton = (Button) findViewById(R.id.contextButton);
        registerForContextMenu(contextButton);
    }

    @Override                          /** Override Parent Class for this Application */
    public void onCreateContextMenu(ContextMenu menu, View view,
                                    ContextMenuInfo menuInfo) {
        super.onCreateContextMenu(menu, view, menuInfo);
        menu.setHeaderTitle("Android Context Menu");
        menu.add(0, view.getId(), 0, "Invoke Context Function 1");
        menu.add(0, view.getId(), 0, "Invoke Context Function 2");
    }

    @Override
    public boolean onContextItemSelected(MenuItem item) {
        if(item.getTitle()=="Invoke Context Function 1") {
                contextFunction1(item.getItemId());
        }
        else if(item.getTitle()=="Invoke Context Function 2"){
                contextFunction2(item.getItemId());
        }
        else {
                return false;
        }
        return true;
    }

    public void contextFunction1(int id){
        Toast.makeText(this, "function 1 invoked!", Toast.LENGTH_SHORT).show();
    }

    public void contextFunction2(int id){
        Toast.makeText(this, "function 2 invoked!", Toast.LENGTH_SHORT).show();
    }
```

```
    public boolean onKeyDown(int keyCode, KeyEvent event) {
        if (keyCode == KeyEvent.KEYCODE_ENTER) {
                textUpdate();
                return true;

        }
        return false;
    }

    public void textUpdate() {
            TextView text = (TextView)findViewById(R.id.testText);
            text.setText("ENTER KEY PRESSED!");
    }
}
```

Figure 9–16. *Adding the Java code to implement a context menu in HandlerExamples.java*

Now let's run our code with **Run As ➤ Android Application** and see how it all works together. A long-click on the button brings up the context menu. A touch or click on one of the buttons highlights it, as shown in Figure 9–17. Once it is clicked, a Toast menu tells us our method has been run. Also notice that our previous section code for onKeyDown() still works perfectly.

Figure 9–17. *Running our application in the Android 1.5 emulator after adding a context menu*

Controlling the Focus in Android

One of the most challenging aspects of UI design and programming is tracking and controlling the focus of your application. The focus is where the UI is paying attention, representing which UI element the user is presently dealing with.

The tough part about focus is that you can't always see it visually. Even as an end user, it is sometimes difficult to see where the focus is within an application. We have all experienced this with our computers at one time or another, most commonly in forms where the active cursor for a field moves from one field to another as the form is filled out or the Tab key is used to jump the focus from field to field.

It is even more difficult to control, track, and implement focus from a programming standpoint. Note that focus is not something that you need to specifically worry about (Android handles it automatically), unless it is somehow tripping up your application's user experience.

Android has an internal algorithm that decides how to hop from one UI element (View) to another based on which View is closest to the previous View, but you can also control how the focus moves from one UI element to the next with your own custom code. Here, we will go over the basics in order to get you started and familiar with the concepts, in case you need to intervene with your own XML or Java code to manually control focus.

First, we will look at how to control focus via XML, as it is easier to understand and implement than the Java route. Later, we will go over Java methods that allow you to take focus or otherwise control the focus based on what the user is doing in the application.

Adding the XML for Focus Control

To start, let's add a couple buttons to the UI we've been developing in this chapter and set the focus to do something that is not standard focus procedure in Android.

The easiest way to do this is to copy our existing Button tag in our *main.xml* file and paste it in twice right underneath our existing Button tag markup (see Figure 9–18).

```xml
<?xml version="1.0" encoding="utf-8"?>
<LinearLayout
xmlns:android="http://schemas.android.com/apk/res/android"
android:orientation="vertical"
android:layout_width="fill_parent"
android:layout_height="fill_parent">

<TextView android:layout_width="fill_parent"
        android:layout_height="wrap_content"
        android:id="@+id/testText"
        android:text="BEFORE KEYSTROKE DETECTED TEXT!"
        android:textColor="#FFDDAA"
        android:textSize="19px"/>

        <Button android:text="Long-Click Here to Access ContextMenu"
            android:id="@+id/contextButton"
            android:layout_gravity="center"
            android:layout_width="wrap_content"
            android:layout_height="wrap_content"/>

        <Button android:text="Second Button"
            android:id="@+id/secondButton"
            android:layout_gravity="center"
            android:layout_width="wrap_content"
            android:layout_height="wrap_content"/>

        <Button android:text="Third Button"
            android:id="@+id/thirdButton"
            android:layout_gravity="center"
            android:layout_width="wrap_content"
            android:layout_height="wrap_content"/>
</LinearLayout>
```

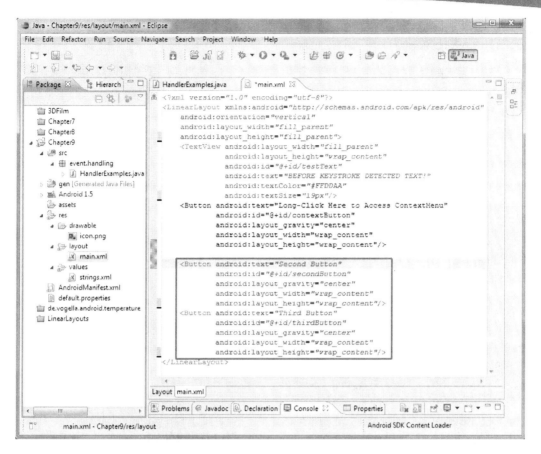

Figure 9–18. *Adding UI buttons to the main.xml file*

To make our Button tags unique, we also need to rename their IDs to secondButton and thirdButton. This way, we can access them in our Java code and also change their display text to reflect that they are the second and third buttons, respectively.

We will leave all of the other Button tag attributes for scaling and centering the same.

Now we will add our android:nextFocus attributes, so that we have control over which UI elements our focus jumps to and from when the user navigates the UI with the arrow keys on the front of the smartphone.

For the existing contextButton tag attributes, we want to add an android:nextFocusUp attribute and point it to the third button. Then, if users hit the up arrow on their Android smartphone when they are on the first button, it will cycle back down to the last button.

Since the ID of the third button is thirdButton, this tag attribute will read as follows:

android:nextFocusUp="@+id/thirdButton"

This is done in order to reference the third button tag we have defined in our XML markup here as the destination UI element for the up arrow focus to go to if users hit the up navigation arrow when they are on (have focus on) the first UI button (contextButton from our prior example).

To control advancement of focus from the contextButton to the secondButton button, we add this:

```
android:nextFocusDown="@+id/secondButton"
```

Now we have defined all of the focus movements that can happen for the contextButton, and we are ready to define the focus movements for the next two buttons.

This will be a very similar process. In fact, you can simply cut and paste the two lines of code that you wrote for the contextButton tag and change the ID attributes after you paste them into the two new Button tags.

For the second Button tag, we will add in another two android:nextFocus attributes. This time, these point to the buttons immediately above and below the second button, so this one is the easiest. The code looks as follows:

```
android:nextFocusUp="@+id/contextButton"
android:nextFocusDown="@+id/thirdButton"
```

For the third Button tag, we will add in another two android:nextFocus attributes, which finally point to the buttons immediately above and back up to the top button in our loop of buttons, as follows:

```
android:nextFocusUp="@+id/secondButton"
android:nextFocusDown="@+id/contextButton"
```

The first attribute is pretty straightforward, as the secondButton button is above our third button. For the nextFocusDown attribute, since there is no button underneath the third button, we actually want the focus to wrap, or loop back, to our first contextButton button, so that is the ID we use in the android:nextFocusDown attribute that we add to the final Button tag.

> **NOTE:** There are nextFocusLeft and nextFocusRight attributes available (one for each arrow key) if you are using a horizontal LinearLayout tag attribute, for instance.

Here are the three blocks of nextFocus attributes that we have added to our three buttons so that you can check your work (see Figure 9–19):

```
<Button android:text="Long-Click Here to Access ContextMenu"
        android:id="@+id/contextButton"
        android:nextFocusUp="@+id/thirdButton"
        android:nextFocusDown="@+id/secondButton"
        android:layout_gravity="center"
        android:layout_width="wrap_content"
        android:layout_height="wrap_content"/>

<Button android:text="Second Button"
        android:id="@+id/secondButton"
        android:nextFocusUp="@+id/contextButton"
```

```
        android:nextFocusDown="@+id/thirdButton"

        android:layout_gravity="center"
        android:layout_width="wrap_content"
        android:layout_height="wrap_content"/>

<Button android:text="Third Button"
        android:id="@+id/thirdButton"
        android:nextFocusUp="@+id/secondButton"
        android:nextFocusDown="@+id/contextButton"
        android:layout_gravity="center"
        android:layout_width="wrap_content"
        android:layout_height="wrap_content"/>
```

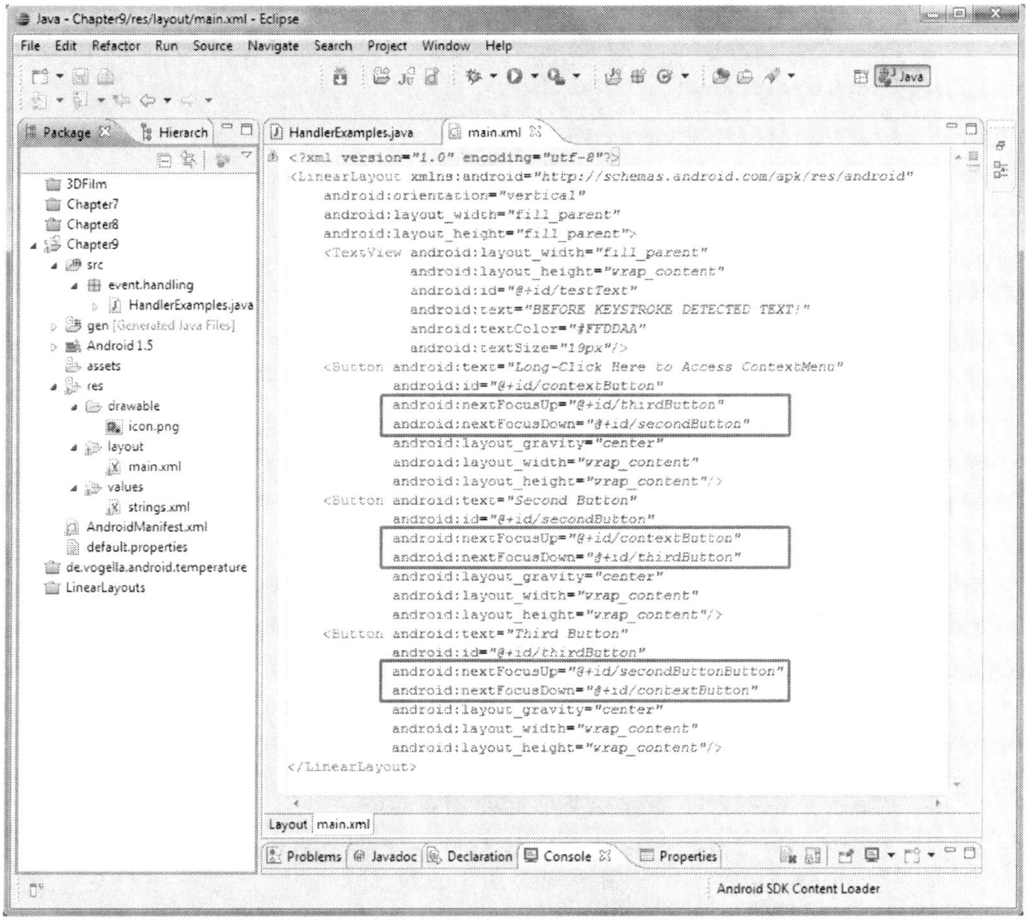

Figure 9–19. *Controlling the focus via XML mark-up in main.xml*

Adding the Java for Focus Control

Now let's declare the two new buttons we defined in our *main.xml* markup in our Java code, and point them toward our ContextMenu code that we wrote in the previous section, so that they actually do something useful.

Here are the four new lines of code that we need to write to support these new buttons (see Figure 9–20):

```
public void onCreate(Bundle savedInstanceState) {
    super.onCreate(savedInstanceState);
    setContentView(R.layout.main);
    Button secondButton = (Button) findViewById(R.id.secondButton);
    registerForContextMenu(secondButton);
    Button thirdButton = (Button) findViewById(R.id.thirdButton);
    registerForContextMenu(thirdButton);
    Button contextButton = (Button) findViewById(R.id.contextButton);
    registerForContextMenu(contextButton);
}
```

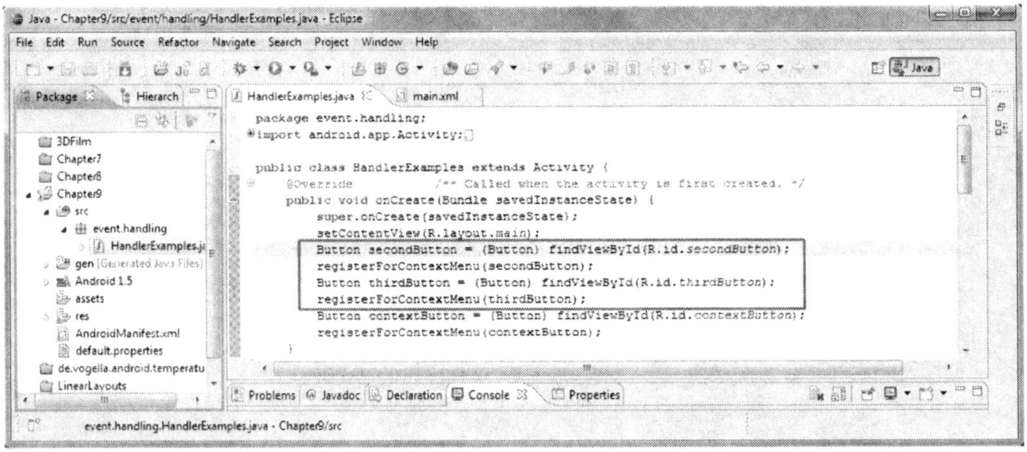

Figure 9–20. *Registering our buttons for the context menu in HandlerExamples.java*

To implement this in the quickest fashion, select the two lines of code that define and point our contextButton object to the registerForContextMenu() method, and paste them twice above or below the original two lines of code.

Change the contextButton reference to secondButton in the first two lines, and to thirdButton in the last two lines. You have now declared all three buttons and set them to actually do something in your code.

Now let's use our familiar **Run As ➤ Android Application** work process to compile and run this application, as shown in Figure 9–21. It now traps or handles onKey events and onContextMenu events, as well as implements control of focus among the usable UI elements, namely the buttons.

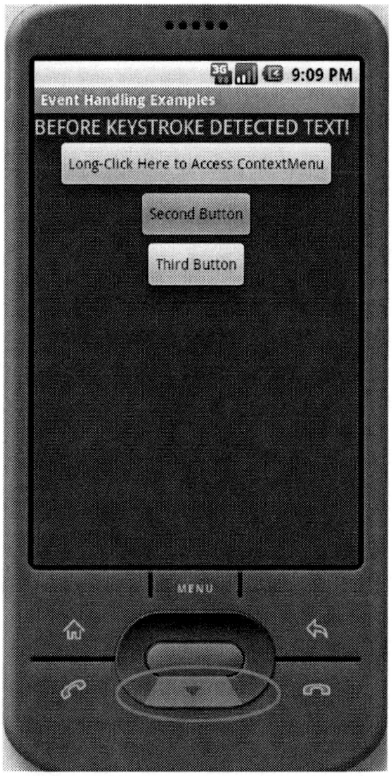

Figure 9–21. *Running our sample application in the Android 1.5 emulator after adding focus control*

You will notice now that when you compile and run this code, all three buttons will call up a ContextMenu. In your own apps, you may want all (or many) of your UI elements to bring up the same context menu selections (say the application default context menu), and this is the way to do that using very few lines of code.

It is important to test your applications vigorously, as some bugs will show up only after the features have been used already once or twice.

To test this application, long-click each of the buttons and select either option. Everything should work as expected and pull up the context menu. To see the cycling focus that we have implemented, use the up or down arrow/keys on the bottom of the Android smartphone (in this case, on the emulator) to cycle the focus among the buttons (focus is shown in orange). You will notice no matter which direction you choose, the focus cycles or loops through the buttons correctly.

> **NOTE:** Remember that Android will handle focus for you as a matter of routine. This includes jumping between UI elements on the screen and even jumping to the next logical UI element if a UI element (a View object) is hidden (or shown) or removed (or added) as a matter of the application programming logic.

Setting Focus Availability

View objects can be defined (in XML or Java) to be able to accept (or deny) focus using the isFocusable() method or the android:focusable (XML) attribute. If you define a View (UI object) to be focusable (or not focusable) in XML, and then want to change this later at runtime (while your application is running), there is also a setFocusable() method that can flip this (Boolean) switch. These focus methods control focus navigation via the smartphone navigation key hardware.

There are separate methods to control the focus in relation to the touchscreen, and these are named very similarly: isFocusableInTouchMode() and setFocusableInTouchMode(). For XML markup coding, you would use the format android:focusableInTouchMode, similar to nontouch focus.

Finally, if you simply want to ascertain if there has been a change of focus on a UI object, you can use the onFocusChanged() method. This method can be called to find out if there is a change in state from true to false, or focused to not focused, that you can use in more advanced programming endeavors that watch focus even more closely. With this method, your software can essentially watch what the user is doing with your UI and respond accordingly. As you can see, Android gives us a huge dose of control over our application's focus.

Summary

This chapter has covered some important and advanced concepts in Java programming, as well as in Android app development. The topics ranged from setting up event listeners and event handlers to controlling the focus of your UI design as the user moves through it, which is a part of your user experience design.

You now know how to handle clicks via navigation keys or touchscreen, long-clicks, and keyboard use. We even covered some advanced features like context menus, the Toast system for user message notifications, and controlling the focus in your XML or Java code, or via both.

We covered a lot of important material in this chapter, so be sure to review it. It includes some clever and new ways to use the Eclipse IDE as well, and that is also important to master by the time you are finished with this book.

Chapter 10

Understanding Content Providers

In this chapter, we are going to take a look at how to provide content within your application. We'll cover how to share that content, and how to access and modify the data that represents that content.

We have gotten significantly more advanced as we have progressed from chapter to chapter, and this chapter is no different. Data access is significantly more complex than event handling and UI design. This is because it involves database design and requesting security permissions for database access. In fact, starting with this chapter, we will need to modify the application's *AndroidManifest.xml* file, so be warned that we are getting into some fairly complicated concepts and code here.

We'll begin with an overview of exactly what Android content providers are, and what they do for your Android user. After that, you will learn how to use SQLite-based content providers for your Android applications although this is beyond the scope of this chapter and book.

An Overview of Android Content Providers

Content provider is a term unique to Android development that means nothing more than a datastore of data values, usually in the form of a SQLite database that is already part of the Android operating system (OS). You can also create your own content providers for your application.

An Android content provider provides you with access to sharable data structures commonly called *databases*. The basic procedure is as follows:

1. Get permission to open the database.

2. Query the data.

3. Access the data.

In accessing data, you might read the data, write the data (i.e. change the values of the existing data), or append new data onto the database structure, based on the type and level of security permissions that have been established in the *AndroidManifest.xml* file.

Data can be in Android internal memory or in external memory such as an SD card, or even on an external server that is remote to the Android device itself.

Databases and Database Management Systems

The usual way for content providers to provide data structures for Android applications is via a database management system (DBMS). A DBMS manages a database by providing ways for users to create databases, as well as to populate them with data via reading and writing operations.

There is a complete open source DBMS right inside the Android OS called SQLite. This is a relational DBMS (RDBMS). An RDBMS is based on relationships that can be drawn between data arranged in tables. Later in this chapter, you will see how to write data into these tables in the RDBMS.

The SQL in SQLite stands for Structured Query Language. The "Lite" or "Light" part delineates that this is a "lightweight" version of the DBMS, intended for embedded use in consumer electronics devices, and not a full blown version of SQL, as would be used on a computer system. Later, we will look briefly at how it allows you to access database data records and the data contained within their individual data fields. All you really need to know about SQLite is that it is a part of Android and that you can use it for data storage. Android takes care of the DBMS functions for you!

In a DBMS, the highest level of data storage is the database itself, which contains tables of data in rows and columns. Each table is two-dimensional, where a row is called a *record*. Within each record are *fields*, organized into columns, which contain the individual data items that make up the records. Fields can contain different data types, such as numbers, text, or even references to data that is stored somewhere else. However, each field must contain the same data type as the other fields in the same column (see Figure 10–1).

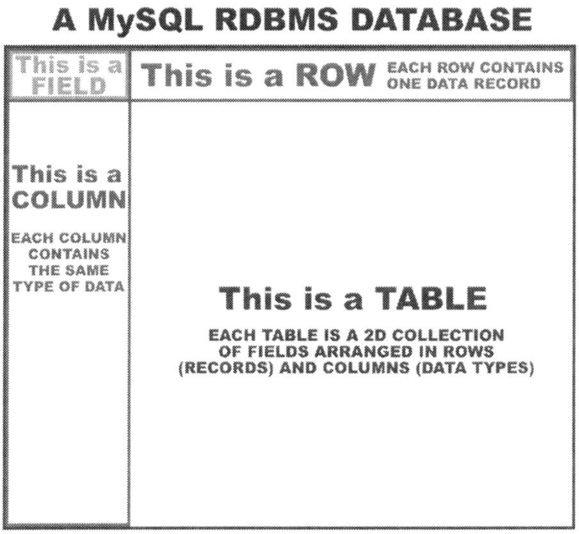

A MySQL RDBMS DATABASE

Figure 10–1. *MySQL RDBMS database*

Note that there can be more than one table in a database (and usually is, for both performance and organizational reasons). As long as there is a key (a unique index) for each record in each table, information for a single data entry can span more than one table. For instance, if your key or ID is 217, your personal information and phone information can be in two different tables stored under that same key value.

> **CAUTION:** After the record structure and data fields that define this record structure are set up, don't change the structure later. This is because the currently loaded records and fields may not fit into the new data structure definition correctly. So, it's best to design what your database structure will be up-front, making the DBMS design process especially critical to the success of the project.

The content providers that are provided with the Android OS all use SQLite, because it is compact and open source, so we are going to focus on those in this chapter.

Android Built-in Content Providers

A significant number of SQLite database structures are hard-coded into Android in order to handle things that users expect from their phones and tablets, such as contact address books, camera picture storage, digital video storage, music libraries, and so forth. The most extensive of these SQLite database structures is the Contacts database.

The base-level interfaces of the `android.provider` package allow us to access those data structures that define the setup and personalization of each user's smartphone. Obviously, the data in each of these structures will be completely different for each user's phone.

Contacts Database Contact Providers

Table 10–1 lists the Contacts database interfaces found on the Android Developer site (http://developer.android.com/reference/android/provider/package-summary.html).

Table 10–1. *The Contacts Interfaces for Android 1.x Support*

Interface	Contents
Contacts.OrganizationColumns	Organization
Contacts.GroupsColumns	Groups
Contacts.PeopleColumns	People
Contacts.PhonesColumns	Phone numbers
Contacts.PhotosColumns	Contact photographs
Contacts.PresenceColumns	IM presences
Contacts.SettingsColumns	Phone settings
Contacts.ContactMethodsColumns	Contact methods
Contacts.ExtensionsColumns	Phone extensions

If you browse the Android documentation, you'll see that the interfaces listed in Table 10–1 are all described as "deprecated." *Deprecated* means that these classes have been replaced by other classes in a newer version of the programming language (such as Java) or API (such as Android). The newer classes that replace older classes are usually more robust or complex, or sometimes they differ only in how they are implemented.

This is what has happened with the Contacts interfaces between Android versions 1.*x* (1.0, 1.1, 1.5, and 1.6) and Android versions 2.*x* and 3.*x* (2.0, 2.1, 2.2, 2.3, and 3.0). So, the database interfaces that work with Android 1.*x* phones are different than the ones that work on the Android 2.*x* phones (more advanced or feature-rich database structures, in this case).

If you are going to support 1.5 and 1.6 phones (as we are doing throughout this book), you will need to use the database interfaces listed in Table 10–1.

The good news is that deprecated does not mean disabled. It more accurately means in this case, "not suggested for general use unless you need to support pre-2.0 versions for your Android users." So, if you need to support Android 1.5 and later phones, you can use the interfaces listed in Table 10–1, and they will still work well on 2.*x* (and 3.*x*) smartphones. However, you may not be able to access data from a few new fields or tables unless you add support for the new 2.x DBMS structures in your code by detecting what OS the user is using, and have code sections that deal with each (1.x and 2.x) structure differently.

> **NOTE:** If you want to be able to access every new feature, you can have your code detect which version of the OS the phone is using, and have custom code that delivers the optimal functionality for each version.

In the case of Android, deprecation (a common problem that developers need to get used to) equates to different versions of the Android OS being able to do different things, and thus having different sets of functionality that can be used for each operating system level or version. With Android this is especially prevalent as different OS versions support different hardware features for new phones and tablets, requiring new APIs and changes to existing APIs in ode to support the new hardware features.

> **NOTE:** Over time, versional functionality gets more and more difficult to keep track of. Indeed, we already have eight (if you count Android 3.0) different OS versions that our code must work across. Keeping track of all the programming constructs and logic mazes is enough of a challenge for most, without a layer on top of that regarding remembering which constructs and interfaces work or do not work with a given OS version. This is one reason why programmers are so well paid.

Table 10–2 lists some of the new version 2.*x* content providers for manipulating contact information. Some of these replace the deprecated versions that are listed in Table 10–1, and are available from the same Android developer site link: (`http://developer.android.com/reference/android/provider/package-summary.html`).

Table 10–2. *Android 2.x Content Providers*

Interface	Contents
`ContactsContract.CommonDataKinds.CommonColumns`	For subclassing databases
`ContactsContract.ContactsColumns`	Contact main information
`ContactsContract.ContactOptionsColumns`	Contact options
`ContactsContract.ContactStatusColumns`	Contact status
`ContactsContract.PhoneLookupColumns`	Phone numbers
`ContactsContract.GroupsColumns`	Group definitions
`ContactsContract.PresenceColumns`	IM presences
`ContactsContract.SettingsColumns`	Account settings
`ContactsContract.StatusColumns`	IM visibility

Android MediaStore Content Providers

The other collections of content providers that are important within the Android OS are the MediaStore content providers. These are listed in Table 10–3.

Table 10–3. *Android MediaStore Content Providers*

Interface	Contents
MediaStore.Audio.AlbumColumns	Album information
MediaStore.Audio.ArtistColumns	Artist information
MediaStore.Audio.AudioColumns	Audio information
MediaStore.Audio.GenresColumns	Audio genre information
MediaStore.Audio.PlaylistsColumns	Audio playlist information
MediaStore.Images.ImageColumns	Digital images
MediaStore.Video.VideoColumns	Digital video
MediaStore.MediaColumns	Generic media store

In the rest of this chapter, we will look at how to declare content providers for use, access them, read them, modify them, and append to them.

Defining a Content Provider

Before a content provider can be used, it must be registered for use by your Android application. This is done by using some XML markup in the *AndroidManifest.xml* file. The **<provider>** tag, so aptly named, allows us to define which content providers we are going to access once our application is launched. Here's a <provider> tag for the Images content provider:

```
<provider android:name="MediaStore.Images.ImageColumns"  />
```

All Android content providers expose to developers a publicly accessible unique reference, or address, if you will, to each database. This address is called a URI, and the Android constant that points to the data location within the database tableis always called CONTENT_URI.

A content provider that provides access to multiple tables will expose a unique URI for each table. Here are a couple examples of predetermined Android URI constants:

```
android.provider.Contacts.Phones.CONTENT_URI
android.provider.Contacts.Photos.CONTENT_URI
```

The first reads "android (the OS) dot provider (the component type) dot Contacts (the database) dot Phones (the table) dot CONTENT_URI (the constant that points to the data location)." Yes, there is a logical method to the madness here.

> **NOTE:** URI objects are used for much more than just Android content providers, as you have seen in Chapter 8. All of the ones that are used to access Android content providers start with `content://`, just like a web address starts with `http://`.

Creating the Content Providers Example Project in Eclipse

Let's set up our *Chapter10* project folder in Eclipse right now, so you can learn a little more about the Android manifest editor and how Eclipse can automate the Android manifest XML coding process for us.

1. If you still have the *Chapter9* project folder open from the previous chapter, right-click that folder and select **Close Project**.

2. Then select **File ➤ New ➤ Project** and choose **Android Project** to open the **New Android Project** dialog.

3. Fill it out as follows (and shown in Figure 10–2).

   - **Project name:** Name the project **Chapter10**.

   - **Build Target:** Set this to Android 1.5.

   - **Application name:** Name the application Android Content Providers.

   - **Package name:** Set this to `content.providers`.

   - **Create Activity:** Check this box and name the activity `DatabaseExamples`.

   - **Minimum SDK Version:** Enter 3, which matches a minimum SDK version of 3.

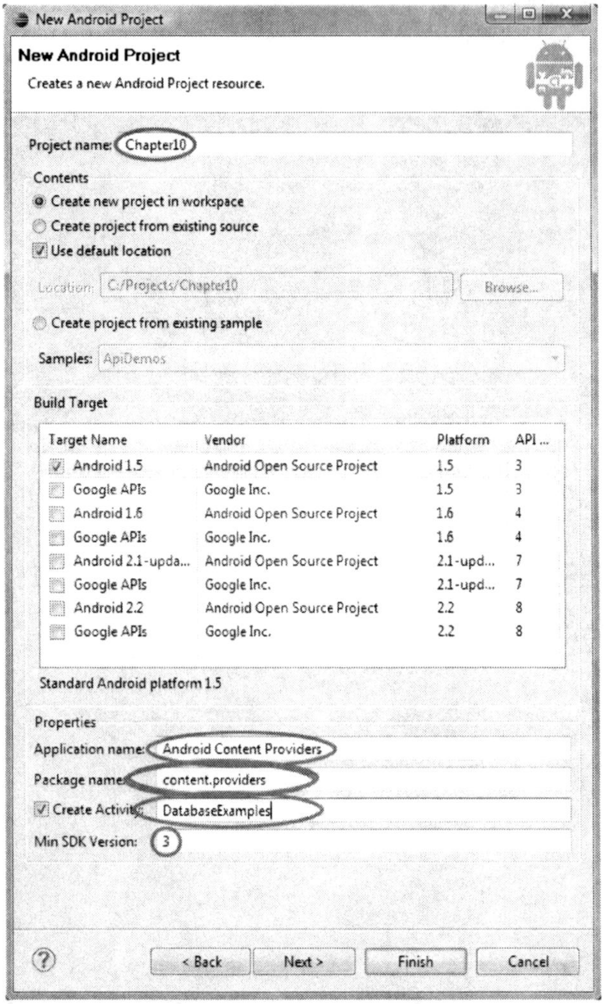

Figure 10–2. *Creating the Chapter10 Android project*

Defining Security Permissions

The *AndroidManifest.xml* file is usually referred to as the manifest for your application, and it tells the Android OS what we intend to do with our application. It is accessed during the initial launch of your application to set up the memory for the application and to boot up any system resources or pointers (addresses to things that we are going to talk with or connect to) that are needed for the application to run successfully.

In this case, that means we will be asking Android for permission to access, and possibly even change (depending on the tags we add), one of the Android databases outlined in the previous tables. We need to get permissions to use certain areas of the OS so that Android can implement a robust level of security within its OS infrastructure.

To define permissions, use the `<uses-permission>` tag:

```
<uses-permission android:name="android.permission.READ_CONTACTS" />
```

This tag allows the application to READ the CONTACTS database. Read-only operations are inherently safe, as we are only looking into these databases and reading from them. A read operation is nondestructive to a database.

If we wish to change (overwrite or update, and append) data in a database, we need to use a different permission tag that tells Android that we are going to write data to an Android OS database. In this case, WRITE_CONTACTS represents the permission and database we will use. As you may have guessed, the WRITE version of the tag looks like this:

```
<uses-permission android:name="android.permission.WRITE_CONTACTS"/>
```

Permission for write operations is a bit more serious matter, due to the fact that we are now able to screw up the database. In this case, we are dealing with the smartphone user's contacts data, and we might overwrite data that was there before our app ever accessed it.

> **TIP:** There are different permission tags that control different levels of access to services or databases that are part of Android. To see a list of all of them, and to get an idea of what Android will let you access with regard to smartphone hardware, features, and databases, check out this link: `developer.android.com/reference/android/Manifest.permission.html`. You will be amazed and empowered.

Now let's see how easy it easy to use Eclipse to add the necessary permissions. Follow these steps:

1. Right-click the *AndroidManifest.xml* file in the Project Explorer navigation pane, as shown in Figure 10–3, and select **Open** or hit the F3 key on the keyboard.

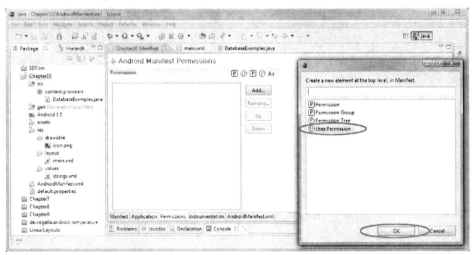

Figure 10–3. *Adding a permission in the Chapter10 manifest using the Eclipse visual editor*

2. In the Chapter10 Manifest tab, click the Permissions tab at the bottom of the window (see Figure 10–3).

3. Click the Add… button in the right pane.

4. Select the Uses Permission entry at the bottom of the list, and then click OK (see Figure 10–4).

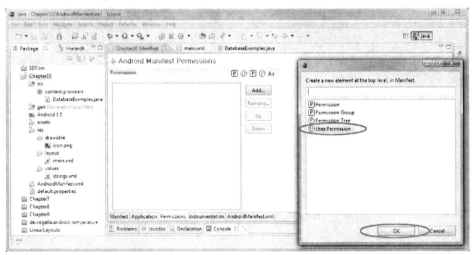

Figure 10–4. *Selecting the Uses Permission entry*

5. You'll see the uses-permission tag in the Permissions pane. From the drop-down menu that lists permissions, select android.permission.READ_CONTACTS (see Figure 10–5). Now it will appear in the left part of the pane.

6. Selecting the Uses Permission type on the right should update the pane at the left, but currently it does not, so we (redundantly, since it's already at the bottom of the list) click the Down button to force the manifest editor to update the left pane with the proper uses-permission tag setting.

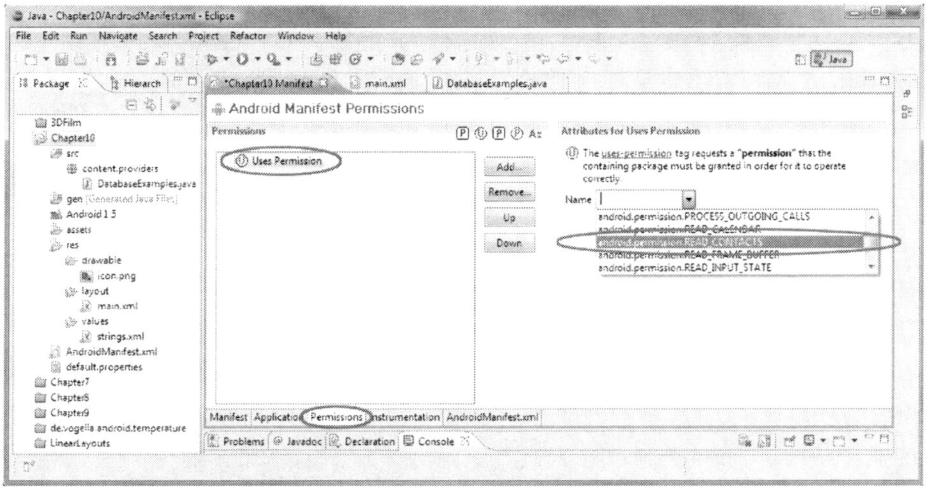

Figure 10–5. *Selecting the READ_CONTACTS permission*

7. Repeat steps 3 through 6 to add another uses-permission tag, this time selecting the android.permission.WRITE_CONTACTS option (see Figure 10–6).

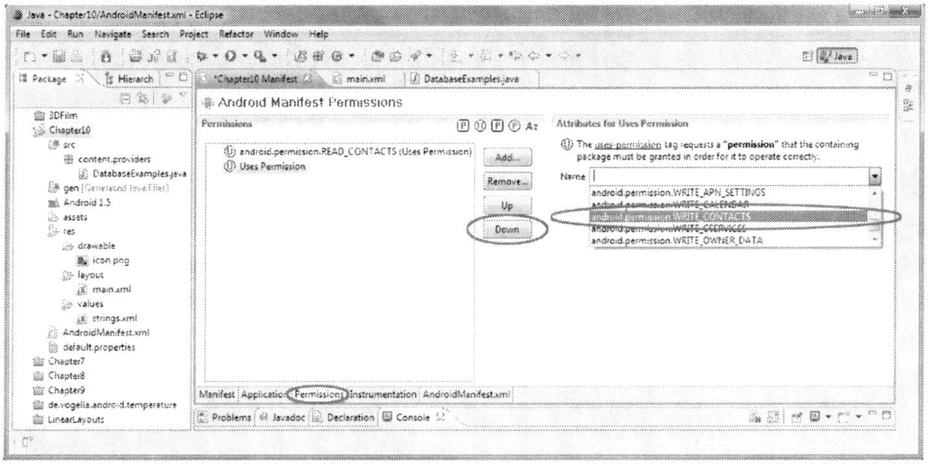

Figure 10–6. *Selecting the WRITE_CONTACTS permission*

That's all there is to adding our read and write permissions. Figure 10–7 shows our *AndroidManifest.xml* file with the two permission tags at the bottom, before the closing tag:

```
<uses-permission android:name="android.permission.READ_CONTACTS"></uses-permission>
<uses-permission android:name="android.permission.WRITE_CONTACTS"></uses-permission>
```

TIP: Anytime you are working with the Eclipse manifest editor, you can click the AndroidManifest.xml tab at the bottom of the window and see what this helper is doing as far as writing the actual XML markup code.

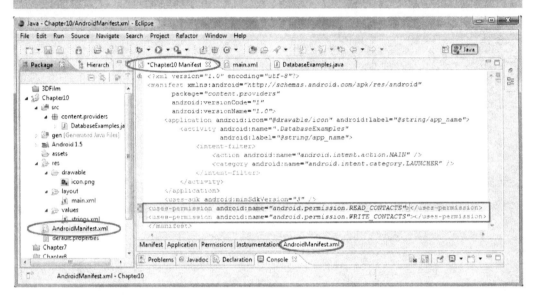

Figure 10–7. *The XML output for the permission additions we made in the visual editor*

Now that we have permissions to read and write to the Contacts database, we can get started working with databases.

Adding Data to the Contacts Database

Android SQLite uses a table-based database model, where rows represent each data record and the columns represent the data fields, each with a constant type. In this way, each piece of data in each column is the same exact type or classification, and each row is a unique collection of data of these types spanning across the row.

In this example, we are going to work with the **Contacts.People** table. After we add some sample data to this table, it will look like Table 10–4.

Table 10–4. *Contacts.People Database Table with Sample Data*

_ID	_COUNT	NAME	NUMBER
44	4	Bill Gates	212 555 1234
13	4	Steven Jobs	425 555 6677
53	4	Larry Ellison	201 555 4433
27	4	Mark Zuckerburg	213-555-4567

The column headers are the names that are used by Android to reference the data held in each column. These are what you use in your Java code to access each field of data within each record. For example, in some Java code we will write, we will refer to People.NAME and People.NUMBER.

The column names prefaced by an underscore character (_ID and _COUNT) are data fields assigned and controlled by Android; that is, you cannot WRITE these values, but you can READ them.

Now let's add the four data records shown in Table 10–4 into our Android emulator. (If you like, you can add more than four records.) We'll do this using the utilities that come on the smartphone. Follow these steps:

1. Run the emulator as usual by choosing **Run As ➤ Android Application**.

NOTE: Another way to start the emulator is to select **Window ➤ Android SDK and AVD Manager**. Select your 1.5 emulator and press Start... and then Launch. Any contacts you enter should be saved for later, even if you close the emulator.

2. Press the Home button. You will see four icons on the home screen (shown in Figure 10–8 on the left side) labeled Messaging, Dialer, Contacts, and Browser. The one called Contacts is a front-end to our Contacts database and will allow us to add in the records shown in Table 10–4.

Figure 10–8. *Adding new contacts to the Android Contacts database via the Contacts utility*

3. Click the Contacts icon to launch the Contacts database, which is initially empty. The screen tells us that we do not yet have any contacts and how to add new contacts to the Contacts database (as shown on the right side of Figure 10–8).

4. Click the Menu button to bring up a menu from the bottom of the screen (similar to the menu we created in Chapter 7) that offers four different options for working with the Contacts database.

5. Select the New Contact option to bring up the new contact data-entry form.

6. Fill out the name (`People.NAME`) and mobile phone number (`People.NUMBER`) fields at the top of the screen (as shown on the left side of Figure 10–9), and then click the Menu button.

7. Select the Done option to add the record to the database. Our addition appears on the screen (as shown in the right side of Figure 10–9).

Figure 10–9. *Adding a record to the Contact database*

8. Repeat steps 4 through 7 to add the three other names in Table 10–4, and maybe a few of your own.

Working with a Database

Let's get started writing our application that will access the Contacts database. We'll do some data queries against it, update the data, add data, and delete data.

Querying a Content Provider: Accessing the Content

First, let's add a button to our example app's *main.xml* file that will trigger our database query via an onClick event (as discussed in Chapter 9 regarding events processing, or, as discussed in the previous chapter).

1. Right-click the *main.xml* file, which is located under the */res/layout* folder. Then open the Eclipse layout editor and add the button via drag-and-drop as you have done in previous examples. Here is the code that shows the changes to the Button and TextView we need to make (see Figure 10–10):

```
<TextView  android:layout_width="fill_parent"
           android:layout_height="wrap_content"
           android:text="Click Button Below to Run a Query" />

<Button    android:text="Click to Query Contacts Database"
           android:id="@+id/queryButton"
           android:layout_width="wrap_content"
           android:layout_height="wrap_content"
           android:layout_gravity="center" />
```

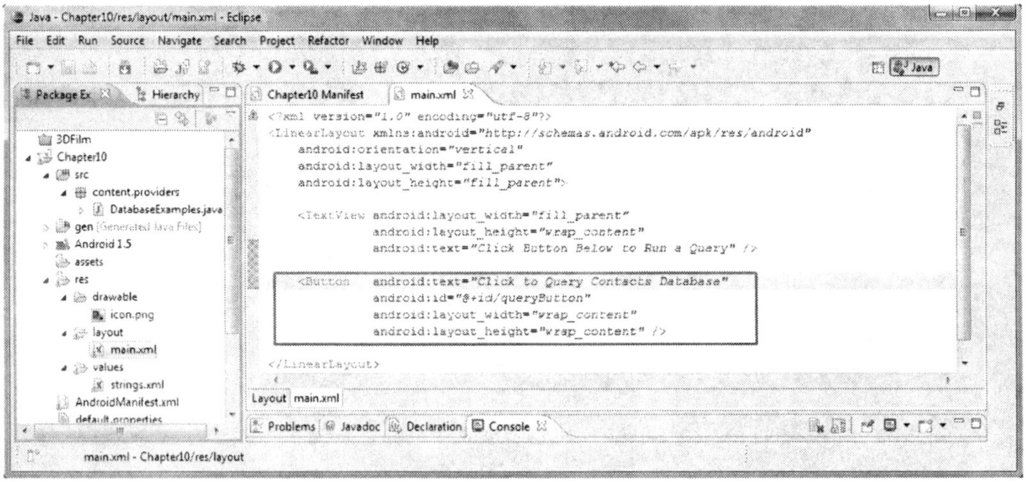

Figure 10–10. *Adding our Button code to main.xml*

2.   Next, right-click the */src/content.providers/DatabaseExamples.java* file and select **Open**.

3.   First, we will add in our Button object declaration and our onClick event handling code, as we did in the previous chapter. Later, we'll write our custom query method, once our UI is in place. To get things going, add the following three import statements that we need to define our Button:

```
import android.widget.Button;
import android.view.View;
import android.view.View.OnClickListener;
```

> **NOTE:** Remember that you use the **import** statement to pull in the classes that you are going to leverage in your code.

4.   Now declare our Button object, like so, with some fairly standard code:

```
Button queryButton = (Button)findViewById(R.id.queryButton);
```

5. Next, use the setOnClickListener() method to add the ability to handle events for this button, using the following lines of code (see Figure 10–11). First, we attach the new OnClickListener to our queryButton, and then inside the onClick event handler, we assign the queryContactPhoneNumber() method (which we will code next), to be run when an onClick event is encountered. Note in Figure 10–11 that queryContactPhoneNumber() is underlined in Eclipse, which tells us that the method we are calling does not (yet) exist.

```
queryButton.setOnClickListener(new OnClickListener() {
        public void onClick(View view) {
                queryContactPhoneNumber();
        }
});
```

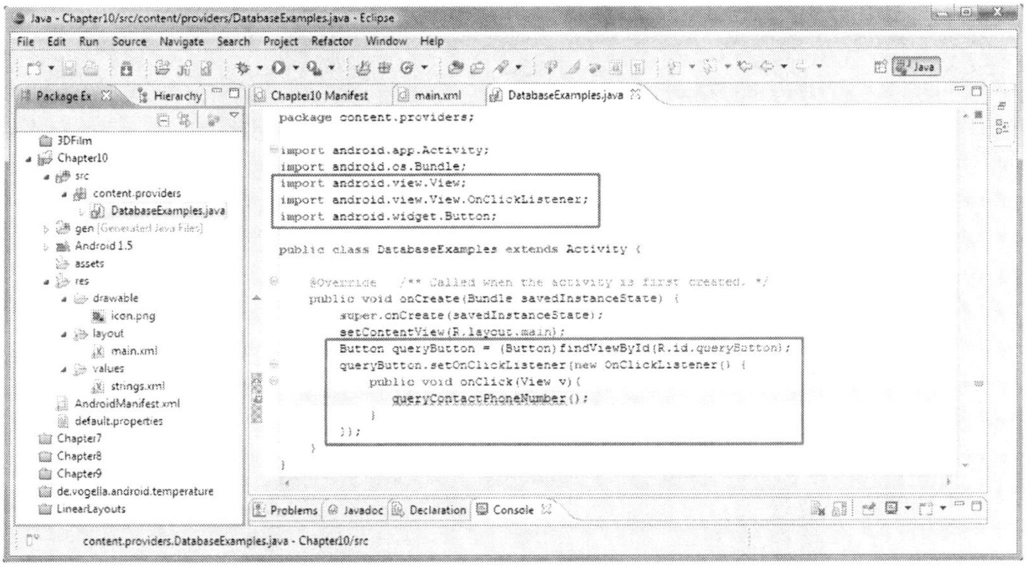

Figure 10–11. *Declaring our import statements and query button in DatabaseExamples.java*

TIP: As you've seen, when a method does not yet exist, Eclipse puts a red *X* in the left margin of the code-editing pane and a red underline under the method name. If you want to remove those error indicators immediately, simply hover your cursor (mouse) over the red underline for a second, and select the Create Method option when the list of possible solutions pops up underneath it. Hovering your mouse this way is a great technique for learning more about Java and Eclipse. Don't be afraid to explore and experiment with the Eclipse IDE as you work through this book.

6. Next, let's add the four new `import` statements that we need (shown in Figure 10–12). The first brings in our familiar `android.widget.Toast` class to easily display our data via the Toast UI widget. The second imports the `android.net.Uri` class that allows us to define the `Uri` object we need to access the database. The third imports the all-important Cursor class `android.database.Cursor` that allows us to traverse the data within all of the Android databases. Finally, `android.provider.Contacts.People` is the table we will be accessing:

```
import android.widget.Toast;
import android.net.Uri;
import android.database.Cursor;
import android.provider.Contacts.People;
```

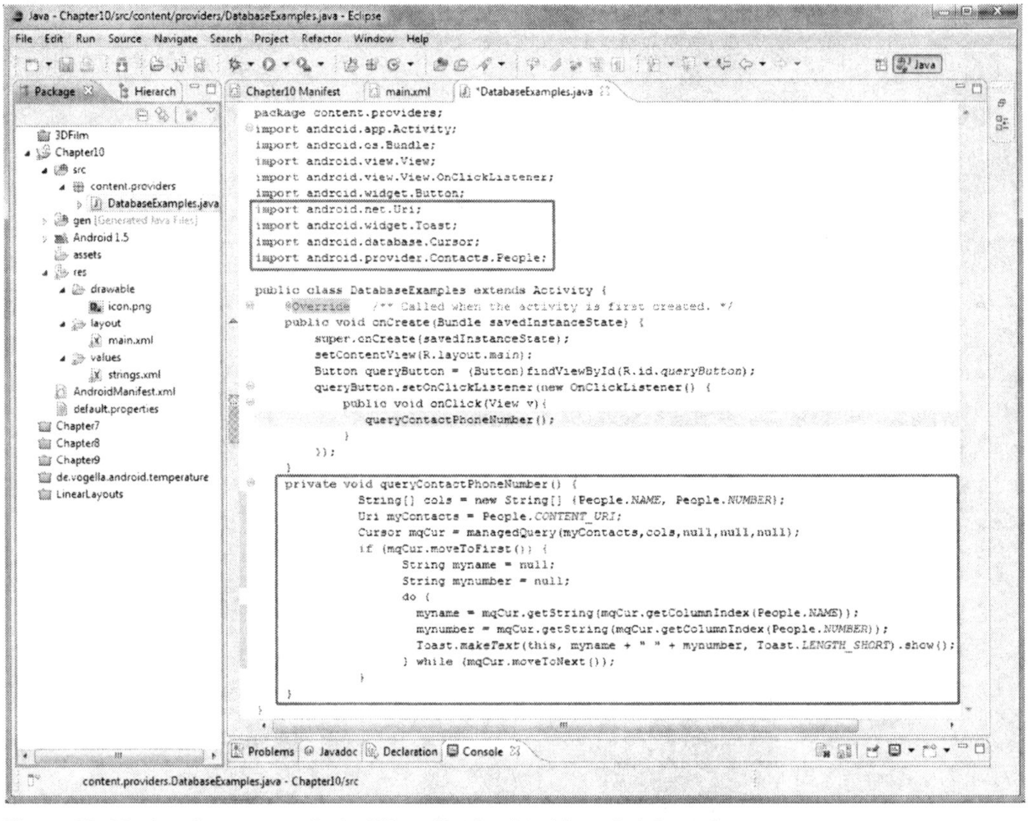

Figure 10–12. *Java for our queryContacttPhoneNumber() and import statements*

7. Now we can write our **queryContactPhoneNumber()** method, to query the database (also shown in Figure 10–12).

```
private void queryContactPhoneNumber() {
    String[] cols = new String[] {People.NAME, People.NUMBER};
    Uri myContacts = People.CONTENT_URI;
    Cursor mqCur = managedQuery(myContacts,cols,null,null,null);
```

```
    if (mqCur.moveToFirst()) {
        String myname = null;
        String mynumber = null;
        do {
            myname = mqCur.getString(mqCur.getColumnIndex(People.NAME));
            mynumber = mqCur.getString(mqCur.getColumnIndex(People.NUMBER));
            Toast.makeText(this, myname + " " + mynumber, Toast.LENGTH_SHORT).show();
        } while (mqCur.moveToNext());
    }
}
```

Let's decipher exactly what is going on in this query method that we have written. Our method is declared `private` (meaning it operates completely inside the class that contains it) and void, as it returns no values. The first line defines a string array variable called `cols` and instantiates it with a new string array loaded with the value of two constants from the `Contact.People` table called `NAME` and `NUMBER`. These are the two data fields from which we wish to access data.

```
    private void queryContactPhoneNumber() {
        String[] cols = new String[] {People.NAME, People.NUMBER};
```

The next line creates a `Uri` object called `myContacts` and sets it equal to the `People.CONTENT_URI` table address that we are going to query.

```
        Uri myContacts = People.CONTENT_URI;
```

We then need to create a `Cursor` object called `mqCur` and assign to it the results of the call to the `managedQuery()` method. This method uses the `myContacts` Uri object, the `cols` column references that we are going to pull data from, and three `null`s (which represent more complex SQLite operations).

```
        Cursor mqCur = managedQuery(myContacts,cols,null,null,null);
```

The `Cursor` object that is now properly populated with our `managedQuery()` results will be used in our iterative code, a do...while loop inside an `if` statement, to traverse the records of our table that `managedQuery()` accesses.

The `if` part of the statement is true when the `mqCur` object has been positioned at the first record of the results via the `moveToFirst()` method. When this happens, the contents of the `if` statement are executed.

```
        if (mqCur.moveToFirst()) {
```

The `myname` and `mynumber` string variables are cleared by setting them to `null` before we enter into the do...while loop. The loop is started on the next line with a do construct containing three logical programming statements. It ends with a `while()` condition that says, "Move `mqCur` cursor object to the next record."

As long as there is a next record that can be moved to, this will equate to true. When it does not (at the end of the last record in the results), it will equate to false and drop out of the loop, which will cease to function, just as we intended. In other words, as long as there is another record to process, we'll do another run of the code in the loop.

```
        do {
            ...
        } while (mqCur.moveToNext());
```

Now let's look at the three things done in the do...while loop while there are records to read.

First, we set the myname variable to the value of the data that is found in the current record of the results (on the first loop entry, this is the first record; on the second loop entry, this is the second; and so on).

```
myname = mqCur.getString(mqCur.getColumnIndex(People.NAME));
```

We do this via two methods of the mqCur Cursor object:

- The getColumnIndex() method gets the internal reference or index number for the People.NAME column for the current record.

- getString() gets the string data from that location in the results and puts it into the myname variable.

We repeat the process in the next line of code for mynumber using People.NUMBER. It is also held in a string format, so you can use dashes or whatever you like between the numbers.

```
mynumber = mqCur.getString(mqCur.getColumnIndex(People.NUMBER));
```

Once our myname and mynumber string variables are loaded with the data values from the database record, we call our familiar Toast widget and display the record on the screen. Notice in this version of the Toast widget we get a little more advanced than just passing a text string in the second argument of the makeText() method. Here, we use our two variables (which contain text strings) and concatenate them (attach them) to a " " space character using the + operator (used for joining strings together):

```
Toast.makeText(this, myname + " " + mynumber, Toast.LENGTH_SHORT).show();
```

Note that this could also be written in two lines of code:

```
Toast.makeText(this, myname + " " + mynumber, Toast.LENGTH_SHORT);
Toast.show();
```

Now right-click your *Chapter10* folder and choose **Run As ➤ Android Project**. Try out the Click to Query Contacts Database button to see it trigger our query method, displaying data we added earlier. Figure 10–13 shows an example.

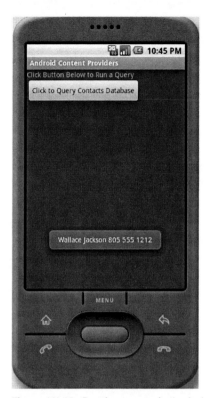

Figure 10–13. *Running a query in the Android 1.5 emulator*

Appending to a Content Provider: Adding New Content

Now you'll see how to add new content to a content provider database. Here, we will add a new contact name and phone number to the Contacts database.

1. First, copy and paste the first Button tag in our *main.xml* file and change the ID to addContactButton. The text of the button should read "Click to add a Contact to the Database" (see Figure 10–14).

```
<Button android:text="Click to add a Contact to the Database"
        android:id="@+id/addContactButton"
        android:layout_width="wrap_content"
        android:layout_height="wrap_content"
        android:layout_gravity="center" />
```

Figure 10–14. *Adding our second button in main.xml*

2. The first stage of the Java code is to add two global objects that all the methods in our class can use. There are two URIs that will contain the locations where we can add data and change data:

```
public class DatabaseExamples extends Activity {
        Uri addUri = null;
        Uri changeUri = null;
```

3. Next, let's add in the code to implement the second button for our UI by copying the Button object declaration and the onClick event handling code and pasting it immediately underneath the existing UI code in our DatabaseExamples activity class.

4. Change the Button variable name to addButton, and change the R.id to point to our new addContactButton. Also, set our method call to the new addContactPhoneNumber() method we are going to write (see Figure 10–15). Here is the new code:

```
Button addButton = (Button)findViewById(R.id.addContactButton);

addButton.setOnClickListener(new OnClickListener() {
    public void onClick(View view) {
        addContactPhoneNumber("Steve Wozniak", "415-555-7654");
    }
});
```

NOTE: This line of code calls our addContactPhoneNumber() method and passes it new database record data so that a new contact entry can be added to the Contacts database.

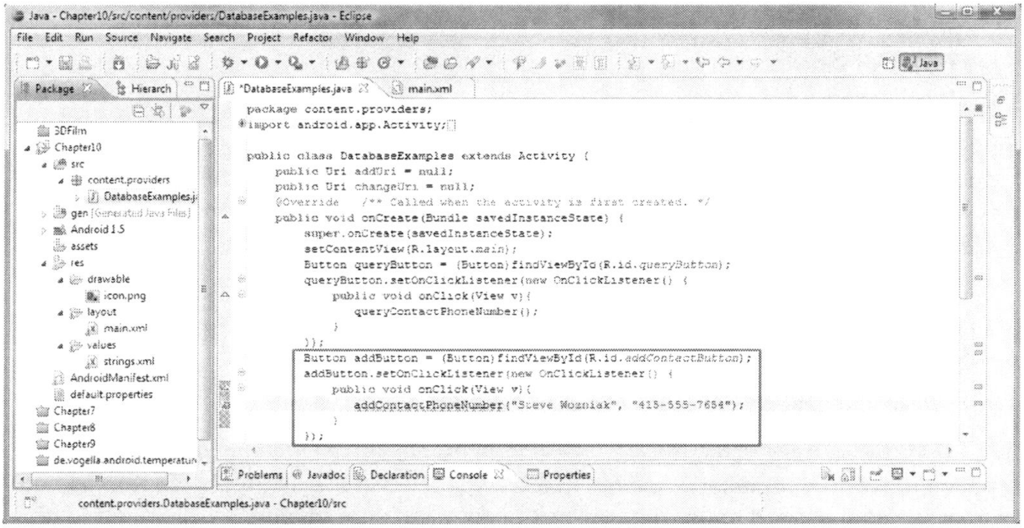

Figure 10–15. *Adding the Java code to add in the second button*

5.   Next, we are going to add the new method addContactPhoneNumber().

```
private void addContactPhoneNumber(String newName, String newPhone) {
    ContentValues myContact = new ContentValues();
    myContact.put(People.NAME, newName);
    addUri = getContentResolver().insert(People.CONTENT_URI, myContact);
    Uri contentUri = Uri.withAppendedPath(addUri, People.Phones.CONTENT_DIRECTORY);
    myContact.clear();
    myContact.put(People.Phones.TYPE, People.TYPE_MOBILE);
    myContact.put(People.NUMBER, newPhone);
    changeUri = getContentResolver().insert(contentUri, myContact);
    Toast.makeText(this, "New Contact: " + newName + " " + newPhone,
                Toast.LENGTH_SHORT);
}
```

We make sure that the addContactPhoneNumber() private method is declared with the correct parameters, as follows:

```
private void addContactPhoneNumber(String newName, String newPhone) {
```

This is a bit different from our queryContactPhoneNumber() method, as we are passing the method two string parameters: a name and a phone number. Since the addContactPhoneNumber() method does not return any values, it is still a void method and is declared as such, just like the others.

Now we are ready to write the code that will add a new name and phone number to the Contacts database. The first thing that we need to do is to create a ContentValues object called myContact that defines the table, column, and data values that need to be passed into the content provider. Since this is a new class that we are using in our code, we also need to add a statement to the end of our list of import statements (see Figure 10–16).

```
import android.content.ContentValues;
```

After we do that, we can instantiate a new `ContentValues` object called `myContact` via the following declaration:

```
ContentValues myContact = new ContentValues();
```

Immediately after that, we need to configure that object with a data pair via the `put()` method. This loads the `ContentValues` object with the table (`People`), the column (or field of data to operate on) `NAME`, and the string variable with the name in it, `newName`.

```
myContact.put(People.NAME, newName);
```

Next, we use the `getContentResolver()` method to insert the `myContact` `ContentValues` object into the `People` table, which is at the location specified by `CONTENT_URI` constant we discussed earlier in the chapter:

```
addUri = getContentResolver().insert(People.CONTENT_URI, myContact);
```

This writes the `newName` variable that we loaded into our `myContact` `ContentValues` object into the `People.NAME` database column that we specified in the same object. So, now our `newName` variable passed to our method has been taken care of, and we just need to do the same thing for our `newNumber` data variable. Then we will be finished. After this call, `addUri` will hold the location of the newly inserted record.

The next line of code declares a `Uri` object named `contentUri` that appends the `People.Phones.CONTENT_DIRECTORY` onto the `addUri` and creates a new, more detailed URI object for the next query. (We are basically setting the location of where to add the phone number by using the location of the new name record as a reference.) Now all we need to do is change the data in the `myContact` `ContentValues` object for the final data-insertion operation.

```
Uri contentUri = Uri.withAppendedPath(addUri, People.Phones.CONTENT_DIRECTORY);
```

The first thing we want to do to the `myContact` object is to clear it, or basically turn it into an empty object with a clean slate. Then, in the next two lines, we use the `put()` method to load the `myContact` `ContentValues` object with the URI and table and column values for the phone number field that we wish to write, and the `newPhone` phone number string variable data (415-555-7654), using the following lines of code:

```
myContact.clear();
myContact.put(People.Phones.TYPE, People.TYPE_MOBILE);
myContact.put(People.NUMBER, newPhone);
```

Finally, we call our powerhouse `getContentResolver()` method to go into our content provider and insert the phone number data into the correct table and data column (data field) location. This is done with the following code:

```
changeUri = getContentResolver().insert(contentUri, myContact);
```

Once our data record is written by the two `getContentResolver()` operations, we can send a Toast to our users in the usual way, telling them that the write has been performed.

```
Toast.makeText(this, "New Contact: " + newName + " " + newPhone, Toast.LENGTH_SHORT);
```

Figure 10–16 shows the code as it appears in Eclipse with the `import` statement, two global `Uri` object variables declared, and our `addContactPhoneNumber()` method highlighted.

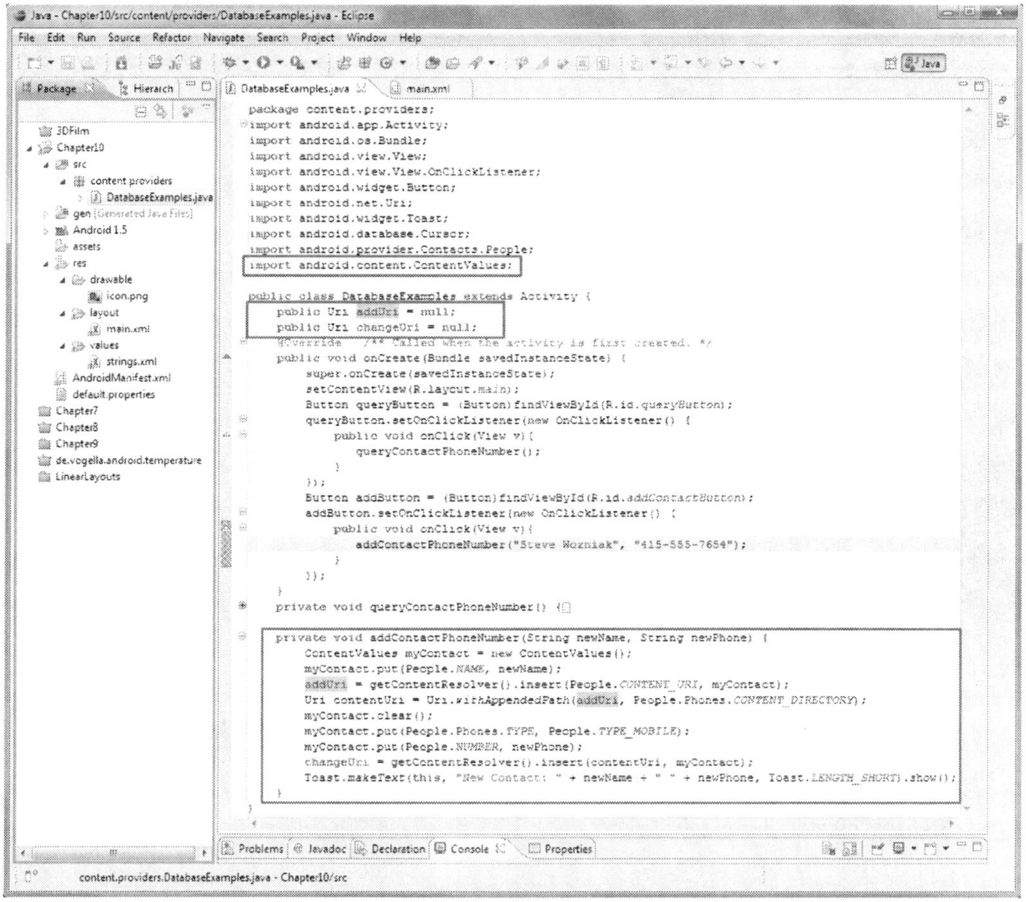

Figure 10–16. *Writing the Java code for our AddContactPhoneNumber method*

We declared the two `addUri` and `changeUri` URI objects at the top of our code outside all of our methods so that they can be used in any of the methods in this class. We will be using them in other methods later in this chapter, so we've made them available for that purpose.

Now right-click your *Chapter10* project folder and select **Run As ➤ Android Application**. As you will see when you click the second button, the name and number in our code is added to the Contacts database and a message confirming this is toasted (isn't that a cool term?) to the screen, as shown in Figure 10–17. Now let's go into our desktop and find the data.

Figure 10–17. *Adding a contact in the Android 1.5 emulator*

To see the new data for Steve Wozniak, select the Contacts icon, hit the Menu button at the bottom of the screen (on the phone), and choose the Search function. Then scroll down the list until you see the Steve Wozniak entry (highlighted on the right in Figure 10–18).

Figure 10–18. *Using the Contacts editor utility in the Android 1.5 emulator*

Now that you've seen how to add data to a contact provider, let's look at how to modify the content provider's data.

Modifying Content Provider Data: Updating the Content

Changing an existing record is another write operation as far as a database is concerned, because new data is written to a database record field, and that data overwrites the existing data that was there.

Let's dive right into our usual work process to see updating content in action.

1. First, in *main.xml*, copy the addContactButton Button tag and paste it right underneath our other Button tags. Change the ID attribute to modifyPhoneButton. This reflects the fact that we are going to modify the phone number to the new phone number, just as we would do in real life (people don't change names quite as often as they change mobile phone numbers).

2. Next, change the text of the button to read "Click to Modify the Contact in the Database". Here's the code in your Eclipse editor's main.xml tab (also shown in Figure 10–19):

```
<Button android:text="Click to Modify the Contact in the Database"
        android:id="@+id/modifyPhoneButton"
        android:layout_width="wrap_content"
        android:layout_height="wrap_content"
        android:layout_gravity="center" />
```

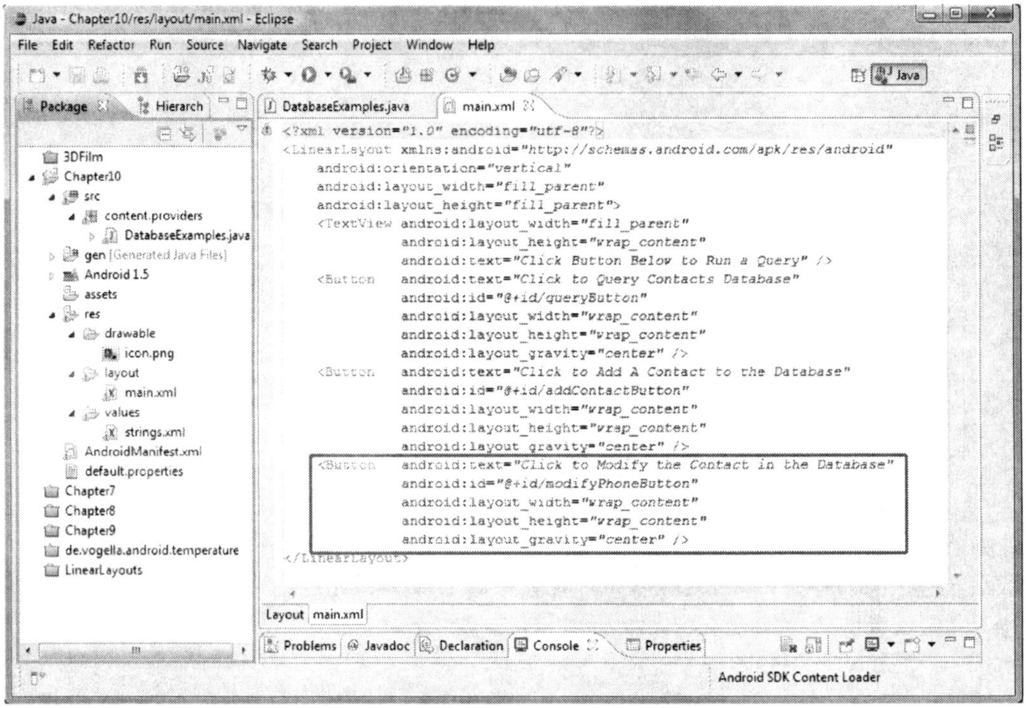

Figure 10–19. *Adding a modify contact button in main.xml*

3. To finish off implementing the UI for this new database operation, let's do a similar cut-and-paste operation in our *DatabaseExamples.java* file. Add the addButton Button object and the addContactPhoneNumber() onClick() method call, and turn them into a modButton Button object and an onClick event handler that calls a modifyPhoneNumber() method (see Figure 10–20):

```
Button modButton = (Button)findViewById(R.id.modifyPhoneButton);
modButton.setOnClickListener(new OnClickListener() {
    public void onClick(View v){
        modifyPhoneNumber("916-555-1234");
    }
});
```

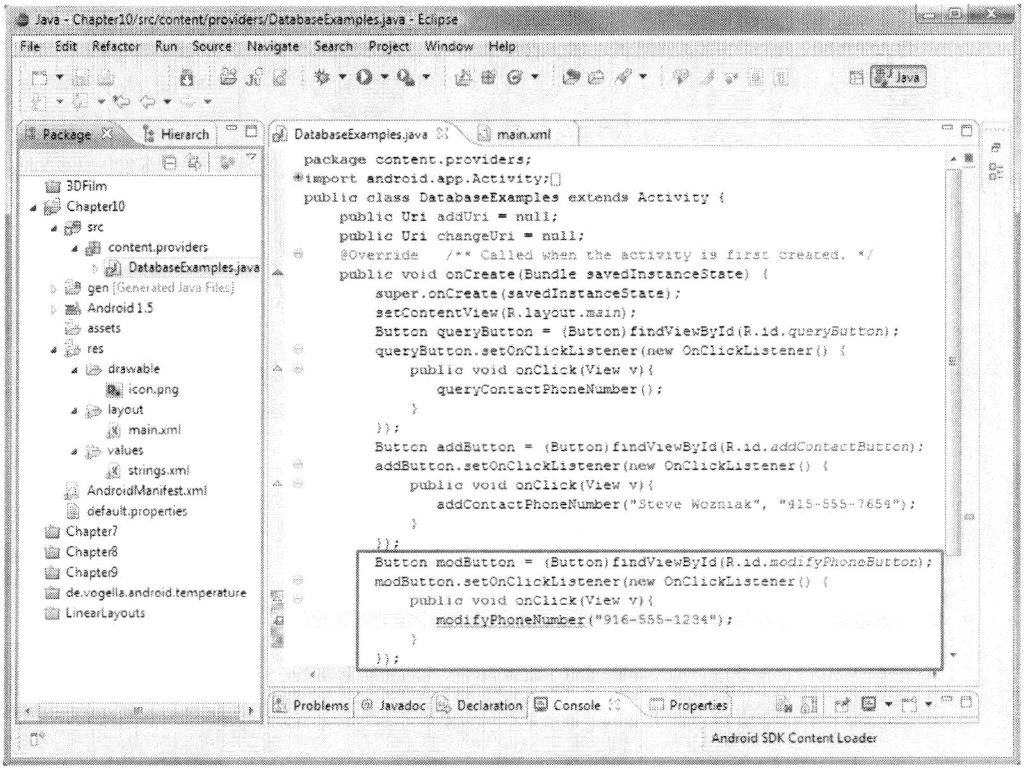

Figure 10–20. *Adding the Java code to implement our modify contact button*

The real heavy lifting is done in our modifyPhoneNumber() method, which will update the phone number in the database record we just added. It takes a single string containing the new telephone number to replace the existing one (see Figure 10–21). Also notice in Figure 10-21 that we have collapsed our previous two methods using the "+" feature in Eclipse that allows us to expand and contract blocks of code for easier viewing of what we are working on currently. This is shown with a small red square at the left of the screenshot.

```java
private void modifyPhoneNumber(String replacePhone) {
    if (changeUri == null) {
        Toast.makeText(this, "You need to create a new contact to update!",
                    Toast.LENGTH_LONG).show();
    } else {
        ContentValues newPhoneNumber = new ContentValues();
        newPhoneNumber.put(People.Phones.TYPE, People.TYPE_MOBILE);
        newPhoneNumber.put(People.NUMBER, replacePhone);
        getContentResolver().update(changeUri, newPhoneNumber, null,null);
        Toast.makeText(this, "Updated phone number to: " + replacePhone,
                    Toast.LENGTH_SHORT).show();
    }
}
```

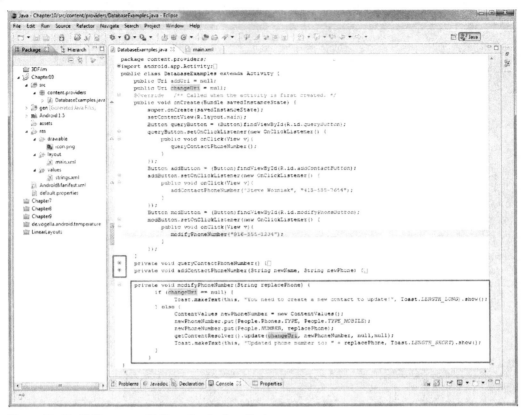

Figure 10–21. *Writing our modifyPhoneNumber() method*

The modifyPhoneNumber() method uses an if...then...else programming loop structure. First, let's make sure there is data in the changeUri data object by comparing the changeUri object to null via the if (changeUri == null) construct.

```
if (changeUri == null) {
    Toast.makeText(this, "You need to create a new contact to update!",
                Toast.LENGTH_LONG).show();
```

If this construct equates to true, we print a Toast message, saying that the add operation has not been done yet, and suggesting that the user use the add method (which we just wrote) to create the record that we want to modify.

If the (changeUri == null) equates to false, it means that the changeUri is loaded with the database and column references needed to access and modify the database record. Then we can continue and execute the database modification via four lines of code and a Toast notification that tells us what was done to the database.

```
        getContentResolver().update(changeUri, newPhoneNumber, null,null);
        Toast.makeText(this, "Updated phone number to: " + replacePhone,
                Toast.LENGTH_SHORT).show();
    }
}
```

The first line of code is the creation of the newPhoneNumber ContentValues object, which will hold our database names and constants that we will use to reference the phone number field in the Contacts database.

```
    } else {
        ContentValues newPhoneNumber = new ContentValues();
```

First, we load the newPhoneNumber ContentValues object with the columns of data we are going to modify. In the second line of code, we state that the People.Phones.TYPE will be People.TYPE_MOBILE (that is, we are updating the mobile number). We then use the People.NUMBER database constant to say we want to update the number with the contents of the replacePhone data variable that we passed into the modifyPhoneNumber() call.

```
        newPhoneNumber.put(People.Phones.TYPE, People.TYPE_MOBILE);
        newPhoneNumber.put(People.NUMBER, replacePhone);
```

In our fourth line of code inside the else section of our loop, we call the getContentResolver().update() method:

```
        getContentResolver().update(changeUri, newPhoneNumber, null,null);
```

We pass it the following objects:

■   changeUri (which we created in the addContactPhoneNumber() method) specifies the location of the last record we worked with, which is the one we want to update.

■   newPhoneNumber is a ContentValues object that specifies which field of that record structure we wish to modify. It also specifies the updated data for that data field (the new mobile number).

Finally, we add in our Toast.makeText() call to display the data we have modified once the getContentResolver().update() is complete.

```
        Toast.makeText(this, "Updated phone number to: " + replacePhone,
                    Toast.LENGTH_SHORT).show();
```

Compile and run the application in the Android 1.5 emulator, and you will see our new Click to Modify the Contact in the Database button, as shown in Figure 10–22.

Figure 10–22. *Modifying a contact in the Android 1.5 emulator*

We can now query the database, add a record to the database, and change the phone number in an existing database record. Let's complete this tour of common database operations by adding an option to delete a record from the content provider database.

Removing Content Provider Data: Deleting Content

Our final example of manipulating the database demonstrates how to delete database records. We'll also make a few final changes in our *main.xml* UI code to make everything look a bit more professional.

1. For the TextView tag, change the text attribute to read "Click Buttons Below to Query, Add, Modify, Delete". Also add 25 dip of padding to the top and 50 dip of padding to the bottom to space out the objects on the application screen and make it more readable. Here's the new code (also shown in Figure 10–23):

```
<TextView
    android:layout_width="fill_parent"
    android:layout_height="wrap_content"
    android:text="Click Buttons Below to Query, Add, Modify, Delete"
    android:paddingTop="25dip"
    android:paddingBottom="50dip"/>
```

2. Use your favorite cut-and-paste work process to copy the modify
Button tag that we just created and paste it underneath the other Button
tags. Change the ID to deleteContactButton and the text to read "Click
to Delete the Contact in the Database". Your code should look like
this (also shown in Figure 10–23):

```
<Button android:text="Click to Delete the Contact in the Database"
        android:id="@+id/deleteContactButton"
        android:layout_width="wrap_content"
        android:layout_height="wrap_content"
        android:layout_gravity="center" />
```

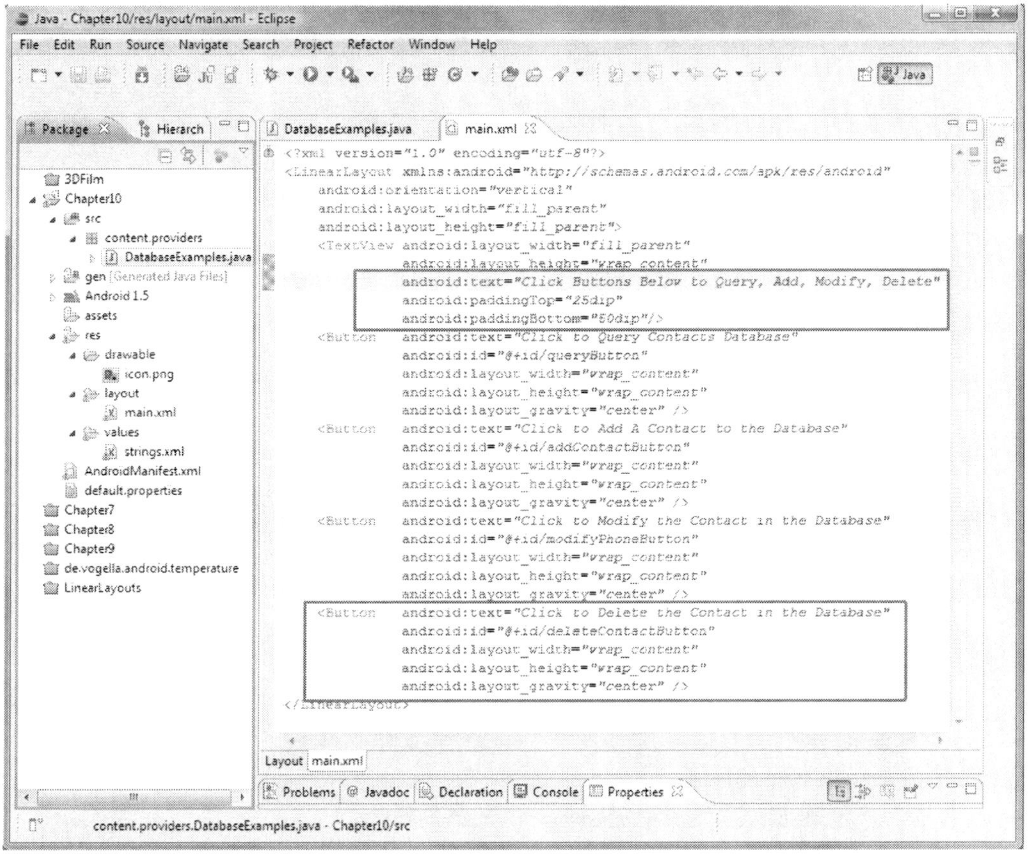

Figure 10–23. *Adding the delete button XML markup to main.xml*

3. Now we will repeat the same copy-and-paste operation in our Java
code. Copy the modButton Button object creation and
setOnClickListener() event handling routine. Change the object name
to delButton and the method call to deleteContactPhoneNumber()
(Figure 10–24 shows what your Java code for your UI definitions should
look like in the Eclipse DatabaseExamples.java tab).

```
Button delButton = (Button)findViewById(R.id.deleteContactButton);
delButton.setOnClickListener(new OnClickListener() {
    public void onClick(View v){
        deleteContactPhoneNumber();
    }
});
```

> **NOTE:** Since we are simply deleting the record, we do not need to pass the method a variable.
> This is because the road map to the database information that we wish to operate on is already
> in our changeUri object, ready to reference.

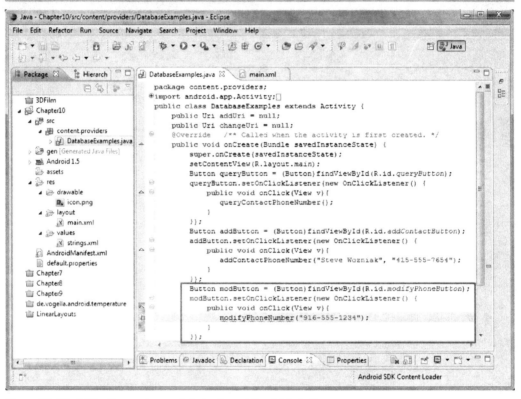

Figure 10–24. *Adding the our Java code to implement the delete button*

4.   Now we will create our new deleteContactPhoneNumber() database
     method. All we need to do is add in the code that makes sure our
     changeUri object is still intact and loaded with reference parameters,
     and then access our ContentResolver object to delete the data record.
     Here's the code (see Figure 10–25):

```
private void deleteContactPhoneNumber() {
    if (changeUri == null) {
        Toast.makeText(this, "You need to create a new contact to delete!",
                    Toast.LENGTH_LONG).show();
```

```
        } else {
            getContentResolver().delete(addUri, null, null);
            Toast.makeText(this, "Deleted contact at: " + addUri.toString(),
                        Toast.LENGTH_SHORT).show();
            addUri = null;
            changeUri = null;
        }
    }
```

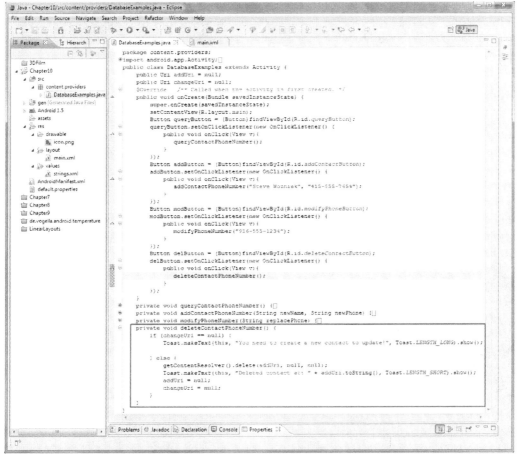

Figure 10–25. *Adding our deleteContactPhoneNumber method to DatabaseExamples.java*

This code uses an if loop that is identical to the one we constructed in the modifyPhoneNumber() method earlier.

```
    if (changeUri == null) {
        Toast.makeText(this, "You need to create a new contact to delete!",
                    Toast.LENGTH_LONG).show();
```

The if statement basically says. "I our changeUri object is not loaded with the data from the add and modify operations, then tell the users that they need to create a new contact first to delete the record; otherwise, perform the following operations."

The meat of our code to delete the database record that we have created is inside the else portion of our if...then...else loop structure. It begins with a call to setContentResolver().delete() to delete the data record whose particulars are referenced in the addUri that we created in the addContactPhoneNumber() routine we coded earlier.

```
    } else {
        getContentResolver().delete(addUri, null, null);
```

In this method, we are referencing the addUri, which references the Contacts database and contact name, rather than the changeUri, which references the phone number and type data fields. This is because we are deleting the top-level database record, and not just the phone number inside it.

Once we have deleted our database record via the ContentResolver, we can Toast to our users a message that it has been deleted. Finally, we set the URIs to null because we have deleted the record.

```
        Toast.makeText(this, "Deleted contact at: " + addUri.toString(),
                    Toast.LENGTH_SHORT).show();
        addUri = null;
        changeUri = null;
    }
```

Now let's select **Run As ➤ Android Application** and see our latest button in action. In the example in Figure 10–26, you can see that our Toast message shows the URI for the Contacts database's People table and record number 13.

Figure 10–26. *Running our final database application in the Android 1.5 emulator*

We now have our finished database-access application. This version is spaced out much better on the screen, and it has all four database operations in place and functioning:

- The Click to Query Contacts Database button shows the entire Contacts database, including the new addition.
- The Click to Add a Contact to the Database button adds a new record.
- The Click to Modify the Contact in the Database button changes the database record to include a new phone number.
- The Click to Delete the Contact in the Database button deletes the new record.

We have successfully written code to manipulate one of Android's internal content provider databases.

Summary

This is probably one of the most complicated chapters in this book, because it combines the following:

- Knowledge of SQLite database design, functionality, and access—in itself a topic that can easily span several books
- The Android concept of content providers
- The Java programming language constructs that are necessary to access and manipulate these database structures

You should feel a great sense of accomplishment from getting through all of this unscathed. You are learning how Android deals with advanced database concepts and structures.

Most of the content providers that you will be working with in Android are already a part of the OS. They provide access to the common functions that users want in their phones, including contacts, music (audio), entertainment (video), and similar. The built-in content providers were listed in this chapter. We also covered the concept of deprecation, because as of Android 2.x, the internal content provider database structures were enhanced, making pre-2.0 OS tables deprecated, although still usable, as you saw in this chapter.

The primary Java classes in Android that handle content providers are (surprise!) the ContentProvider class, the ContentResolver class, and the ContentValues class. Each plays a critical role in defining (ContentProvider), accessing (ContentResolver), and addressing (ContentValues) a SQLite database structure.

Although there are other ways to pull in data to your Android application, such as off your SD card or off a remote server, the SQLite DBMS is the most robust approach and the only one that can be accessed between applications. Furthermore, this is the most useful content provider type to learn, because *all* of Android's user data is stored and accessed via these SQLite databases. Unfortunately, it's also the most difficult way to implement content providers (database access) within the Android OS.

Chapter 11

Understanding Intents and Intent Filters

This chapter will delve into intents, which are messaging objects that carry communications between the major components of your application—your activities, services, and broadcast receivers, which handle Android messaging. We have seen that Android development is highly modularized, and intents provide a way to wire these modules together to form a cohesive yet flexible application with secure, fluid communication among all of its components.

This is a fairly complex and important topic, and we are going to cover intents as they pertain to activities, services, and broadcast providers in detail. In fact, by the time we get to the end of the chapter, we will have an application that has three XML files and four different Java files open in the Eclipse IDE. Lucky we are close to the end of the book, because for a book on Android for absolute beginners, this chapter is going to seem a bit advanced. We'll chalk it up to a rapid learning process and dive right in.

What Is an Intent?

An intent is represented by the `android.content.Intent` class. It is in the `content` package because intents can be used to quickly access content providers, as we will see in this chapter. But its use is much broader than that; in fact, the Android Developer Reference says, "An intent is an abstract description of an operation to be performed," so intents can be used to quickly accomplish many tasks that would otherwise take more programming code. An intent is a sort of a programming shortcut that's built into the Android OS and programming environment.

An Intent object is basically a passive data object (a bundle of instructions, if you will) that both provides a description of some sort of standard operating system or developer created "action" that needs to be performed and passes the data which that action needs to operate on to the code receiving the intent.

In addition to a specified action, the Intent object can also contain relevant data needed to complete that action, as well as data type specifications, constants, flags, and even extra data related to the data needed by the action.

Because intents provide a detailed data and process communication structure among Android application components, they can also be rather complex data structures (objects). We'll see the various parts of an intent's structure in the next section.

There are three types of Intent objects that can be used inside the Android OS to communicate with activities, services, and broadcast receivers. In fact, there is one intent type for each of these. None of these types of Intent objects are allowed to intersect with (i.e., interfere with, or collide with, or mistakenly be used with or by) any of the other types of Intent objects. For this reason, we will cover each type of Intent object separately, so we can see how intent-based communication with activities, services, and broadcast messages differ from each other.

Android Intent Messaging via Intent Objects

Essentially, intents carry messages from one module of your application to another (activity to activity, activity to service, broadcast to activity, etc.). Intents can be sent to and from background processing services or intra-application activities or even inter-application broadcast messages. Intents are similar to the events that are found in other programming languages, except that intents can reach outside your application whereas events can't. Events are used to process user interface elements, as we have seen in previous chapters, and are internal to the blocks of programming logic you write. Intents can be passed to other applications written by other programmers, allowing them to be connected as modules of each other, if needed.

Intent object-based messages can contain up to seven different kinds of informational parts:

- **Component name**. The name of the class that the intent and its action are targeting, specified by using the package name and the class name.

- **Action**. A predefined type of action that is to be performed, such as ACTION_DIAL to initiate a phone dialing sequence or ACTION_VIEW to view records in a database.

- **Data**. The actual data to be acted upon, such as the address of the database records to view or the phone number to dial.

- **Category**. Android has predefined intents that are part of the OS that are divided into various types or categories for easy access and use. The category name tells what area of the OS the action that follows it is going to affect. For instance, CATEGORY_HOME deals with the Android Home screen. An ACTION_MAIN following a CATEGORY_HOME would cause the Home screen to be launched in the smatphone.

- **Type**. This attribute specifies the type of the data using a MIME format. It's often left out as Android is usually able to infer the data type from analyzing the data itself.

- **Flags**. This allows on/off flags to be sent with the intent. Flags are not used for typical intents, but allow more complicated intents to be crafted if needed by advanced developers.

- **Extras**. This parameter allows any extra information that is not covered in the above fields to be included in the intent. This allows very complex intents to be created.

With these seven different types of information, the messaging construct that an Intent object communicates can become quite an intricate data structure, if you need it to be, it can also be quite simple, depending on the application use that is involved.

The first thing an Intent object usually specifies is the name of the application component you are targeting (usually a class you create); this is specified via the package and class name, like so:

```
ComponentName(string package, string class)
```

The component name is optional. If it is not specified, the Android OS will utilize all of the other information contained within the Intent object to infer what component of the application or Android OS the Intent object should be passed to for further processing. It is safer to always specify this information. On the other hand, intents are intended to be used as programming shortcuts, and for many standard or common instances, Android is designed to properly infer how to process them.

The most important part of the Intent object is the action specification. The action defines the type of operation that the intent is requesting to be performed. Some of the common action constants are listed in Table 11–1, along with their primary functions, so you can get an idea of where these intents might be utilized in the Android OS.

Table 11–1. *Examples of Action Constants and Their Primary Functions*

Action Constant	Target Activity	Function
ACTION_DIAL	Activity	Displays the phone dialer
ACTION_CALL	Activity	Initiates a phone call
ACTION_EDIT	Activity	Display data for user to edit
ACTION_MAIN	Activity	Start up an initial task activity
ACTION_BATTERY_LOW	Broadcast Receiver	Battery low warning message
ACTION_HEADSET_PLUG	Broadcast Receiver	Headset plug/remove message
ACTION_SCREEN_ON	Broadcast Receiver	The screen turned on message
ACTION_TIMEZONE_CHANGED	Broadcast Receiver	Time zone has changed

It is important to note that in many cases the action constant that is specified determines the type and structure of the data of the Intent object. The data parameter is as important to the overall result of the intent resolution as the specified action to be performed. Without providing the data for the action to operate on, the action is as useless as the data would be without any action to be performed on it!

The ACTION_DIAL action constant is a good example; it targets an activity and displays the smartphone dialing utility with the phone number (the data passed to it) to be dialed. The data is the phone number the user entered into the user interface, and since the action constant is ACTION_DIAL, Android can infer that the data passed to it is the phone number to be dialed.

Thus, the next most important part of the Intent object is the data component, which contains the data that is to be operated on. This is usually done via a URI object that contains information about where the data can be found.

As we learned in the previous chapter, this often turns out to be a database content provider; for instance, a SQLite database can be the target of an ACTION_VIEW or ACTION_EDIT intent action. So, to edit database record information about a person in your contacts list with the database ID of 1, we would use the following intent data structure:

ACTION_EDIT content://contacts/people/1

A closely related part of the Intent object specification is the data's MIME type, which explicitly tells Android what type of data the intent should be working with so that, for example, audio data doesn't encounter an image processing routine.

The type part of the Intent object allows you to specify an explicit MIME data definition or data type that, if present, overrides any inference of the data type by the Android OS. You may already be familiar with the MIME data type declarations, as they are quite common on web servers and other types of data servers.

MIME TYPES

MIME stands for "Multipurpose Internet Mail Extensions" and was originally designed for e-mail servers to define their support for different types of data. It has since been extended to other server definitions of supported data and content types, and to communication protocols (such as HTTP) data type definitions, and now to Android OS to define content data types as well. Suffice it to say that MIME has become a standard for defining content data types in a myriad of computing environments. Examples of MIME definition include the following:

- Content-Type: text/plain
- Content-Type: image/jpeg
- Content-Type: audio/mp3
- Content-Type: video/mp4
- Content-Type: application/msword

Another important parameter of an Intent object is the category, which is meant to give additional or more fine-tuned information about the action that is specified to execute. This is more useful with some actions than with others.

A good example of how categories help define what to do with a given action is launching the home screen on a user's Android phone via an Intent object. You use the Action constant ACTION_MAIN with a category constant CATEGORY_HOME and voila! Android launches the phone's Home screen and shows it on the display.

Finally, the extras parameter allows additional data fields to be passed with the Intent object to the activity, service or broadcast receiver. This parameter uses a Bundle object to pass a collection of data objects.

This is a slick way to allow you to piggyback any additional data or more complex data structure you wish to pass along with the Action request/message.

Intent Resolution: Implicit Intents & Explicit Intents

Intents, like events, need to be resolved so that they can be processed properly. Resolution in this case means ascertaining the appropriate component to handle the intent and its data structure.

There are two broad categories of intents—explicit intents and implicit intents. We will look at explicit intent resolution first, as it is much more straightforward. Then, we'll cover implicit Intents and see how they need to be filtered so that Android knows how to handle them properly.

Explicit Intents

Explicit intents use the component portion of the Intent object via the ComponentName data field. You'll generally use these when working with applications you have developed, as you'll know which packages and classes are appropriate for the Intent object to send an action message and data to be acted on. Because the component is specified explicitly, this type of intent is also safer as there is zero room for error in interpretation. Best programming practices dictate that you thoroughly document your code and thereby give other programmers using your intent code the proper component name information. However in the real world, this best case does not always happen and thus Android also has implicit intents and intent filters to handle other scenarios.

Other developers may not know what components to explicitly declare when working with your application, and thus explicit intents are a better fit for non-public inter-application communication. In fact, developing your application so that other developers can use the intents is what implicit intents and intent filters are all about. As noted earlier, if there is a component name specified, it will override all of the other parts of the Intent object as far as determining what code will handle the intent resolution.

There are two ways to specify a component. One way is via the `setComponent()` method, which uses the `ComponentName` object:

`.setComponent(ComponentName);`

The other way is using the `setClass(Context, Class)` method to provide the exact class to use to process the intent. Sometimes this is the only information in the intent, especially if the desired result from using the intent is simply to launch parallel activities that are internal to the application when they are needed by the user.

Implicit Intents

Implicit intents are those that don't specify the component within the intent object. This means that Android has to infer from the other parameters in the intent object what code it needs to pass the intent message to for successful processing.

Android does this inference based on a comparison of the various actions, data, and categories defined in the intent object with the code components that are available to process the intent. This is usually done via intent filters that are defined in the `AndroidManifest.xml` file.

Although designing classes that utilize implicit intents and intent filters is beyond the scope of an introductory book on Android programming, we will go over the concept here just to give you an idea of what can be done in Android and in what situations you would use implicit intents and intent filters. You can find more information at

`developer.android.com/reference/android/content/IntentFilter.html`.

Intent filters are declared in `AndroidManifest.xml` using the `<intent-filter>` tag, and they filter based on three of the seven attributes of the Intent object; action, data, and category.

Intent filters provide a description of intent object structures that need to be matched as well as a `priority` attribute to be used if more than one match is encountered. If no action filters are specified, the action parameter of the intent will not be tested at all, moving the testing on to the data parameter of the intent. If no data filters are specified, then only intents that contain no data will be matched. Here is an example `intent-filter` definition from an `AndroidManifest.xml` file that specifies that video MPEG4 and audio MPEG3 can be retrieved from the internet via HTTP:

```
<intent-filter>
<data android:mimeType="video/mp4" android:scheme="http" />
<data android:mimeType="audio/mp3" android:scheme="http" />
</intent-filter>
```

For Intent filtering based on data characteristics, the data parameter gets broken down into four subcategories:

- **Data type;** This is the MIME data type, for instance, `image/jpeg` or `audio/mp3`,

- **Data scheme:** This is written as `scheme://host:port/path`

- **Data authority:** This is the server host and the server port (see the data scheme format above) specified together.

- **Data path:** A data path is an address to the location of the data, for instance, `http://www.apress.com/datafolder/file1.jpg`.

Any of these you specify will be matched precisely to the content of the intent itself, for example:

```
content://com.apress.project:300/datafolder/files/file1
```

In this example, the scheme is `content`, the host is `com.apress.project`, the port is `300`, and the path is `datafolder/files/file1`.

Since we can specify intents explicitly, we can use intent objects productively via the methodologies outlined in the rest of this chapter without having to learn the convoluted hierarchy of how to match unspecified intents. If you wish to delve into the complexities of how to set up levels of intent filters for implicit intent matching, visit the Android developer site and get ready to wrap your mind around some intense global logic structures.

Using Intents with Activities

Enough theory, let's write an Android application that uses intents to switch back and forth between two different activities— an analog watch activity and a digital clock activity—so you can see how intents are sent back and forth between more than one `Activity` class.

1. First, let's close our `Chapter10` project folder (via a right-click and Close Project) and create a new `Chapter11` Android project with the following parameters, as shown in Figure 11–1:

    - Project name: Chapter11
    - Application name: Intents and Intent Filter Examples
    - Package name: intent.filters
    - Create activity: IntentExamples
    - Build Target: Android 1.5
    - Min SDK Version: 3

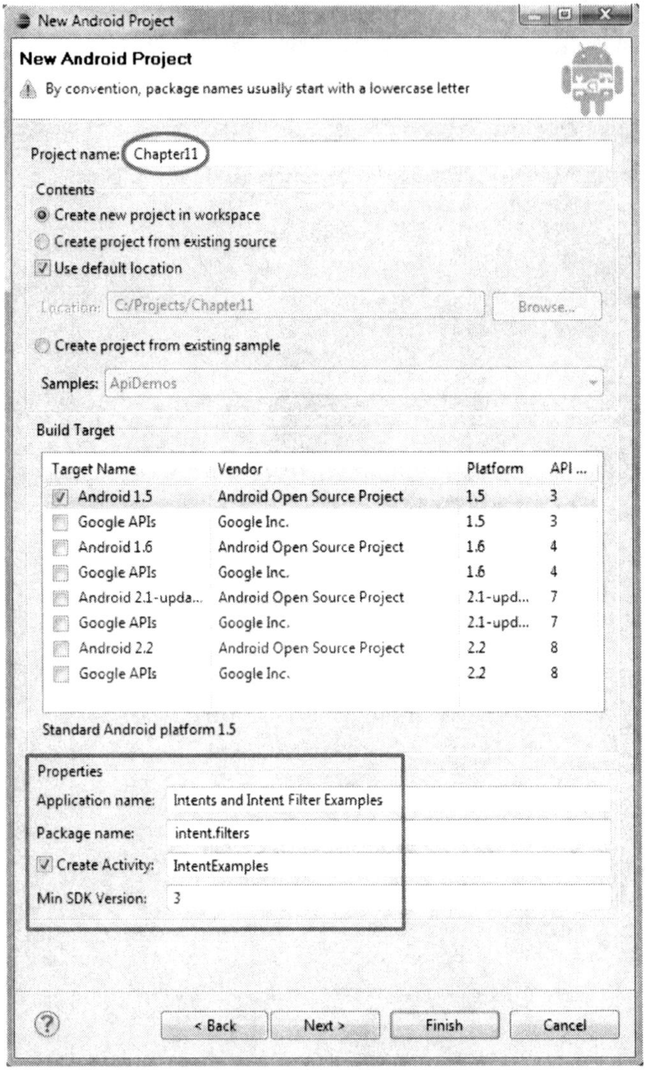

Figure 11–1. *Creating our IntentExamples project in Eclipse*

2. Now we are going to create a second `Activity` class, so we can switch
   back and forth between the two activities using an intent. To do this, we
   need to right-click on the Chapter11 folder, and select **New ➤ Class**,
   which opens a dialog (Figure 11–2) that will create a new Java activity
   class in the same folder as the `IntentExamples.java` class our New
   Android Project dialog just created.

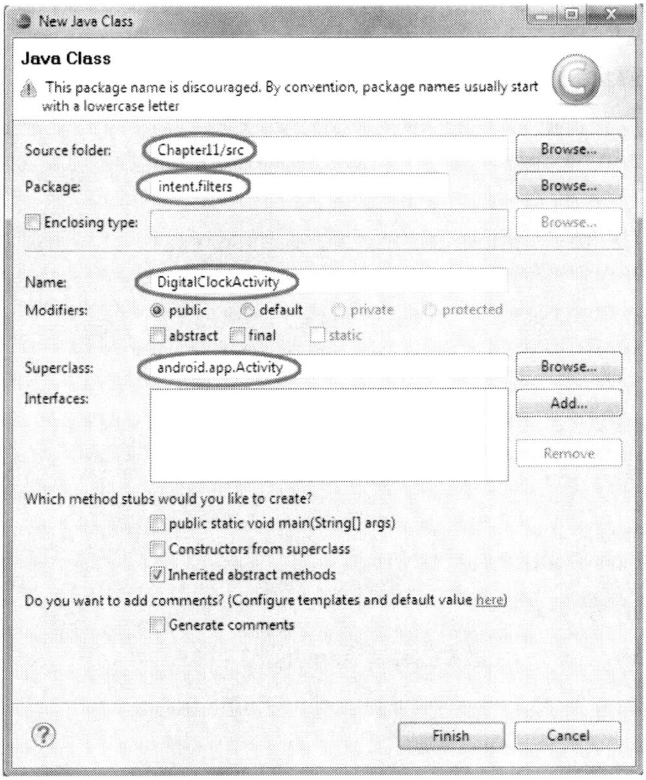

Figure 11–2. *Creating a new Java activity class*

3. If you right-clicked on the Chapter11 folder to do the **New ➤ Class** operation, the dialog will already have the first field filled out, with the **Source folder** field set to Chapter11/src. In the next field, you can either type in the intent.filters package name we created in our **New Android Project** dialog, or you can click the **Browse** button to the right of the field, and select this package from the list.

4. Next we need to fill out the **Name** field, which will name our class. Let's use DigitalClockActivity since that's one of the activities we'll use in this exercise.

5. Leave the **Modifiers** as set. Since we are creating an Activity class, we need to extend the superclass android.app.Activity. This is the full pathname to the Activity class, which is part of the app package in Android OS.

Now let's create our user interface for our first activity, which we will leave in its default main.xml file container (shown in Figure 11–3).

1. Let's expand our `TextView` tag with some new attributes:

    a. Start with text that reads "You Are Currently in: Activity #1"

    b. Use the `android:textColor` attribute to set the color to **#FEA**, which is the equivalent to hexadecimal #FFEEAA, a light orange-gold color.

    c. Let's use the `android:textSize` attribute to increase the text size to 22 device-independent pixels, so it's large and readable.

    d. Finally, let's use the `android:paddingBottom="20dip"` attribute to push the button user interface object down and away from the text title a little bit.

```
<TextView   android:layout_width="fill_parent"
            android:layout_height="wrap_content"
            android:text="You Are Currently in: Activity #1"
            android:textColor="#fea"
            android:textSize="22dip"
            android:paddingBottom="20dip"/>
```

2. Next, let's edit the `Button` tag attributes:

    a. Change its `text` label to "Go To Digital Clock: Activity #2"

    b. Set the `textSize` attribute to 18 pixels so we have readable text on our button.

    c. Now let's define our button size in pixels: `android:layout_width="280px"` and `android:layout_height="60px"` .

    d. Finally, we'll center our UI button with the familiar `android:layout_gravity="center"` and we are done creating the button UI attributes.

```
<Button android:id="@+id/Button01"
        android:text="Go To Digital Clock: Activity #2"
        android:textSize="18px"
        android:layout_width="280px"
        android:layout_height="60px"
        android:layout_gravity="center"/>
```

3. Now we'll add an `AnalogClock` tag, so we can create a cool watch. Use the **Layout** tab at the bottom of the Eclipse editor (circled in Figure 11–3) and drag the AnalogClock View element icon out of the Views List on the left, and drop it under the `Button` in the UI layout view.

4. Then, either go into the **Properties** tab at the bottom of Eclipse, find the **Misc** section, and add in **Layout gravity** and **Layout margin top** values of **center** and **30dip**, respectively, or click the **main.xml** tab at the bottom of the editor, and add in the tags yourself by hand.

> **NOTE:** If Eclipse is not showing the **Properties** tab at the bottom, simply go into the **Window** menu and select **Show View ➤ Other...** and select **Properties** and then **OK**.

5. Next, copy the `image1.png` file from our earlier `Chapter7/res/drawable` folder to your `Chapter11/res/drawable` folder, then right-click on the `Chapter11` folder and use the **Refresh** option so that Android can see this image file inside our project.

6. Go into the **Properties** tab again and find the file using the **Background** option, then click on the search ellipses ... to open a dialog where you can select `image1.png` in the drawable folder to use as a background. Here's the final `AnalogClock` tag:

```
<AnalogClock    android:id="@+id/AnalogClock01"
                android:layout_width="wrap_content"
                android:layout_height="wrap_content"
                android:layout_gravity="center"
                android:layout_marginTop="30dip"
                android:background="@drawable/image1" />
```

And here is the final code, which is also shown in Figure 11–3 for context:

```
<?xml version="1.0" encoding="utf-8"?>
<LinearLayout xmlns:android="http://schemas.android.com/apk/res/android"
    android:orientation="vertical"
    android:layout_width="fill_parent"
    android:layout_height="fill_parent">
    <TextView    android:layout_width="fill_parent"
                 android:layout_height="wrap_content"
                 android:text="You Are Currently in: Activity #1"
                 android:textColor="#fea"
                 android:textSize="22dip"
                 android:paddingBottom="20dip"/>
    <Button android:id="@+id/Button01"
            android:text="Go To Digital Clock: Activity #2"
            android:textSize="18px"
            android:layout_width="280px"
            android:layout_height="60px"
            android:layout_gravity="center"/>
    <AnalogClock    android:id="@+id/AnalogClock01"
                    android:layout_width="wrap_content"
                    android:layout_height="wrap_content"
                    android:layout_gravity="center"
                    android:layout_marginTop="30dip"
                    android:background="@drawable/image1" />
</LinearLayout>
```

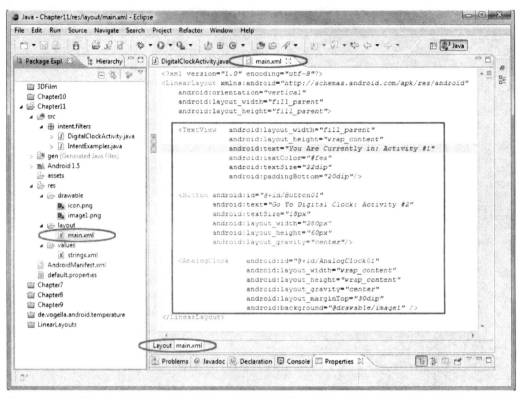

Figure 11–3. *Adding user interface elements to our main.xml file*

Writing the Digital Clock Activity

Now let's copy the user interface we just developed in our main.xml to use for our second activity, which we've already created a DigitalClockActivity.java class for.

1. The easiest way to do this is to right-click on the main.xml file under the /res/layout folder and select **Copy** from the pop-up context menu, then right-click on the /res/layout folder in the Package Explorer pane (right above the file name) and select **Paste,** which will paste a copy of main.xml right alongside main.xml in the same folder. When you do this you will get a **Name Conflict** dialog like the one in Figure 4.

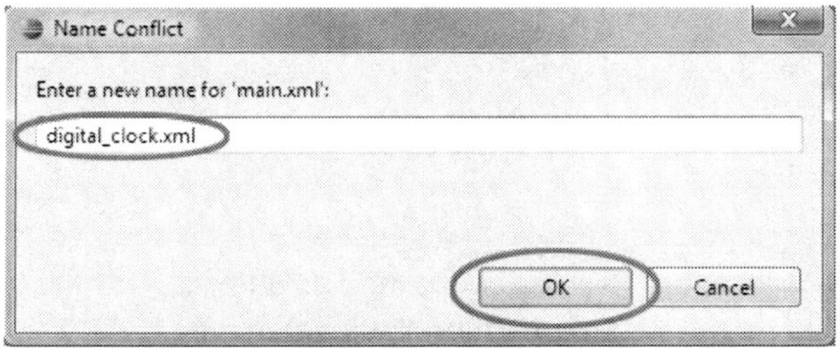

Figure 11–4. *Specifying digital_clock.xml as the new name for main.xml*

2. Eclipse sees the duplicate file names and automatically provides a simple dialog box that allows you to change the name. Change it to digital_clock.xml and click **OK**.

3. We are ready to right-click on digital_clock.xml and select **Open**, or hit the F3 key to open the copied file in its own editor pane, so we can change some of the key tag attributes and quickly craft a user interface for our second (digital clock) activity. Do this now.

4. Edit the AnalogClock tag as follows:

    a. Change it to a DigitalClock tag.

    b. Remove the background image reference to image1.png.

    c. Change the id to DigitalClock01 .

    d. Add a textSize attribute of 32dip.

    e. Add a textColor attribute of #ADF to add some nice blue sky coloring.

    f. Finally, add an android:typeface="monospace" attribute for readability, and we're ready to change our TextView and Button UI objects.

```
<DigitalClock    android:id="@+id/DigitalClock01"
                 android:layout_width="wrap_content"
                 android:layout_height="wrap_content"
                 android:layout_gravity="center"
                 android:layout_marginTop="30dip"
                 android:textSize="32dip"
                 android:textColor="#adf"
                 android:typeface="monospace"/>
```

5. Change the button text to "Go to Analog Watch: Activity #1" and leave the ID at Button01. Why? Because these two different XML files are going to be called by two different Activity classes, and thus the ID does not conflict. If one Activity class referenced both these XML files, we might have a naming conflict.

```xml
<Button android:id="@+id/Button01"
        android:text="Go to Analog Watch: Activity #1"
        android:textSize="18px"
        android:layout_width="280px"
        android:layout_height="60px"
        android:layout_gravity="center"/>
```

6. Finally, we change the TextView object text to read "You are Currently in: Activity #2" and change the android:textColor to the #ADF value we are using with the digital clock tag.

```xml
<TextView    android:layout_width="fill_parent"
             android:layout_height="wrap_content"
             android:text="You Are Currently in: Activity #2"
             android:textColor="#adf"
             android:textSize="22dip"
             android:paddingBottom="30dip"/>
```

When you're done, the whole UI layout should look like this (also shown in Figure 11–5):

```xml
<?xml version="1.0" encoding="utf-8"?>
<LinearLayout xmlns:android="http://schemas.android.com/apk/res/android"
    android:orientation="vertical"
    android:layout_width="fill_parent"
    android:layout_height="fill_parent">

    <TextView    android:layout_width="fill_parent"
                 android:layout_height="wrap_content"
                 android:text="You Are Currently in: Activity #2"
                 android:textColor="#adf"
                 android:textSize="22dip"
                 android:paddingBottom="30dip"/>

    <Button android:id="@+id/Button01"
            android:text="Go to Analog Watch: Activity #1"
            android:textSize="18px"
            android:layout_width="280px"
            android:layout_height="60px"
            android:layout_gravity="center"/>

     <DigitalClock    android:id="@+id/DigitalClock01"
                      android:layout_width="wrap_content"
                      android:layout_height="wrap_content"
                      android:layout_gravity="center"
                      android:layout_marginTop="30dip"
                      android:textSize="32dip"
                      android:textColor="#adf"
                      android:typeface="monospace"/>
</LinearLayout>
```

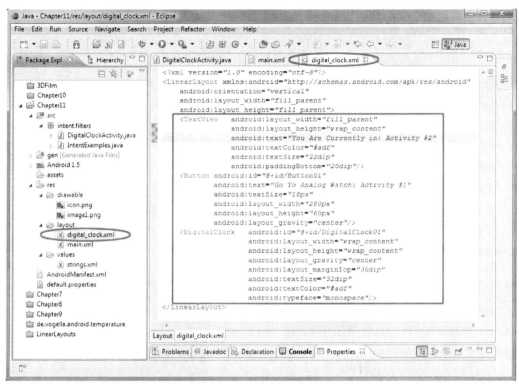

Figure 11–5. *XML mark-up for the digital_clock.xml user interface activity*

Wiring up the Application

While we're working with XML files, let's add an `activity` tag in our
`AndroidManifest.xml` file so our second activity can be recognized by Android, before
finishing off the configuration.

Right-click on the `AndroidManifest.xml` file name under your Chapter11 folder (at the
bottom of the list), and select **Open** or hit F3. Add a second `activity` tag after the first
tag (which our New Android Project dialog has already created) that points to the new
`DigitalClockActivity.java` class we created earlier (see Figure 11–6). Here is the code:

```
<activity android:name=".DigitalClockActivity"></activity>
```

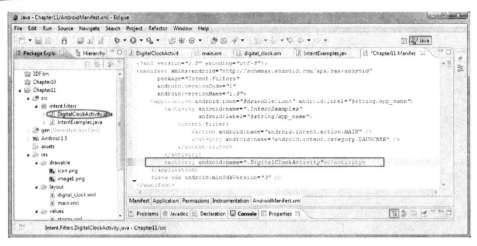

Figure 11–6. *Adding the DigitalClockActivity tag to our AndroidManifest.xml file*

Now let's make sure both Activities have user interfaces. Thanks to our handy **New Android Project** dialog, our IntentExamples class is ready and pointing to the main.xml file so that the Activity #1 side of the equation is already taken care of. So all we have to worry about is the DigitalClockActivity class.

Copy the import android.os.Bundle statement and the onCreate() method over to the DigitalClockActivity.java class and change the R.layout specification to point to the digital_clock XML user interface specification. Now we've implemented our user interface logic for each of our two Activity classes as follows (and as shown in Figure 11–7):

```
public void onCreate(Bundle savedInstanceState) {
    super.onCreate(savedInstanceState);
    setContentView(R.layout.digital_clock);
}
```

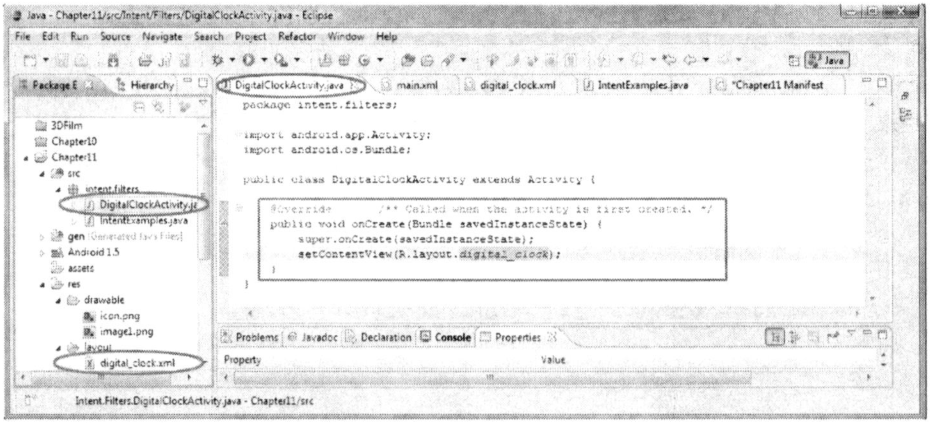

Figure 11–7. *Adding the digital clock user interface layout*

Sending Intents

Now we need to add in our Button object and Intent object code to the onClick() event handler in each activity so each can send an intent to the other activity, allowing us to switch between the two activities using the button.

So let's get started with the main IntentExamples activity class first, and add in our familiar Button object instantiation and an onClick() event handler that will contain the code that creates our Intent object. Remember to also add in (or have Eclipse add in for you using the hover-over-redline method we learned earlier) the import statements for the android.view.View and android.widget.Button packages, as well as a new import we haven't used before called android.contact.Intent, which defines our Intent object class.

Since we've already covered adding a button and attaching it to an onClick() event handler routine, we'll get right into the two lines of code that create our Intent object and send it over to the second activity. Here is the code, which you'll also see in Figure 11–8. The screenshot shows what your Eclipse editor pane for IntentExamples.java will look like when we are finished.

```java
Button Activity1 = (Button) findViewById(R.id.Button01);
Activity1.setOnClickListener(new View.OnClickListener() {
    public void onClick(View view) {
        Intent myIntent =
          new Intent(view.getContext(), DigitalClockActivity.class);
        startActivityForResult(myIntent, 0);
    }
});
```

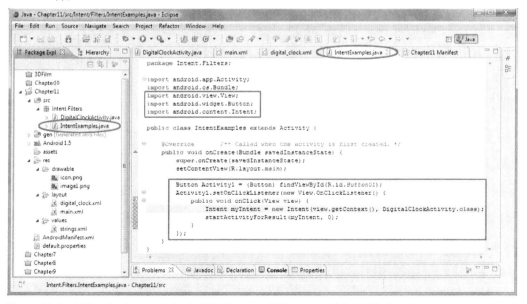

Figure 11–8. *Adding the Java code for the UI button, event listener, and Intent object*

To create an Intent object, we use the now familiar structure where we declare the object type (Intent) and our name for it (myIntent). We set it equal to a new Intent object using the new keyword, along with a call to the Intent class's constructor. The constructor takes the context this intent is created in (in this case, a button obtained from the View via a view.getContext() method call) and the activity class (DigitalClockActivity.class) into which we want to pass our Intent object.

We then use the startActivityForResult() method (part of the android.content.Intent class we imported) to pass the intent object we just created, myIntent, and a parameter of zero; this is what we are sending to the other activity to be acted on. This would typically consist of data that your application wants to pass from one activity class to another via the Intent object for further processing. In this case, we are simply calling (switching to) the other user interface activity.

Now let's look at the code in our DigitalClockActivity class and see how the second activity talks back to the first activity. We will skip over the Button instantiation and onClick() event handling explanations, and get right into the intent declaration and the Java code that returns a result to the calling activity class via yet another Intent object. Here's the code (also shown in Figure 11–9).

```java
Button activity2 = (Button) findViewById(R.id.Button01);
activity2.setOnClickListener(new View.OnClickListener() {
    public void onClick(View view) {
        Intent replyIntent = new Intent();
        setResult(RESULT_OK, replyIntent);
        finish();
    }
});
```

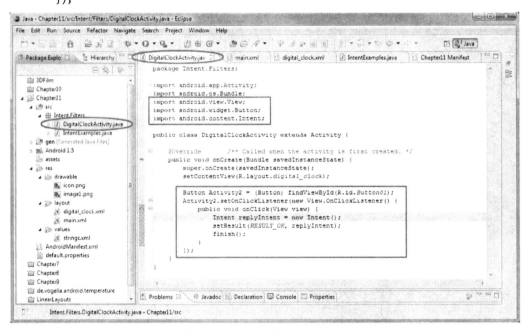

Figure 11–9. *Java Code for the DigitalClockActivity, event listener, and intent object*

In this activity class, in the onClick() listener we create a new (empty) intent object called replyIntent, then load it with the setResult() method, which loads a constant called RESULT_OK. When we have finished handling the intent (in this case by loading a new intent with the reply data), we call the finish() method to send the intent back, after the button in the second activity is clicked on to send us back to the first activity.

Now let's right-click on our Chapter11 folder and then **Run As ➤ Android Application** so we can see that we can now switch back and forth between the two activities that contain the two different time utilities we created in one application. As you can see in Figure 11–10, we can switch between the two activities by clicking on the respective buttons, and we can do this as many times as we like, and the application performs as expected and does not crash. That is important, by the way, that the app does not crash under repeated use.

Figure 11–10. *Running our app in the Android 1.5 emulator and switching back and forth between activities*

Next we will use an intent object to call a service, the MediaPlayer, to play some music in the background and allow us to start the music and stop the music.

To do this we first must learn what services are and how they can help us do things in the background without affecting our application's user interface functionality. We will then get into an example that uses intents with both services and activities.

Android Services: Data Processing in its own Class

Android has an entire Service class dedicated to enabling developers to create services that run apart from the main user interface program logic. These services can either run in a separate process (known as a **thread** in Java programming as well as in other programming languages) or the same process as the user interface activities.

A thread is an area of the operating system's memory where a program function has its own resources and can run in parallel with other applications or other application components or functions. For instance, a video player can run in a different thread from the rest of the application so that it doesn't hog all of the main application thread resources.

Threads were originally devised for multitasking operating systems like Mac, Linux, and Windows, so that if a program or task crashed, it would not bring down the entire operating system. Instead, just that thread or process could crash or lock-up, and the others that were running wouldn't be affected adversely.

A service is a type of Android application component that needs to run asynchronously (not in step with the usual flow of the user interface). For example, if you have some processing that takes a bit longer than the user is willing to wait for, you can set off the processing asynchronously in the background while the main program continues. When the processing has finished, the results can be delivered to the main program and dealt with appropriately. A service can also be used by other Android applications, so it is more extensible than an activity.

To create your own service class to offload programming tasks like calculating things or playing media such as audio or video in real-time, you need to subclass the Service class and implement at least its onCreate(), onStart(), and onDestroy() methods with your own custom programming logic. You also must declare the Service class in your AndroidManifest.xml file using the <service> tag, which we'll get into a bit later on.

Using Intents with Services

To see how to control a service class via intent objects, we will need to add some user interface elements to our Chapter11 IntentExamples activity, namely two button objects that will start and stop our service. In this case, the service is the Android MediaPlayer, which needs to run in the background, independently of our user interface elements.

1. First, let's add a Button tag to our main.xml file by copying the Button01 tag and pasting it underneath the AnalogClock tag.

2. Change the id to startButton and the android:text to "Start the Media Player Service" and leave the other attributes in the tag the same.

```
<Button android:id="@+id/startButton"
    android:text="Start the Media Player Service"
    android:textSize="18px"
    android:layout_width="280px"
    android:layout_height="60px"
```

```
android:layout_gravity="center"/>
```

3. Next, copy this `startButton` tag and paste the copy immediately below the `startButton` tag.

4. Change the id of the copy to `stopButton` and the `android:text` to read "Stop the Media Player Service" so that we now have a stop button and a start button. Figure 11–11 shows both buttons in place in the **Layout** tab of Eclipse and Figure 11–12 shows the code in context.

```
<Button android:id="@+id/stopButton"
    android:text="Stop the Media Player Service"
    android:textSize="18px"
    android:layout_width="280px"
    android:layout_height="60px"
    android:layout_gravity="center"/>
```

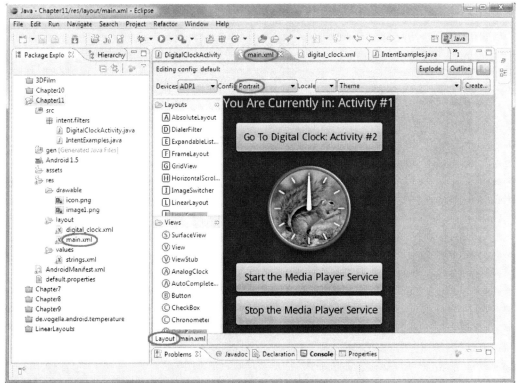

Figure 11–11. *Designing our media player user interface in the Eclipse Layout Editor in Portrait mode*

5. Now let's change the `AnalogClock` tag attribute `android:layout_marginTop` to use `20dip` rather than `30dip`. Copy the attribute to the line below and change it to `android:layout_marginBottom` so that we have an even 20 pixels of spacing around the analog watch.

```
<AnalogClock    android:id="@+id/AnalogClock01"
                android:layout_width="wrap_content"
                android:layout_height="wrap_content"
                android:layout_gravity="center"
                android:layout_marginTop="20dip"
                android:layout_marginBottom="20dip"
                android:background="@drawable/image1" />
```

6. Click the **Layout** tab at the bottom of the `main.xml` pane to make sure the user interface layout looks good and check Figure 11–12 to see that your XML looks right.

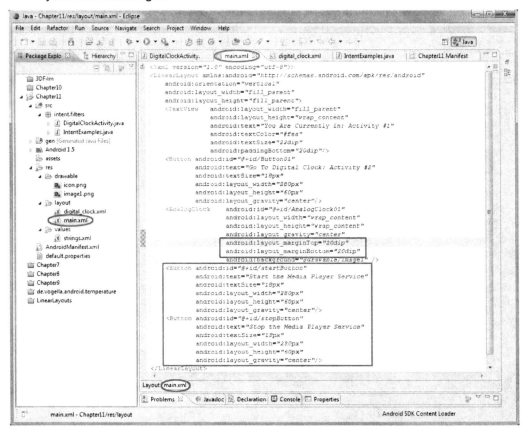

Figure 11–12. *Adding start and stop buttons for our media player in main.xml*

Next we need to let our Android application know that we are going to be calling a service, and this is done via the `AndroidManifest.xml` file. We will edit that file next to add a `service` tag that points to our `MediaPlayerService` class, which we are going to code next. We will add this `service` tag right after the second `activity` tag we added in the previous example (see Figure 11–13 for context). This is how the `service` tag is structured:

```
<service android:enabled="true" android:name=".MediaPlayerService" />
```

The first attribute of the `service` tag `android:enabled` indicates that the service is enabled for use. If you set this attribute to `false`, the service is still declared to Android for the application and can later be enabled via Java code. As we have seen, everything that can be done in XML can also be accessed and changed in our Java code.

The second attribute, `android:name`, specifies the name of the service class that we will code. We are going to name it `MediaPlayerService.java` so we specify that in XML as `.MediaPlayerService`. Now we are ready to start coding the service that will play media files without interfering with the user interface code in our activity class.

Note that if you haven't created the `MediaPlayerService.java` class before you add the `service` tag, Eclipse may highlight this fact with a red X in the margin to the left of the `service` tag, as shown circled in Figure 11–13.

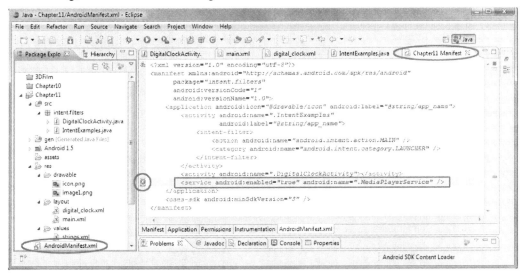

Figure 11–13. *Adding a Media Player Service Tag to the AndroidManifest.xml file in Eclipse*

Now that we've added the XML mark-up, let's create the `MediaPlayerService.java` class, extending the Android `Service` class to create our own custom service class that we'll call from our `IntentExamples` Activity class.

Creating a Service

To do this, we will use the same work process as before:

1. Right-click on your Chapter11 folder in the Eclipse Package Explorer pane on the left and select **New ➤ Class**.

2. Fill out the **New Java Class** dialog as follows:

    ▪ Source folder: Chapter11/src. Default entry, as specified by Eclipse

- Package: intent.filters. Click **Browse** button and select from list

- Name: MediaPlayerService

- Modifiers: public

- Superclass: android.app.Service

3. When everything is filled out, select **Finish**.

The completed dialog is shown in Figure 11–14. It will create an empty class where we can put our media player logic for creating, starting, and stopping the media player.

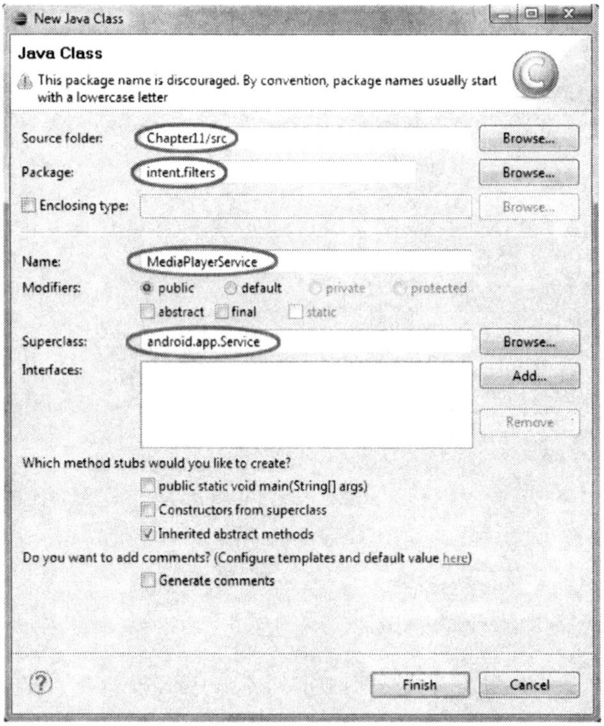

Figure 11–14. *Creating the MediaPlayerService.java class via the New Java Class dialog*

Below (and in Figure 11–15) is the empty class that the **New Java Class** dialog created for us, complete with the import statements that let us use the Service class, the Intent class, and the IBinder interface. We won't actually be using the IBinder interface in this example but will leave in the code. This won't affect how the app runs because it is used by a null method, onBind(). We need to keep this method here because Android expects it to be implemented when we extend the Service class, but we'll just leave it as is.

```
package intent.filters;

import android.app.Service;
import android.content.Intent;
import android.os.IBinder;
```

```java
public class MediaPlayerService extends Service {
    @Override
    public IBinder onBind(Intent intent) {
        // TODO Auto-generated method stub
        return null;
    }
}
```

> **NOTE:** Binding is a concept in services where your activity can talk with the Service class while it is running, and more than one time; but our example simply needs to start and stop the service, so the complexity of binding is not needed.

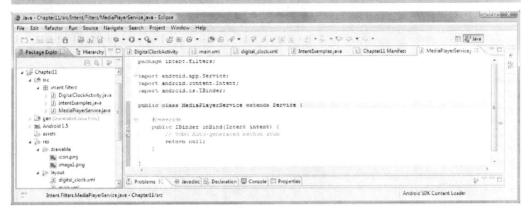

Figure 11–15. *Android-created MediaPlayerService base service class*

Here is the code that lets our MediaPlayerService class do things. I'll show you each of the bold sections in turn as I describe what they do, so you can type them in as we go:

```java
package intent.filters;

import android.app.Service;
import android.content.Intent;
import android.os.IBinder;
import android.media.MediaPlayer;

public class MediaPlayerService extends Service {
    MediaPlayer myMediaPlayer;

    @Override
    public IBinder onBind(Intent intent) {
        // TODO Auto-generated method stub
        return null;
    }

    @Override
    public void onCreate() {
        myMediaPlayer = MediaPlayer.create(this, R.raw.mindtaffy);
        myMediaPlayer.setLooping(true);
    }
```

```
@Override
public void onStart(Intent intent, int startid) {
    myMediaPlayer.start();
}

@Override
public void onDestroy() {
    myMediaPlayer.stop();
}
}
```

The results are shown in Figure 11–16.

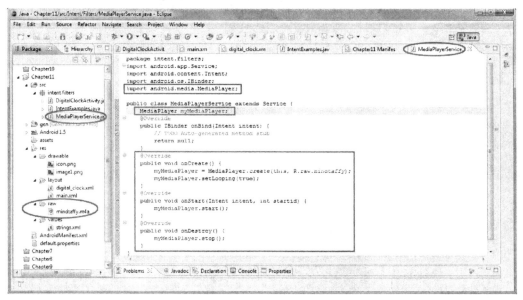

Figure 11–16. *Adding our MediaPlayer onCreate, onStart and onStop methods*

The first code structure we always add to a new class is the onCreate() method, which tells the class what to do to set itself up when it is called the first time (i.e., created).

We will use the onCreate() method to instantiate and configure our MediaPlayer object and load it with our audio file. Since the audio file is an MP3 file and already optimized for compression, we will put it in the /res/raw folder. Files in the /raw folder are left alone by the Android app compression process and are simply put into the .apk file as is. We'll do that now before explaining the code in detail.

1. Let's create a Chapter11/res/raw folder to hold the mindtaffy.m4a file that we will call in our MediaPlayerService class. You can either create the new /raw folder under the /Chapter11/res folder using your operating system's file manager or you can right-click on the /res folder in the Eclipse Package Explorer pane and select **New ➤ Folder** and enter **raw** in the **Folder name:** field.

2. Copy `mindtaffy.m4a` into the new `/raw` folder

3. Right-click on the `Chapter11` folder and select **Refresh** and, if necessary, **Validate** to remove any error flags you might get in Eclipse. Usually if **Refresh** does not make something visible to Android and get rid of error flags in Eclipse, the **Validate** procedure will. If it doesn't, you may have a problem and need to examine your overall application structure.

Implementing Our MediaPlayer Functions

Now it's time to go into the code so you can add the media player functionality to your own app:

1. First, at the top of the `MediaPlayerService` class, declare a public global variable called `myMediaPlayer` of object type `MediaPlayer`. This will be accessed in one way or another by each of the methods that we'll be coding here, so we declare it at the top of the class to make it visible to the whole class.

    ```
    MediaPlayer myMediaPlayer;
    ```

2. In the `onCreate()` code block, let's set the **myMediaPlayer** object to contain the results of a **create()** method call with the `mindtaffy.m4a` file passed as a parameter using the `R.raw.mindtaffy` reference. The `create()` method call creates an instance of the media player and loads it with the audio file that we are going to play.

3. Next we call the `setLooping()` method on the `myMediaPlayer` object and set a `true` parameter so that the audio file loops while we are testing the rest of the code.

    ```
    @Override
    public void onCreate() {
        myMediaPlayer = MediaPlayer.create(this, R.raw.mindtaffy);
        myMediaPlayer.setLooping(true);
    }
    ```

4. Now that our `myMediaPlayer` object has been declared, loaded with MP3 data, and set to loop when started, we can trigger it with the `start()` method, which we will code next in the `onStart()` method (`onStart()` is called when the service is started by our activity).

    ```
    @Override
    public void onStart(Intent intent, int startid) {
        myMediaPlayer.start();
    }
    ```

5. In the onDestroy() method we use the stop() method to stop the myMediaPlayer object. onDestroy() is called when the service is closed and disposed of by Android, so we release memory containing the media player and the audio file when we exit the application.

```
@Override
public void onDestroy() {
    myMediaPlayer.stop();
}
```

Wiring the Buttons to the Service

Now let's go back into our IntentExamples.java class using the Eclipse editor tab and add our Button objects, associated onClick() event handlers for each button, and the necessary calls to our Service class onStart() and onDestroy() methods, as shown in Figure 11–17.

Figure 11–17. *Implementing the start and stop buttons to control the media player*

First we have the start button.

```
Button startButton = (Button) findViewById(R.id.startButton);
startButton.setOnClickListener(new View.OnClickListener() {
    public void onClick(View view) {
        startService(new Intent(getBaseContext(), MediaPlayerService.class));
    }
});
```

As usual, we declare our `startButton` Button object with the `startButton` ID reference, then use the `setOnClickListener()` method to add `onClick()` event handling to the `startButton`. We are now ready to call the `startService()` method inside the `onClick()` programming construct.

`startService()` calls the `onStart()` method of the Service class we just wrote, and requires an intent object; this intent object tells Android what service to start and call the `onStart()` method on. We will get a little tricky here and create a new intent object inside of the `startService()` call using the following code structure:

```
startService(new Intent(getBaseContext(), MediaPlayerService.class));
```

To create a new intent object, we need to declare the current context as the first parameter and then pass the name of the service class we wish to call as the second parameter. In a third level of nesting (inside the new intent creation), we use another method called `getBaseContext()` to obtain the current context for the new intent object. As the second parameter, we will declare the name of the `MediaPlayerService.class` to complete the creation of a valid intent object.

Now let's go through the same procedure with the `stopButton` Button object, inserting the `stopButton` ID reference and then using the trusty `setOnClickListener()` method to add `onClick()` event handling to our new `stopButton`. Now we're ready to call the `stopService()` method in our newest `onClick()` programming routine.

```
        Button stopButton = (Button) findViewById(R.id.stopButton);
        stopButton.setOnClickListener(new View.OnClickListener() {
            public void onClick(View view) {
                stopService(new Intent(getBaseContext(), MediaPlayerService.class));
            }
        });
```

The `stopService()` method calls the `onDestroy()` method of our Service class and requires an intent object that tells Android what service to stop (destroy) and call the `onDestroy()` method on.

We will create yet another new intent object in the `stopService()` call, using the following code structure:

```
stopService(new Intent(getBaseContext(), MediaPlayerService.class));
```

To create our final intent object, we will declare the current context as our first parameter and then pass the name of our `MediaPlayerService()`class as our second parameter.

Running the Application

Now we are ready to right-click our Chapter11 folder and **Run As ➤ Android Application** to run our app. You'll find when you test the application that everything works perfectly with everything else; you can start and stop the media player as many times as you like, the music plays smoothly in the background without faltering, and you can switch back and forth between the two activities as many times as you want without affecting the media playback of the audio file. See Figure 11–18.

Figure 11–18. *Running our media player service inside the Android 1.5 emulator*

Next we are going to take a look at using Intent objects with broadcast receivers, and then we will have covered all three areas of Intent use within Android.

Using Intents with Broadcast Receivers

The final type of intent object we will look at in this chapter is the broadcast receiver, which is used for communication between different applications or different areas of Android, such as the MediaPlayer or Alarm functions. These intents send, listen to, or receive messages, sort of like a head's up notification system, to let your application know what's going on around it during the ongoing operation of the smartphone, whether that's a phone call coming in, an alarm going off, or a media player finishing a file playback.

Since we already have an analog watch and a digital clock, let's add a timer and alarm function to finish off our suite. Since our analog clock user interface screen is full of UI elements, let's add the alarm functions to our digital clock user interface, as that's the most logical place to add an alarm anyway. Figure 11–19 shows a basic diagram of what we will do in XML and Java to create the intent and alarm in our next application segment.

```
DEFINE USER INTERFACE (XML)
<EditText> User Enters Timer Duration
<Button> Click Start Timer Countdown
            ↓
ENABLE USER INTERFACE (Java)
Button startTimer.setOnClickListener()
onClick(View view) { timerAlert(view); }
            ↓
CREATE INTENT & ALARM (Java)
timerIntent = new Intent(this, timerBroadcastReceiver.class);
AlarmManager = (AlarmManager) getSystemService(ALARM_SERVICE);
            ↓
RECEIVE INTENT & NOTIFY (Java)
onReceive (Context context, Intent intent)
Toast.makeToast(context, "ALARM NOTIFICATION!")
```

Figure 11–19. *What we have to do in XML and Java to create the intent and alarm*

Creating the Timer User Interface via XML

So, first, let's add an EditText tag so we can let users enter their own custom timer duration. Place the following markup in your digital_clock.xml file after the DigitalClock tag:

```
<EditText android:layout_width="wrap_content"
        android:layout_height="wrap_content"
        android:id="@+id/timeInSeconds"
        android:layout_gravity="center"
        android:hint="Enter Number of Seconds Here!"
        android:inputType="numberDecimal"
        android:layout_marginTop="30dip"
        android:layout_marginBottom="30dip" />
```

The EditText tag has an ID of timeInSeconds and a layout gravity of center for consistency with our prior UI design. Since EditText is a new user interface object for us, we will add an android:hint attribute that says "Enter Number of Seconds Here!"

NOTE: The hint attribute is text you enter to appear in the text field when it is created by Android and placed on the screen in the layout container. This hint tells the user what to type in the field, which, in this case, is the number of seconds the timer should count down.

Next we have an important android:inputType attribute, which tells us what data type the field will contain, in this case a real number that is represented by the numberDecimal constant. The timer uses milliseconds, so if we want the timer to count 1534 milliseconds, we can type 1.534 in this field and achieve this precise result. Finally, we add two margin attributes (top and bottom) of 30dip each to space the user interface out and to make it more visually attractive to the end user.

We'll also add a Button tag called startTimer to, well, start the timer. Let's use an ID of startTimer and an android:text value of "Start Timer Countdown" to prompt the user. And we'll also use our familiar android:layout_gravity="center" to center our button, so that the UI remains consistent.

```
<Button android:layout_width="wrap_content"
        android:layout_height="wrap_content"
        android:layout_gravity="center"
        android:id="@+id/startTimer"
        android:text="Start Timer Countdown" />
```

Figure 11–20 shows how our digital_clock.xml file should look in the Eclipse IDE.

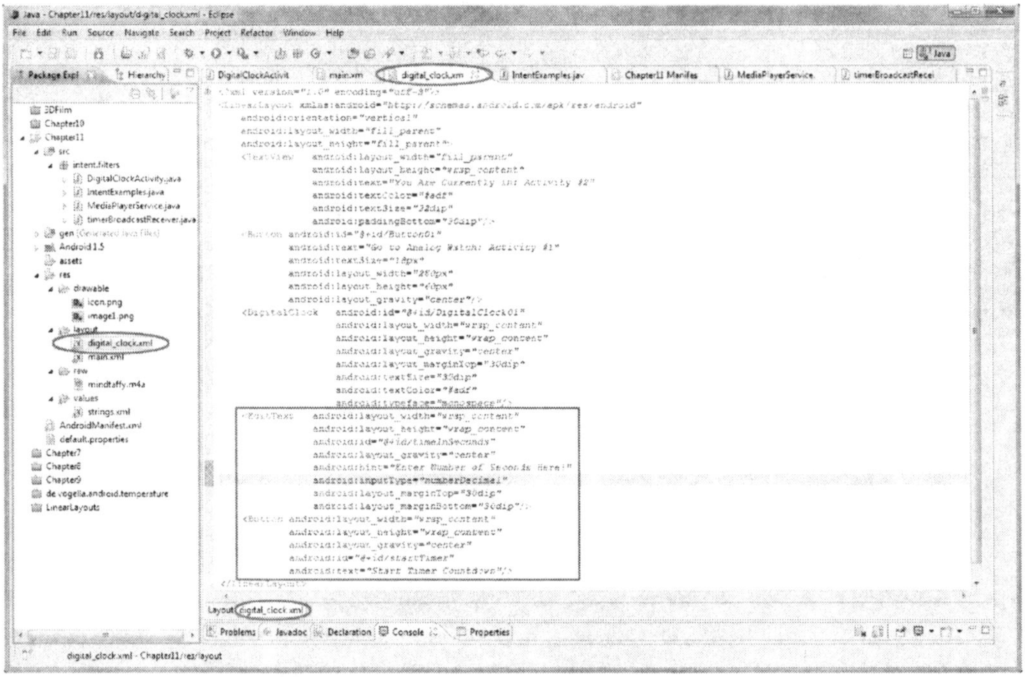

Figure 11–20. *Adding our timer user interface elements to the digital_clock.xml file*

Creating a Timer Broadcast Receiver

Now let's create our TimerBroadcastReceiver class, which is a subclass of the BroadcastReceiver class.

1. As we are now used to doing, let's create a new class using **New ➤ Class**, and use the following parameters:

    ▪ Source folder: Chapter11/src. Default entry, as specified by Eclipse

- Package: intent.filters. Click **Browse** button and select from list
- Name: TimerBroadcastReceiver
- Modifiers: public
- Superclass: android.content.BroadcastReceiver

2. When everything is filled out, select **Finish**.

Figure 11–21 shows what your **New Java Class** dialog should look like when you've entered all of the relevant new Java class information.

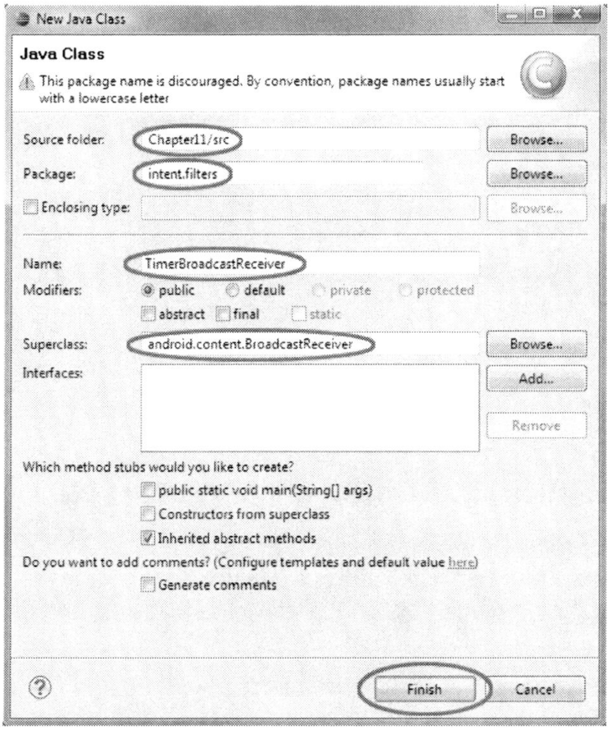

Figure 11–21. *Creating a new TimerBroadcastReceiver class via the New Java Class dialog in Eclipse*

Now we have an empty class shell with all of the import statements that we need for our BroadcastReceiver class and an empty onReceive() method for us to fill out with our programming logic. The onReceive() method will receive our intent and broadcast a message via the Toast class, which will notify us regarding the alarm status.

Let's add an import statement for the Toast widget so we can use it to broadcast a message to the user when the broadcast receiver is used. It is important to note that this Toast message could be replaced by anything we want to happen when our timer goes off, including but not limited to playing a song, playing a ringtone, vibrating the phone, playing a video, or anything else you can think of.

```
import android.widget.Toast;
```

The Toast widget's makeText() method can be coded as follows:

```
public void onReceive(Context context, Intent intent) {
    Toast.makeText(context, "Alarm Notification", Toast.LENGTH_LONG).show();
}
```

We first pass the Toast widget the context parameter received along with the onReceive() call and then tell it what to write to the screen (our "Alarm Notification" string) and how long to show it on the screen (the LENGTH_LONG constant). We then append the show() method to makeText() to draw the message to the screen.

Figure 11–22 shows how all of this should look on the TimerBroadcastReceiver tab in the Eclipse IDE.

Figure 11–22. *Our TimerBroadcastReceiver class*

Configuring the AndroidManifest.xml file <receiver> Tag

Now we need to declare our broadcast receiver using the receiver tag in our AndroidManifest.xml file so it is registered for use with Android. We will do this right after the service tag that we added in the previous section, entering the following line of XML mark-up code:

```
<receiver android:name=".TimerBroadcastReceiver" android:enabled="true" />
```

This is fairly straightforward. We use the name attribute to assign our TimerBroadcastReceiver class name to the receiver declaration tag and then enable it for use in our application by setting the android:enabled attribute to true so that the broadcast receiver is live (Figure 11–23).

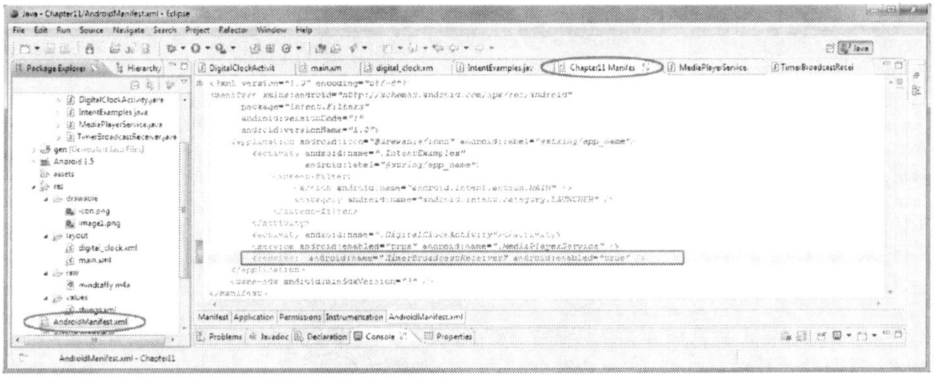

Figure 11–23. *Adding a <receiver> tag to our AndroidManifest.xml file*

Now our broadcast receiver is set up to notify users via a Toast message when the broadcast receiver is utilized. The next thing we need to do is add the code to our `DigitalClockActivity` class to implement an alarm clock function that triggers this Broadcast Receiver class via an intent object, so we can see how all this works together.

Implementing our Intent

The modifications to our `DigitalClockActivity` class will be done via several new `import` statements, an event handler for a click on our start timer countdown button, and the `timerAlert()` method that we will write to do all the heavy lifting to implement the new timer functionality to our application and to trigger our broadcast receiver class using intent objects.

Let's start with the `onCreate()` method:

```
public void onCreate(Bundle savedInstanceState) {
    super.onCreate(savedInstanceState);
    setContentView(R.layout.digital_clock);

    Button activity2 = (Button) findViewById(R.id.Button01);
    activity2.setOnClickListener(new View.OnClickListener() {
        public void onClick(View view) {
            Intent replyIntent = new Intent();
            setResult(RESULT_OK, replyIntent);
            finish();
        }
    });

    Button startTimer = (Button) findViewById(R.id.startTimer);
    startTimer.setOnClickListener(new View.OnClickListener() {
        public void onClick(View view) {
            timerAlert(view);
        }
    });
}
```

Now let's see how to add the highlighted code, starting with the import statements needed.

1. We need to import the two new widgets that we are going to use to implement editable text and a toast notification message. Both of these classes are from the android.widget package:

```
import android.widget.EditText;
import android.widget.Toast;
```

2. Next let's create our startTimer Button object for the start timer countdown button and use the findViewById() method to set it to the new startTimer button tag we previously added to our digital_clock.xml file. Place the following in the onCreate() method after the existing button code:

```
Button startTimer = (Button) findViewById(R.id.startTimer);
```

3. Now we'll add a setOnClickListener() method to handle events generated by the startTimer button. Inside of that construct we will create an onClick() method that calls a timerAlert() method, which holds all of the relevant program logic to set up intents and construct the alarm feature for our digital clock activity:

```
startTimer.setOnClickListener(new View.OnClickListener() {
    public void onClick(View view) {
        timerAlert(view);
    }
});
```

We will pass the view variable (the onClick view or button that was passed from the onClick() method) to the timerAlert() method so that it has the context needed for the PendingIntent. Here is the code for the timerAlert() method, which we will go over line by line:

```
public void timerAlert(View view) {
    EditText textField = (EditText) findViewById(R.id.timeInSeconds);
    int i = Integer.parseInt(textField.getText().toString());
    Intent timerIntent = new Intent(this, TimerBroadcastReceiver.class);
    PendingIntent myPendingIntent =
      PendingIntent.getBroadcast(this.getApplicationContext(), 0, timerIntent, 0);
    AlarmManager myAlarmManager = (AlarmManager) getSystemService(ALARM_SERVICE);
    myAlarmManager.set(AlarmManager.RTC_WAKEUP, System.currentTimeMillis() +
      (i * 1000), myPendingIntent);
    Toast.makeText(this, "Alarm is set for " + i + " seconds!",
                Toast.LENGTH_LONG).show();
}
```

1. First, we need two import statements for two new classes from the android.app package.

   ▪ android.app.AlarmManager is a class that manages alarm functions for the Android OS.

- android.app.PendingIntent is a class that allows intents to be pending, which means they can be scheduled. This means they can be handled by classes in Android even if the calling class is paused, missing, asleep, stopped, or destroyed before the called intent has been processed. This is important for an alarm, especially if the timer is set to hours rather than minutes or seconds, because the phone could run out of charge before the Intent was ever satisfied.

```
import android.app.AlarmManager;
import android.app.PendingIntent;
```

2. The `timerAlert()` method is void because it just performs some tasks relating to setting up intents and alarm functions. It takes a `View` object named `view` as its passed parameter.

```
public void timerAlert(View view) {
```

3. The first thing we do in this method's code block is to declare the `EditText` object, name it `textField`, and locate it in our `digital_clock.xml` layout definition via its `timeInSeconds` ID parameter.

```
EditText textField = (EditText) findViewById(R.id.timeInSeconds);
```

4. Once we have the `textField` object we can use the `getText()` method along with the `toString()` method to get the string that the user types into the field. We then use the `parseInt()` method to convert that string value into an integer value and store it in the `i` variable of type `int` (or integer). Later we will use this integer value with our `set()` method to set the alarm.

```
int i = Integer.parseInt(textField.getText().toString());
```

5. In the third line of code we declare an `Intent` object that we name `timerIntent` and set it to a new `Intent` object with the context of `this` and the class of `TimerBroadcastReceiver.class` as we have done in the previous sections of this chapter. We will use this `timerIntent` object in the `PendingIntent` object.

```
Intent timerIntent = new Intent(this, TimerBroadcastReceiver.class);
```

6. Now let's create a `PendingIntent` object called `myPendingIntent` and set it to the result of the `getBroadcast()` method call; this takes four parameters:

- The context
- Code
- The intent object we want to use as a `PendingIntent`
- Any constants

> **NOTE:** In this case we need no code or constants so we simply pass the current context, which we get using the `getApplicationContext()` method and the `timerIntent` object we created just prior in the previous line of code.

```
PendingIntent myPendingIntent =
  PendingIntent.getBroadcast(this.getApplicationContext(), 0, timerIntent, 0);
```

7. Now we are ready to create our alarm using the `AlarmManager` class. To do this we declare an `AlarmManager` object named `myAlarmManager` and call the `getSystemService()` method with the `ALARM_SERVICE` constant to specify that we want to get the alarm system service and set it to the `myAlarmManager` object. Once we have defined `myAlarmManager` as an alarm service object we can use the `set()` method to configure it for our use in the application.

```
AlarmManager myAlarmManager = (AlarmManager) getSystemService(ALARM_SERVICE);
```

8. The next line in the code block is the one that ties everything else together. The `set()` method we will use on our `myAlarmManager` object has three parameters:

   ■ **TYPE**: The type of alarm trigger we wish to set.

   ■ **TRIGGER TIME:** The alarm will trigger when it reaches this system time.

   ■ **OPERATION**: The `PendingIntent` object containing the context and target intent code we wrote in `TimerBroadcastReceiver.java`, as specified using the `getBroadcast()` method.

```
myAlarmManager.set(AlarmManager.RTC_WAKEUP, System.currentTimeMillis() +
  (i * 1000), myPendingIntent);
```

In our incarnation of the `set()` method on the `myAlarmManager` object, we first specify the `AlarmManager.RTC_WAKEUP`, which uses the Real Time Clock (RTC) method and wakeup constant to specify that we want to wake up the phone (if it is asleep) to deliver the alarm. The RTC method uses the system clock in milliseconds as its time reference.

Using RTC only (without the `_WAKEUP`) will not wake the phone up if it triggers while the phone is asleep, and thus will be delivered only when the phone wakes up again. This makes it not nearly as accurate as the `RTC_WAKEUP` constant. You can imagine how handy it is to be able to wake up your phone at a certain discreet time *even if it is asleep*, so it's a good thing we are exposing you to this handy class here.

The next parameter we need to specify is the precise system time, in milliseconds, to trigger the alarm. We will wax a bit tricky here, and we will specify this middle parameter using a bit of inline programming logic.

We call the `currentTimeMillis()` method on the Android `System` object to get the current system time in milliseconds, then we add to the system time the number of seconds specified by our user in milliseconds, by multiplying the number of seconds in variable i by 1000, since there are 1000 milliseconds in one second. The system time is calculated in milliseconds since 1970, so it is a discrete number that we can simply add our timer milliseconds value to.

This numeric result gives us the exact system time in milliseconds when the alarm needs to be triggered, and puts it into the `set()` method's second parameter, when our inline code is evaluated at runtime. As we have seen, Java allows some fairly powerful programming constructs to be created using just a single line of programming code.

Finally, we will specify the `myPendingIntent` object as our third parameter. This object, created earlier with two lines of code, was loaded with the current context and the `timerIntent` object that we created earlier with three lines of code. The `timerIntent` object references our `TimerBroadcastReceiver` class, which will ultimately be called when the alarm is triggered, and will send a Toast to the screen to tell our end user that the time is up.

The final line of code sends a familiar Toast message to the end user, confirming that the alarm has been set for the proper number of seconds. This is done by passing the Toast `makeText()` method the current context (this) along with the `Toast.LENGTH_LONG` constant and two strings with the i variable between them like this:

```
Toast.makeText(this, "Alarm is set for " + i + " seconds!", Toast.LENGTH_LONG).show();
```

As we've seen here, Java is very flexible in how it allows us to mix different data types. Figure 11–24 shows our newly enhanced `DigitalClockActivity` class with the new import statements, `onCreate()` method and `timerAlert()` method modifications shown. Notice along the top of the IDE that we now have *seven* open tabs with XML and Java code that we have either modified or written. This is the most robust application we've written so far! Now we will run and test our new app.

Figure 11–24. *Adding the startTimer button UI code and timerAlert() method*

Running the Timer Application via the Android 1.5 Emulator

Let's right-click on our Chapter11 folder and select **Run As ➤ Android Application** and get right into our final intent examples application. You'll find when you run the application that all three sections we've added work perfectly together.

This shows us that all of the different types of intents can work seamlessly together in Android and that they don't interfere with each other, as we noted at the beginning of the chapter.

We can now go back and forth between the analog and digital activities using the intents we created; turn on the music and go back and forth while it is playing; and use the timer function while the digital audio is playing back as a service.

In the digital clock activity, we can use the editable text field to set our timer value and the start timer countdown button to trigger the broadcast intent, which broadcasts a Toast to the screen when the specified number of seconds has passed.

Figure 11–25 shows the application running in the Android 1.5 emulator displaying the digital clock, the timer function, and the button that allows us to switch back and forth between our two different activities and their user interfaces.

Figure 11-25. *Running our timerAlert() method in the Android 1.5 emulator to show broadcast receiver intents*

Summary

In this chapter, we've seen how different parts of the Android OS and the developer's application components communicate to form a cohesive and seamless application. From user interface activities to background processing services and systems utilities, intent objects are used in integral ways to pass requests for processing actions on data structures between different types of application components.

This serves to enforce a modular, logical programming work process on the Android applications developer, which ultimately increases security, decreases bugs and poorly constructed code, and attempts to facilitate the kind of optimization that will be needed in the mobile embedded environment of smartphones.

Ultimately, the proper use of intents and the creative structuring of application components is what set the successful Android developer apart from the crowd, so be sure to practice using intents and delve deeper into this area of the Android developer documentation whenever you get a chance.

Chapter 12

The Future

There are a number of advanced Android topics that are beyond the scope of this book, but it's good for you to know about them so you can continue learning on your own.

This chapter will cover the more specialized areas of programming for Android, and give a summary of what is available and how it is implemented, as well as provide some resources for finding more information on implementing these attributes in your future Android applications. The examples, where given, will be short and sweet, to give you a taste of what is to come.

Widgets: Creating Your Own Widgets in Android

As we discussed in Chapter 7, Android has its own collection of user-interface widgets that can be used to easily populate your layouts with functional elements that allow your users to interface with the program logic that defines what your application does. These widgets have their own package called `android.widget` that can be imported into your application and used without further modification.

Android extends this widget capability to its programmers by allowing us to also create our own widgets that can be used by Android as mini-application portals or views that float on the Android home screen, or even in other applications (just like the standard UI widgets). If you remember, user interface elements are Widgets that are sub-classed from `View` objects.

Widgets can be used to provide cool little extras for the Android homescreen, such as weather reports, MP3 players, calendars, stopwatches, maps, or snazzy clocks and similar micro-utilities.

To create an app widget, you utilize the Android `AppWidgetProvider` class, which extends the `BroadcastReceiver` class. To create your own app widget, you need to extend this class and override one or more of its key methods in order to implement your custom app widget functionality. Key methods of the `AppWidgetProvider` class include the following:

- onUpdate(Context, AppWidgetManager, int[])

- onDeleted(Context, int[])

- onEnabled(Context)

- onDisabled(Context)

- onReceive(Context, Intent)

To create an app widget, you need to create an AppWidgetProviderInfo object that will contain the metadata and parameters for the app widget. These are details such as the user interface layout, how frequently it is updated or refreshed, and the convenience class that it is sub-classed from (AppWidgetProvider). This can all be defined via XML, which should be no surprise.

The AppWidgetProvider class defines all of the methods that allow your application to interface with the app widget class via broadcast events, making it a broadcast receiver. These broadcast events, as we discussed in Chapter 11, will update the widget, with some frequency if required, as well as enabling (turning it on), disabling (turning it off), and even deleting it if required.

App widgets also (optionally) offer a configuration activity that can launch itself when the user first installs your app widget. This activity adds a user interface layout that allows your users to modify the app widget settings before (or at the time of) its launch.

The app widget must be declared in the AndroidManifest.xml file, so that the application has registered it with the OS for communications, as it is a broadcast receiver, so we need the following code in our manifest:

```
<receiver android:name="ExampleAppWidgetProvider" >
    <intent-filter>
        <action android:name="android.appwidget.action.APPWIDGET_UPDATE/>
    </intent-filter>
    <meta-data  android:name="android.appwidget.provider"
                android:resource="@xml/example_appwidget_info />
</receiver>
```

Notice that the receiver tag specifies an XML file in the /res/xml folder that sets the parameters for the look and operation of the widget, in a file called example_appwidget_info.xml, which contains the following XML mark-up code:

```
<appwidget-provider
    xmlns:android=http://schemas.android.com/apk/res/android
    android:minWidth="294dp"
    android:minHeight="72dp"
    android:updatePeriodMillis="80000000"
    android:initialLayout="@layout/example_appwidget"
    android:configure="com.example.android.ExampleAppWidgetConfigure" >
</appwidget-provider>
```

- The minWidth and minHeight attributes define the size of the widget.

- updatePeriodMillis defines the update period in milliseconds.

The updatePeriodMillis value should be set as high as possible, as updates consume battery power, and are called even if the smartphone is in sleep mode, which means that the phone is powered on to make the update. The initialLayout attribute calls the XML file that defines the app widget layout itself. You need to define an initialLayout XML file for your app widget in the /res/layout folder, or your app widget will be empty. This should all be old hat to you now after Chapter 6.

The last android:configure attribute is optional, and calls the activity that is needed to configure the UI layout and options settings for the widget on start-up. App widget layouts are based on remote views, which support only the main the following three layout classes in Android:

- LinearLayout
- RelativeLayout
- FrameLayout

The following widget classes are also supported in the initialLayout XML file:

- AnalogClock
- Button
- Chronometer
- ImageButton
- ImageView
- ProgressBar
- TextView

More information can be found at the App Widget Design Guidelines page at:

http://developer.android.com/guide/practices/ui_guidelines/widget_design.html

General Information on App Widgets can be found at:

http://developer.android.com/guide/topics/appwidgets/index.html

Location-Based Services in Android

Location-based services and Google Maps are both very important OS capabilities when it comes to a smartphone device. You can access all location and maps related capabilities inside of Android via the android.location package, which is a collection of classes or routines for dealing with maps and locations, and via the Google Maps external library, which we will cover in the next section.

The central component of the location services network is the LocationManager system service. This Android system service provides the APIs necessary to determine the location and (if supported) bearing of the underlying device's GPS and accelerometer hardware functionality.

Similar to other Android systems services, the LocationManager is not instantiated directly, but is instead requested as an instance from the system by calling the getSystemService(Context) method, which then returns a handle to the new LocationManager instance, like this:

getSystemService(Context.LOCATION_SERVICE)

Once a LocationManager has been established inside of your application, you will be able to do the following three things in your application:

- Query for a list of all LocationProviders for the last known user location.

- Register (or unregister) for periodic updates of the user's current location.

- Register (or unregister) for a given Intent to be fired once the device is within certain proximity of a specified latitude or longitude specified in meters.

Google Maps in Android

Google provides an external library called Google Maps that makes it relatively easy to add powerful mapping functions to your Android applications. It is a Java package called com.google.android.maps, and it contains classes that allow for a wide variety of functions relating to downloading, rendering, and caching map tiles, as well as a variety of user control systems and display options.

One of the most important classes in the maps package is MapView class, a subclass of ViewGroup, which displays a map using data supplied from the Google Maps service. Essentially this class is a wrapper providing access to the functions of the Google Maps API, allowing your applications to manipulate Google Maps through MapView methods that allow maps and their data to be accessed much as though you would access any other View object.

The MapView class provides programmers with all of the various user interface assets that can be used to create and control Google Maps data. When your application passes focus to your MapView object, it automatically allows your users to zoom into, and pan around, the map using gestures or keypresses. It can also handle network requests for additional map tiles or an entirely new map.

Before you can write a Google Maps-based application, you must obtain a Google Maps API key to identify your app:

1. To begin with, you need to provide Google with the signature of your application. To do so, run the following at the command line (this is again a Windows example):

keytool -list -keystore C:\users\<username>\.android\debug.keystore

NOTE: The signature of your application proves to Google that your application comes from you. Explaining the niceties of this is beyond the scope of the book, but for now just understand that you are proving to Google that you created this application.

2. When prompted, the password is android. Here is what you should see:

```
Enter keystore password:
Keystore type: JKS
Keystore provider: SUN
Your keystore contains 1 entry
androiddebugkey, 21-Jan-2011, PrivateKeyEntry,
Certificate fingerprint (MD5): <fingerprint>
```

3. Copy the fingerprint. You'll need it in the next step.

4. Go to http://code.google.com/android/maps-api-signup.html and enter the fingerprint in the "My certificate's MD5 fingerprint:" box.

5. Accept the terms and conditions, then click Generate API Key.

6. On the next page, note your API key.

Now that we have our key, here are the basic steps for implementing a Google Maps app:

1. First you would want to create a new project and Activity called MyGoogleMap, with a Project Build Target of **Google APIs** for version 1.5. We need to do this to use the Google Maps classes.

NOTE: You may have to install the Google APIs using the Android SDK and AVD Manager. They are listed as Google APIs by Google Inc.

2. In the AndroidManifest.xml file within the `<application>` tag use the `<uses-library>` tag to point to the Google Maps library address specified above as follows:

```
<uses-library android:name="com.google.android.maps" />
```

3. Also in the AndroidManifest.xml file and within the `<application>` tag, use the `<uses-permission>` tag to request permission to access the Internet as follows:

```
<uses-permission android:name="android.permission.INTERNET" />
```

4. Next you would want to define some simple user interface elements within your main.xml layout definition, using a basic linear layout with a vertical parameter specified, and then a Google Maps MapView user interface element with the clickable parameter set to true, allowing the user to navigate the map, as follows:

```xml
<?xml version="1.0" encoding="utf-8"?>
<LinearLayout xmlns:android="http://schemas.android.com/apk/res/android"
    android:id="@+id/mainlayout"
    android:orientation="vertical"
    android:layout_width="fill_parent"
    android:layout_height="fill_parent" >
    <com.google.android.maps.MapView
        android:id="@+id/mapview"
        android:layout_width="fill_parent"
        android:layout_height="fill_parent"
        android:clickable="true"
        android:apiKey="Your Maps API Key"
    />
</LinearLayout>
```

5. Now enter your unique Google Maps API key that was assigned to you in the apiKey parameter in the last parameter of the MapView tag.

6. Next open your MyGoogleMap.java activity and extend your class to use a special sub-class of the Activity class called the MapActivity class, as follows:

```java
public class MyGoogleMap extends MapActivity {...}
```

7. One of the primary methods of the MapActivity class is the isRouteDisplayed() method, which must be implemented, and once it is, you will be able to pan around a map, so add this little bit of code as follows to complete your basic map:

```java
@Override
protected boolean isRouteDisplayed() {
    return false;
}
```

8. At the top of your MyGoogleMap class instantiate two handles for the MapView and the ZoomTool controls (LinearLayout) we are going to add next, as follows:

```java
LinearLayout linearLayout;
MapView mapView;
```

9. Next in your onCreate() method, initialize your MapView UI element and add the ZoomControls capability to it via the setBuiltInZoomContols() method as follows:

```java
mapView = (MapView) findViewById(R.id.mapview);
mapView.setBuiltInZoomControls(true);
```

Note that we are using the built-in `MapView` zoom controls so we do not have to write any code and yet when we run this basic application the user will be able to zoom the `MapView` via zoom controls that will appear when the user touches the map and then disappear after a short time-out period (of non-use).

10. Compile and run your `MyGoogleMap` application in the Android emulator.

It is important to note that the external Google Maps library is not an integral part of the Android OS, but is actually something that is hosted externally to the smartphone environment and requires access externally via a Google Maps key that you must apply for and secure before your applications utilize this service from Google. This is the same way that this works for using Google Maps from a web site; it's just that the `MapView` class fine-tunes this for Android usage. To learn more about the Google Maps external library visit:

`http://code.google.com/android/add-ons/google-apis`

Google Search in Android

Google has built its business model on one major service that it has always offered: search. It should be no surprise that search is thus a well-supported core service in Android. Android users can search for any data that is available to them on their Android handset or across the Internet.

Android, not surprisingly, provides a seamless, consistent search experience across the board, and Android provides a robust search implementation framework for you to implement search functions inside of your Android applications.

The Android search framework provides an interface for search that includes both the interaction and the search itself, so that you do not have to define a separate Activity in Android. The advantage of this is that the use of search in your application will not interrupt your current Activity.

Using Android search puts a search dialog at the top of the screen, pushing other content down on the screen as it is utilized. Once you have everything set up to use this capability in Android, you can integrate your application with search by providing search suggestions based on your app or recent user queries, offer you own custom application specific search suggestions in the system-wide quick search function, and even turn on voice search functions.

Search in Android is handled by the `SearchManager` class; however, that class is not used directly, but rather is accessed via an Intent specified in XML or via your Java code via the `context.getSystemService(context.SEARCH_SERVICE)` code construct. Here are the basic steps to set-up capability for a search within your AndroidManifest.xml file.

1. Specify an `<intent-filter>` in the `<activity>` section of the AndroidManifest.xml:

```
<intent-filter>
    <action android:name="android.intent.action.SEARCH" />
```

```
</intent-filter>

<meta-data android:name="android.app.searchable"
        android:resource="@xml/searchable" />
```

2. Next, create the res/xml/searchable.xml file specified in the <meta-data> tag in step 1.

3. Inside searchable.xml, create a <searchable> tag with the following data:

```
<searchable xmlns:android="http://schemas.android.com/apk/res/android"
        android:label="@string/search_label"
        android:searchSuggestAuthority="dictionary"
        android:searchSuggestIntentAction="android.intent.action.VIEW">
</searchable>
```

4. Now in res/values/strings.xml, add a string called search_label.

Now you are ready to implement a search in your application as described here:

`http://developer.android.com/guide/topics/search/search-dialog.html`

Note that most Android phones and devices come with a search button built in, which will pop up the search dialog. You can also provide a button to do this, in a menu maybe. That's for you to experiment with.

Data Storage in Android

Android has a significant number of ways for you to save data on your smartphone, from private data storage for your application, called shared preferences, to internal storage on your smartphone device's memory chips, to external storage via your smartphone device's external storage (HD card or mini HDD), to network connection (Network Attached Storage) via your own network server, to an entire DBMS (Database Management System) via open source SQLite private databases.

Shared Preferences

Shared preferences are persistent data pairs that remain in memory even if your application is killed (or crashes), and thus this data remains persistent across multiple user sessions. The primary use of shared preferences is to store user preferences for a given user's Android applications and this is a main reason why they persist in memory between application runs.

To set your application's shared preferences Android provides us with the SharedPreferences class. This class can be used to store any **primitive data types**, including Booleans (on/off, visible/hidden), floats, integers, strings, and longs. Note that the data created with this class will remain persistent across user sessions with your application even if your application is killed (the process is terminated or crashes).

There are two methods in the SharedPreferences class that are used to access the preferences; if you have a single preference file use getPreferences() and if you have more than one preference files, you can name each and use getSharedPreferences(name) and access them by name. Here is an example of the code in use, where we retrieve a screen name. The settings.getString() call returns the screenName parameter, or the name Android Fan if the setting is not set:

```
public static final String PREFS_NAME = "PreferenceFile";
…

    @Override
    public void onCreate(Bundle savedInstanceState) {
        super.onCreate(savedInstanceState);
        setContentView(R.layout.main);

        SharedPreferences settings = getSharedPreferences(PREFS_NAME, 0);
        String screenName = settings.getString("screenName", "Android Fan");
        // do something with the screen name.
    }
```

We can set the screen name with the following:

```
SharedPreferences settings = getSharedPreferences(PREFS_NAME, 0);
SharedPreferences.Editor editor = settings.edit();
editor.putString("screenName", screenName);
editor.commit();
```

Internal Memory

Accessing internal memory storage on Android is done a bit differently, as that memory is unique to your application and cannot be directly accessed by the user or by other applications. When the application is uninstalled these files are deleted from memory. To access files in memory use the openFileOutput() with the name of the file and the operation needed, which will return a FileOutputStream object which you can use the read(), write() and close() methods to manipulate the data into and out of the file. Here is some example code showing this concept:

```
String FILENAME = "hello_file";
String string = "hello world!";
FileOutputStream fos = openFileOutput(FILENAME, Context.MODE_PRIVATE);
fos.write(string.getBytes());
fos.close();
```

External Memory

The method that is used for accessing external memory on an Android device is getExternalStorageState(). It checks to see whether the media (usually an SD card or internal micro HDD) is in place (inserted in the case of an SD card) and available for usage. Note that files written to external removable storage media can also be accessed outside of Android and applications by PCs or other computing devices that can read the SD card format. This means there is no security in place on files that are written to external removable storage devices.

Using SQLite

The most common way to store data for your application, and the most organized and sharable, is to create and utilize a MySQL Lite database. This is how Android stores and accesses its own data for users who utilize its internal applications such as the Contacts list or Database. Any private database you create for your application will be accessible to all parts of your application, but not to other parts of other developer's applications unless you give permission for them to access it. I will briefly outline how it would be done here, and you can research these methods on the developer.android site for more details.

The way to create a new SQL database in Android is to create a subclass of the SQLiteOpenHelper class and then override the onCreate() method. This method allows one to create a tabular structure within the desired database format that will support your application's optimal data structure. Here is some example code from the Android Developer site showing the SQLiteOpenHelper implemented.

```
public class DictionaryOpenHelper extends SQLiteOpenHelper {
    private static final int DATABASE_VERSION = 2;
    private static final String DICTIONARY_TABLE_NAME = "dictionary";
    private static final String DICTIONARY_TABLE_CREATE =
                "CREATE TABLE " + DICTIONARY_TABLE_NAME + " (" +
                KEY_WORD + " TEXT, " +
                KEY_DEFINITION + " TEXT);";
    DictionaryOpenHelper(Context context) {
        super(context, DATABASE_NAME, null, DATABASE_VERSION);
    }
    @Override
    public void onCreate(SQLiteDatabase db) {
        db.execSQL(DICTIONARY_TABLE_CREATE);
    }
}
```

To write and read from the custom database structure, you would utilize the getWritableDatabase() and getReadableDatabase() methods, which both return a SQLiteDatabase object that represents the database structure and provides methods for performing SQLite database operations.

To perform SQLite database queries on your new SQLite database you would use the SQLiteDatabase_Query methods, which accept all common data query parameters such as the table to query and the groupings, columns, rows, selections, projection, and similar concepts that are mainstream in database programming.

Device Administration: Security for IT Deployments

As of Android version 2.2 (API Level 8), Google has introduced support for secure enterprise applications via its Android Device Administration API. This API provides developers with employee device administration at a lower system level, allowing the creation of "security aware" applications that are necessary in MIS enterprise applications that require that IT maintain a tight level of control over the employees Android Smartphone devices at all times.

A great example of this is the Android e-mail application, which has been upgraded in OS version 2.2 to implement these security features to provide more robust e-mail exchange security and support. Exchange Administrators can now implement and enforce password protection policies in the Android e-Mail application spanning both alphanumeric passwords and simpler numeric PINs across all of the devices in their organization.

IT administrators can go as far as to remotely restore the factory defaults on lost or stolen handsets, clearing sensitive passwords and wiping clean proprietary data. E-mail Exchange End-Users can now sync their e-Mail and calendar data as well.

Using the Android Camera Class to control a Camera

The Android Camera class is used to control the built-in camera that is in every Android smartphone. This Camera class is used to set image capture settings and parameters, start and stop the preview modes, take the actual picture and retrieve frames of video in real-time for encoding to a video stream or file. The Camera class is a client for the camera service, which manages the camera hardware.

To access your Android device's camera, you need to declare a permission in your AndroidManifest.xml that allows the camera features to be included in your application. You need to use the <uses-feature> tag to declare any camera features that you wish to access in your application so that Android knows to activate them for use in your application. The following XML AndroidManifest.xml entries allow the camera to be used and define it as a feature along with the auto-focus capabilities:

```
<uses-permission android:name="android.permission.CAMERA" />
<uses-feature android:name="android.hardware.camera" />
<uses-feature android:name="android.hardware.camera.autofocus"/>
```

The developer.android website has plenty of Java code for you to experiment with.

3D Graphics: Using OpenGL ES 1.x in Android

One of the most impressive capabilities of the Android OS is its ability to "render" 3D graphics in real-time using only the open source OpenGL (Open Source Graphics Language) ES 1.0 API, and in later releases of Android, the OpenGL ES 1.1 and 1.2 APIs. OpenGL ES stands for OpenGL for Embedded Systems.

OpenGL ES is an optimized embedded devices version of the OpenGL 1.3 API that is used on Computers and Game Consoles. OpenGL ES is highly optimized for use in embedded devices, much like the Android Dalvik Virtual Machine optimizes your code by making sure there is no "fat" that the Smartphone CPU and memory need to deal with, a streamlining of sorts. OpenGL ES 1.0 is feature parallel to the full OpenGL 1.3 standard, so if what you want to do on Android is doable in OpenGL 1.3, it should be possible to do it in OpenGL ES 1.0.

The Android OpenGL ES 1.0 is a custom implementation but is somewhat similar to the J2ME JSR239 OpenGL ES API, with some minor deviations from this specification due to its use with the Java Micro Edition (JavaME) for cell phones.

To access the OpenGL ES 1.0 API, you need to write your own custom subclass of the View Class and obtain a handle to an OpenGL Context, which will then provide you with access to the OpenGL ES 1.0 functions and operations. This is done in the onDraw() method of the custom View class that you create, and once you have a handle to the OpenGL Object, you can use that object's methods to access and call the OpenGL ES functional operations.

More information on OpenGL ES can be found at www.khromos.org/opengles/

Information about version 1.0 can be found at www.khronos.org/opengles/1_X/

Android Developer Documents do in fact exist for OpenGL ES 1.0 and 1.1 at

http://developer.android.com/reference/javax/microedition/khronos/opengles/pack age-summary.html

FaceDetector

One of the coolest and most advanced concepts in the SDK is a facial recognition class called FaceDetector.

FaceDetector automatically identified faces of subjects inside of a Bitmap graphic object. I would suggest using PNG24 (24-bit PNG) for the highest quality source data for this operation.

You create a FaceDetector object by using the public constructor FaceDetector:

public FaceDetector (width integer, height integer, maxFaces integer)

The method you use to find faces in the bitmap file is findFaces(Bitmap bitmap, Face[] faces), which returns the number of faces successfully found.

SoundPool

The SoundPool class is great for game development and audio playback applications on Android because it manages a pool of Audio Resources in an optimal fashion for Android Apps that use a lot of audio or where audio is a critical part of the end-user's overall experience.

A SoundPool is a collection of audio "samples," such as sound effects or short songs which need to be loaded into Android memory from an external resource either inside the application's .APK file or from an external file or the internal file system.

The cool thing about the SoundPool is that it works hand in hand with the MediaPlayer Class that we looked at in Chapter 8 to decode the audio into a raw PCM mono or stereo 16-bit CD quality audio stream. This makes it easier for an application to include compressed audio in it's APK and then decompress it on application start-up, load it into memory, and then play it back without hiccups when it is called or triggered within the application code.

It gets even more interesting. It turns out that SoundPool can also control the number of audio assets that are being simultaneously "rendered" or turned from data values into audio sound waves. Essentially this means that the SoundPool is an Audio "Mixing Console" that can be used to layer audio in real-time to create custom mixes based on your gameplay or other applications programming logic.

SoundPool defines a maxStreams parameter that limits the number of parallel audio streams that can be played so that you can put a "cap" on the amount of processing overhead that is used to mixdown audio in your application, in case this starts to affect the visual elements that are also possibly rendering in real-time on the screen. If the maxStreams value is exceeded then the SoundPool turns off individual audio streams based on their priority values, or if none are assigned, based on the age of the audio stream.

Individual audio streams within the SoundPool can be looped infinitely (a value of -1) or any number of discreet times (0 to ...) and also counts from zero so a loop setting of three plays the audio loop four times. Playback rates can also be scaled from 0.5 to 2.0, or at half the pitch to twice the pitch, allowing real-time pitch shifting and with some clever programming one could simulate effects such as Doppler via fairly simple Java code. Samples can also be pitch shifted to give a range of sound effect tones or create keyboard-like synthesizers.

SoundPool also lets you assign a Priority to your individual audio samples, with higher numbers getting higher priority. Priority only comes into play when the maxStreams value specified in the SoundPool Object is hit and an audio sample needs to be removed from the playback queue to make room for another audio sample playback request with a higher priority level. Be sure to prioritize your audio samples so that you can have complete control of your audio and effects mixing during real-time playback.

MediaRecorder

In Chapter 8 we discussed the Android `MediaPlayer` class, which is commonly used to play back audio or video files. Android can also record audio and media files at a high level of fidelity and the counterpart to the `MediaPlayer` class for this is, logically, the `MediaRecorder` class. It is important to note that `MediaRecorder` does not currently work on the Android smartphone emulators.

There are five main `MediaRecorder` classes that control the process of media recording. They are as follows (note that these are defined inside the `MediaRecorder` class, hence the dot notation):

- `MediaRecorder.AudioEncoder`
- `MediaRecorder.AudioSource`
- `MediaRecorder.OutputFormat`

- MediaRecorder.VideoEncoder
- MediaRecorder.VideoSource

You construct a MediaRecorder object and operate on it using the public methods such as prepare(), release(), reset(), setAudioChannels(), setCamera(), setOutputFile(), and a plethora of other methods that control how the new media data is captured and stored on your Android device.

More information on the MediaRecorder class can be found at

http://developer.android.com/reference/media/MediaRecorder.html

Summary

There are a lot of great features in Android that we simply do not have enough time to cover in one book, or that are too high complex for an absolute beginners' book. That doesn't mean that you should not investigate all the cool features that Android has to offer on your own, however, so this chapter introduced some that are very powerful and advanced for a mobile phone operating system.

Where graphics are concerned there is no more powerful open source graphics library than OpenGL and Android implements the latest OpenGL ES 1.2 technology just like HTML5 does currently. Since Android phones have guilt-in GPU hardware, this means that you can render real-time 3D on the fly to visualize just about anything you want to within your application and in three dimensions to boot!

There are many other interesting areas to be discovered in Android as well, from creating your own widgets to creating your own MySQLite databases to using the SmartPhone Camera to the Face Recognition to the SoundPool Audio Engine for games and the Media Recorder to capture your own new media assets. All of this is covered in detail on the developer.android.com website be sure to explore there at length to enhance your knowledge of the thousands of interesting features in Android OS with many more to come!

Index